TRUMP'S
★ WAR ★

TRUMP'S
★WAR★

HIS BATTLE FOR AMERICA

MICHAEL SAVAGE

CENTER
STREET.

NEW YORK   NASHVILLE

Center Street
Hachette Book Group
1290 Avenue of the Americas, New York, NY 10104
centerstreet.com
twitter.com/centerstreet

First Edition: March 2017

Center Street is a division of Hachette Book Group, Inc. The Center Street name and logo are trademarks of Hachette Book Group, Inc.

The publisher is not responsible for websites (or their content) that are not owned by the publisher.

The Hachette Speakers Bureau provides a wide range of authors for speaking events. To find out more, go to www.HachetteSpeakersBureau.com or call (866) 376-6591.

Library of Congress Cataloging-in-Publication Data has been applied for.

ISBNs: 978-1-478-97667-7 (hardcover), 978-1-478-97668-4 (ebook)

Printed in the United States of America

LSC-C

10 9 8 7 6 5 4 3 2 1

CONTENTS

CONTENTS

CONTENTS

CHAPTER ONE

TRUMP'S WAR AGAINST THE ENEMIES WITHIN

I am not a guru. I am not a leader. I am a broadcaster and a writer who can think. In that sense, what you see is what you get: a man of the people, who helped lead this revolution that gave us Donald Trump. In that sense, I am much like the thinkers and writers who helped lead the revolution 241 years ago. That first American Revolution was as much a revolution of ideas as political institutions, just like ours today. And it wasn't led by peasants, like the disastrous French Revolution which immediately followed it. It was led by men of ideas.

THE SHOT HEARD ROUND THE WORLD

When British subjects fired on British troops at Lexington and Concord, they called it the shot heard round the world. That's because it didn't just send a message to King George III. It sent a message to tyrants and the smug intelligentsia all over the world: the workingman, the oppressed citizenry, had had enough.

Donald Trump's startling victory last November was another shot heard round the world. Obama and Clinton had been confident in their ivory tower—if power-mad pols can even have ivory towers. But I saw the revolution coming. I saw it before President Trump did. The people—I call them "the Eddies and the Ediths," the common men and women—were quietly restless. They called me on *The Savage Nation* to express their concerns and discontent. Whenever then-candidate Donald Trump came on the show, I told him: listen to the people and you can't go wrong. He had already used my philosophy of "borders, language, culture" to build his own electoral base. He heeded the advice I gave him and now he is president of the United States. In fact, many people have told me that President Trump's entire campaign sounded like he was reading my books off a teleprompter.

So, we fired a shot but we also dodged a bullet, friends. Not a bullet from the guns Hillary Clinton would have taken from us, but a national disaster, one that went far beyond the tragedy of four more years of the progressive Obama agenda. You see, the Boston Tea Party was all about a crooked trade deal. The colonists were being taxed without representation so they let the king, Parliament, and the complicit East India Tea Company know that they weren't going to stand for it.

Did you ever wonder why "free trade" agreements like North American Free Trade Agreement (NAFTA) and Trans-Pacific Partnership (TPP) are thousands of pages long? It's because they're not about free trade. They're about granting privileges to government-connected special interests, just like the king granted them to his corporations. But the corruption goes far beyond cronyism. For all Americans who lost their manufacturing jobs because of these deals, Hillary Clinton offered to put them on welfare. She and the Establishment wanted to make them dependent, wanted to make them perpetual Democrat voters—something that exceeded the ambition of even the autocrats in eighteenth-century London.

The upshot of that would have been something straight out of Orwell, with an anesthetized populace controlled by an elite ruling class. And the progressives had the nerve to call Republicans trickle-down fascists? The bullet we dodged was a permanent move to European-style socialism and the destruction of our once-robust national character.

So, the leftward march has been halted for now, and none too soon. When the Supreme Court told Americans of every state it was overturning their laws concerning gay marriage, it was no different than the English Parliament telling Massachusetts its local legislature could no longer make its own laws. From then on, Washington was going to decide how marriage is governed in all fifty states. It's not a matter of whether gay marriage itself is right or wrong. It's a matter of who decides.

Prior to the Court's unprecedented overreach, states were deciding the matter on their own, which was as it should be. The Civil War wasn't only about slavery, it was about this core concept of the American ideal: states' rights. Choice. Why should a woman get to "choose" what to do with her body while a state cannot decide what to do with its own body politic?

Some states made gay marriage legal; others prohibited it.

That was done by democratic vote according to long-standing local values. Yet for all their talk about "diversity," liberals would brook no diversity on this matter. Anyone who had reservations was branded a bigot or a rube whose views were to be ignored as an impediment to "progress." Unless, of course, you were a Muslim, in which case Imam Obama would look the other way. He and his fellow progs also averted their watery eyes when gays and women were abused by "friendly" nations like Saudi Arabia. This was by no means the first or the last time Obama's Washington had forced its will upon average Americans. They did the same thing when they passed Obamacare without a single Republican vote. Obama did it himself when he wrote executive orders to nullify immigration laws, regulate the coal industry out of business, and force public schools to allow confused boys to use the girls' restroom and vice versa.

For eight long years, the people suffered this long train of abuses, along with the insults and accusations of racism and bigotry whenever they objected. Until last November, when all of us pushed back.

The war for independence wasn't won at Lexington and Concord in 1775. That was only the beginning. The colonists would have to fight the mightiest empire in the world for eight long years before their independence was finally secured.

Trump and the patriots who elected him are going to have to fight their own eight-year war as well. The question is, what will that war look like? How is Donald Trump going to make good on all his campaign promises?

To begin with, he has already made good on some essentials. The First Amendment will be safe under Trump. No matter what else he does or doesn't do, Donald Trump is never going to attack talk radio, as Hatchet Hillary promised to do. I can guarantee you there will be no return to the "Fairness Doctrine," which was abolished in 1987. That bit of idiocy was enacted by the Federal Communications Commission, which sought to guarantee a diversity of viewpoints.

Neither is a Trump administration going to touch your guns. By appointing the next three judges to the Supreme Court, Trump may very well save the Second Amendment for the next forty years.

Perhaps most important, we're not going to be at war with Russia. As I said in my last book, *Scorched Earth*, it's "life under Trump, death under Clinton." President Trump is going to repair our relationship with Russia in a way Hillary Clinton and Barack Obama's community destroyers like Secretary of Misstate John Kerry could never achieve. Trump decided to speak with Russian president Vladimir Putin before he even took office. Why? Because on October 17, 2016, less than a month before Election Day, Trump appeared on my show and I got that commitment from him.

The liberal media went insane. They all wanted war with Russia. It would have sold newspapers. It would have been good for defense contractors, who are all in bed with the politicians and media in the swamp. But it wouldn't have been good for America.

So, there is much to be thankful for. But now that Donald Trump has won the election, it's our job to make sure he does what we sent him to Washington to do: drain the swamp.

It's not going to be easy. There are armies of special interests on the right and on the left who stand to lose trillions as the forty-fifth president rolls up his sleeves. It's time for all of us to prepare for Trump's War.

I decided to write this book as a battle plan. I was curious myself about how President Trump could make good on his promises, not just because they were big and unprecedented, but because he would face opposition to so many of them.

The "big and unprecedented" part doesn't worry me. Americans are at their best tackling the previously impossible, whether it is throwing off a tyrant or going to the moon. I am more concerned with the steps, the map, the how-to. Not just for the president, but for all of us. Though I will say this about Donald Trump. His biggest fight will not be keeping his promises but avoiding the pitfall of almost every public servant from small-town first selectman to commander in chief: temptation. The temptation to be assimilated into the Washington morass is powerful. Surrounded by "yes" men and women who will say anything you want to hear, possessing more power than any human being in history, you become convinced of your own—dare I say it?—your own divinity.

That's right. Obama succumbed. So did the Clintons. They didn't learn from the history they were supposedly taught in school. Maybe Barry Obama was busy doing "a little blow" during those classes, as he once admitted. In Imperial Rome, generals riding through the city in a triumphant celebration were accompanied by an *auriga*, a slave, who repeatedly whispered in their ear, "*Memento homo.*"

"Remember, you are only a man."

THE ENEMIES WITHIN

No it's not going to be easy. There are armies of special interests on the right and the left that have trillions to lose if we succeed in restoring this nation. They're going to fight hard to hold on to their ill-gotten gains, just as the British tried to hold on to their colonies. The celebration ends today. It's time to prepare for Trump's War.

Only we won't be fighting on battlefields with rifles. We will be fighting an entrenched Establishment whose weapons of mass destruction are far more devious than those of King George III. Instead of cannons and muskets, the Establishment uses a corrupt media and an insidious network of violent agitators to wage a psychological war, instead of a military one. Instead of shelling your town, they seek to imprison your mind with political correctness, envy politics, and intimidation.

The riots started before Trump even took office. Just days after his election, the George Soros–funded network of brownshirts took to the streets to block traffic,[1] loot businesses,[2] and assault anyone suspected of having voted for Trump.[3] It was just a continuation of the street violence that has proliferated under Emperor Barry's anti-police, anti-American regime.

You may not realize how bad it was, because the lying media didn't call any of this rioting. No, these brownshirt street thugs were "protesters."[4] They were "exercising their First Amendment rights." Can you believe that? For weeks after the third presidential debate, all we heard from the News Klux Klan (NKK) was the potential for violence from Trump supporters if he didn't accept the results of the election. Now, when Hatchet Hillary's supporters actually commit violence in the streets, they're called protesters instead of rioters. It's like something out of Orwell.

Let's not forget these aren't spontaneous, grassroots uprisings by honestly concerned liberals. These are organized, criminal mobs, funded by George Soros[5] to wreak chaos on American cities. NKK conspirator *USA Today* tried to discredit claims the protests were organized professionally, but WikiLeaks showed it were lying.[6] They named three different people who were supposedly just "concerned citizens from all walks of life." But they were all people John Podesta identified as professional activists and Democratic Party operatives in his leaked e-mails.

Violence is an integral part of the left-wing worldview. As I've said for decades, including in many of my books, their only vision is "Burn it down, baby." They haven't changed since the French Revolution in 1789, a bloody reign of terror that lasted a decade.

But Trump isn't just fighting the Jacobin left. He's also fighting the Establishment in his own party, which in many ways is even more dangerous than the Democrats. We know what we're up against with the Democrats. They're honest about their hatred of American culture and their desire to "transform" America from a free country of capitalism, individual liberty, and Western values to a totalitarian state of socialism, collectivism, and multicultural chaos.

Republicans claim to oppose all of this, but what have they actually done? Did George W. Bush make any effort to secure our borders? No. Did he stand up for free markets? No. When corporate thieves ripped off investors with fraudulent accounting early in his presidency, Bush responded with the Sarbanes-Oxley Act, saying it was "the most far-reaching reforms of American business practices since the time of Franklin Delano Roosevelt."[7]

When the Federal Reserve blew up the housing bubble, exacerbated by the Community Reinvestment Act, did Bush put the blame where it belonged? No. He said, "Wall Street got drunk,"[8] and then bailed out all his friends with TARP, instead of letting them go bankrupt and get taken over by the people who didn't gamble on risky securities.

What about all those young, true conservatives we elected in 2012? Do you remember them? I have a list of their names. Did the Republican leadership support them? No. They got stabbed in the back by Boehner and McConnell, who went along with the Democrats on virtually everything. Now their altar boy Rinso Priebus is chief of staff.

Immediately following Trump's acceptance speech, Mitch McConnell was in front of the media saying the Republican

Senate was not going to support any of Trump's First 100 Days Agenda, except for repealing Obamacare.[9] Term limits for Congress? Forget it. The border wall? No. TPP? Too late. NATO? We like it just fine how it is.

DRAINING THE SWAMP

There's an old legend that Washington, D.C., was built on a swamp. The enlightened ones over at the *Washington Post* say[10] that's not literally true. But it sure is true figuratively. In addition to all the horrible idealogues, from insane liberals to bloodthirsty neoconservatives to ivory tower academics, there is also the oozing sludge of plain old corruption, drowning any honest attempt to represent the people in its filthy slime.

McConnell doesn't want to drain the swamp. Why would he? He's a swamp dweller, like his co-conspirators John "the Deranged Drunk" Boehner and Paul "Obama's Beard" Ryan. They're all part of the bought-and-sold Republican Party, which is wholly owned by Wall Street and corporate America.

We found out just how deep the swamp water was on the very first day of business for the new Republican Congress. Was their first order of business to introduce a bill cutting taxes, or authorize funds to build the border wall Americans elected Trump to build, or even to repeal Obamacare, the one thing even Turkey Gobbler McConnell said the RINOs would work with Trump to do?

No. Before the echoes from the first gavel had even subsided, they had moved to weaken the independent Office of Congressional Ethics (OCE), an office created in 2008 to address widespread scandals and corruption in Congress. They sought to turn the independent board into a review panel that answered to the House Ethics Committee, whose ineffectiveness was the whole reason the OCE was created in the first place.

Perhaps you don't remember how bad things had become before the board was created. I do. I remember when the FBI raided Louisiana Democrat representative William Jefferson's home and found $90,000 in his freezer.[11] Jefferson was convicted of eleven counts of corruption, including soliciting bribes and other crimes.[12]

But those convicted are only the tip of the iceberg. They are the ones arrogant, unlucky, or stupid enough to get caught. The entire capital is a self-serving cesspool of graft, quid pro quo, and backroom deals. It's corporations offering future jobs to regulators in exchange for the privilege of writing the regulations that give them an artificial advantage in the market. It's the revolving door between Wall Street and Washington, where certain bankers become high-ranking government officials and then return to reap the rewards of the deals they did while in public office.

The good news is Trump won the first skirmish against the RINOs seeking to give themselves a Get-Out-of-Jail-Free card on their first day in office. Using his signature response weapon, the well-timed tweet, Trump called the Republican Congress to task for making this the first order of business in a year where the people's expectations were so high. And the RINOs backed down[13]—this time. The OCE was kept intact and operating just as it has for the past eight years.

But it's a sign Trump and his supporters are going to have to be vigilant. We're going to have to watch these snakes every minute for four to eight long years because they've already shown whose side they're on—their own.

In addition to the liberals, the neocons, the war profiteers, the corporate lobbyists, and the evil of the place itself, Donald Trump must fight what, again, might be the most formidable enemy he faces: temptation. The temptation to be assimilated into the Washington swamp, instead of draining it, is powerful. How many conservatives in the past have gone to Washington intending to change it and ended up being changed themselves instead? How many have heard the siren song of easy money and privilege, if only they would go along to get along?

Trump doesn't need the money, but he's a businessman. As he's said himself during the campaign, he gets along with everyone. That's how you build a successful business in the private sector, because the private sector works on cooperation and mutual benefit. Business owners get wealthier when they please customers.

Washington works on precisely the opposite incentives. The insiders cooperate with each other, but to the detriment of the public, not its benefit. Getting anything done at all usually means compromising your principles and betraying your constituents. Trump not only has the opposing party to deal with; he has lifelong insiders in his own administration who don't know another way to play the game.

Two days after Trump's election, the consummate insider, Newt Gingrich, was already equivocating on Trump's first promise: to build a wall on the southern border and get Mexico to pay for it. Getting Mexico to pay was just a "great campaign device," according to Gingrich.[14] The following Saturday, Trump was backing up on the wall itself.[15] Now, the wall might just be a fence. What does that mean? A cyclone fence? A picket fence? Maybe the Mexicans will carry the pickets with them into Arizona and put them where they want.

There was more backpedaling from Trump's appointees during their confirmation hearings. Secretary of state nominee Rex Tillerson said he supported the Trans-Pacific Partnership (TPP), even though opposing it was a key plank of Trump's economic platform. Defense secretary nominee James Mattis sounded more like Hillary Clinton on NATO and Russia and said he thought the Iran deal was "workable."[16]

Tillerson and CIA director nominee Mike Pompeo were also hawkish on Russia, sounding more like neocon ventriloquists than Trump nominees with their comments on Ukraine, hacking, and the nonexistent Russian threat to Europe.[17]

Homeland security secretary nominee John Kelly said "undocumented children who are part of the Deferred Action for Childhood Arrivals (DACA) program would 'probably not be at the top of the list' and that he would 'keep an open mind.'"[18]

Keep an open mind on illegal immigration? Who appointed this man, Trump or Obama?

There were too many departures from Trump's platform for me to list them all. They were so striking that Trump himself apparently felt he had to cover for them on Twitter.

A January 13 tweet read, "All of my Cabinet nominee [sic] are looking good and doing a great job. I want them to be themselves and express their own thoughts, not mine!"[19]

Trump erased all doubt that he personally would follow through on his key promises by signing several executive orders during his very first week, including withdrawing from TPP, building the wall, a freeze on nonmilitary federal employees, defunding international organizations who perform abortions, banning cabinet members from lobbying for life, and suspending immigration from countries already identified as hotbeds of radical Islamic terrorism. He faced opposition on all of them, the most hostile regarding his suspension of immigration from Iraq, Syria, Iran, Libya, Somalia, Sudan, and Yemen.[20]

Not surprisingly, the executive action most beneficial to U.S. citizens is the one most resisted by the globalists in the swamp. Immediately, the ACLU got a federal judge to partially undermine Trump's order on a legal technicality that may eventually be overturned.[21] In general, the executive order follows the 1952 Immigration and Nationality Act, the relevant sections of which were never overturned by subsequent immigration law. In fact, contrary to what is being reported by many of the fake news outlets lined up against Trump, Obama signed legislation extending the president's authority in this area.[22]

Still, these were huge victories for us. We just need to maintain our resolve because the enemies within are going to try to overturn every one of these actions by Trump by any means possible. And the liberal media will wage a nonstop propaganda war to weaken our commitment.

We can't expect one hundred percent of what he promised, but we must ensure the main campaign promises are fulfilled. they include the wall, jobs, deporting illegal alien prisoners, banning Muslims from certain countries where radical Islamic terrorism is prevalent, lowering taxes, protecting our right to bear arms, dumping Obamacare, rebuilding our military, protecting our religious beliefs from radicals, stopping late-term abortion, just to name a few key promises. I will continue to do my job as a member of the Fourth Estate: to be a thorn in the government's side, even Donald Trump's government, if it goes off course. I will need your help. The Savage Nation put Donald Trump in office. That was just the first battle. Now we're going to have to win the war.

In the ensuing chapters of this book, I am going to be examining the initial appointments, speeches, tweets, and history of Donald Trump and offering my insights and analysis. But analysis is not enough. We need to take action. At the beginning of each chapter, I am going to summarize the "Savage Solutions" needed to restore and reclaim this nation, which is presently teetering on the edge of the abyss. We need to stand behind Trump and, when necessary, hold his feet to the fire, to ensure the vital work gets done. As with the election, it's the Savage Nation that can make the difference.

SAVAGE SOLUTIONS

★ Cut taxes, unshackle American
corporations and citizens.

★ Quit NAFTA at once, just as
he did with TPP.

★ Employment mandate for America:
foreigners need not apply.

★ Immediately rebuild infrastructure
through private investment.

CHAPTER TWO

TRUMP'S ECONOMIC WAR

Donald Trump and Bernie Sanders agree on one thing: The economy is rigged. It's rigged for rich special interests and against the rest of America. Wall Street keeps getting richer and Main Street is, for the first time in American history, getting poorer. On that much, Donald Trump, Bernie Sanders, and even Michael Savage agree.

We disagree on what to do about it. Comrade Bernie thinks we need even more socialism. Unfortunately, a lot of young people agree with him. Donald Trump and I believe exactly the opposite.

What we need is more *true* capitalism, as opposed to the pro-big-business, crony capitalism we have now. Pro-business and capitalism are not the same thing. Capitalism has open competition and people suffer losses when they make bad decisions. What we have now are sellout deals that restrict competition and bailouts whenever the gamblers make a bad bet.

The elites like to call Trump a "populist," implying he's an anti-capitalist demagogue promising to protect uneducated rubes from the natural consequences of the free market. That's a lie. It's the special interests who get protection from natural market forces and Trump's coming to take it away. He's going to try to restore the one thing the elites fear most: a level playing field for every American.

TRADE TRAITORS

On Donald Trump's first business day as president of the United States, he signed an executive order pulling the United States out of the Trans-Pacific Partnership (TPP) trade deal. He immediately faced criticism for keeping this promise to his supporters from Democrats and Republicans, who were all suddenly academic free-market purists when Trump sided with the American people over the special interests.

Let me let you in on some more history they didn't have time to teach you while you were studying climate change in school. In addition to government-funded roads and infrastructure, the Republican Party originally supported high tariffs. Like infrastructure, they inherited this idea from the Whig Party, but it really started all the way back with Alexander Hamilton and the Federalists. The Federalists, Whigs, and Republicans all wanted high tariffs to give American manufacturing a chance to grow out of its infancy, without having to compete with more established manufacturing abroad.

So, when you hear Republicans opposing Trump on his America-first trade policies, you should know it's Trump who is being true to the GOP's founding principles, not the sell-outs. But Trump isn't even proposing the kind of protection-ism Republicans in the past proposed. America isn't in the same position it was back then.

Trump has said many times he's all for "free trade," but it must be fair. This has been my position for decades. A true free-trade deal would only have to be a sentence or two long. It would simply say all signatories agree they will not impose tar-iffs or quotas on imports and won't subsidize domestic manu-facturers nor manipulate their currency to give them an artifi-cial advantage. Period. That's free trade.

That's not what the North American Free Trade Agree-ment (NAFTA) or the Trans-Pacific Partnership (TPP) is. If you haven't read them, I'll give you a hint. They're a little more than two sentences long. They're thousands of pages long because they're full of all sorts of backroom deals for estab-lished corporations to get rich and leave American workers behind. And they don't offer the same benefits to the United States that they do to the other trading partners.

For example, when NAFTA was signed, it eliminated tar-iffs on half of all Mexican imports into the United States, but only one-third of U.S. exports into Mexico.[1] Right off the bat the United States agreed to an unequal exchange, based on Mexico being a poorer country that needed America's help to catch up.

This is a recurring theme with the progressive globalists. They believe wealth should be redistributed from First World countries to the Third World through all sorts of schemes.[2]

You wouldn't find Democrats backing a "free trade" deal unless there was a welfare component. For them, it's all about redistributing wealth from rich countries like the United States to destitute countries, which are of course all nobler than evil white America, no matter why they are destitute.

Even the climate change hoax is largely about international wealth redistribution,[3] but that is a subject for another chapter.

Even with NAFTA fully implemented, it's still slanted toward the poorest of the three trading partners. American exporters must comply with rigorous environmental, safety, and quality regulations. Certainly, the United States is vastly overregulated, but trading partners like Mexico represent the other extreme. NAFTA protects Mexico from scrutiny of its compliance with emission tests, quality controls, and other regulations.[4]

That's why multinationals are so eager to move to Mexico to do their manufacturing. They can do it for a fraction of the cost, partially because poor Mexicans will work for nothing and partially because they don't have to comply with any regulations, or at least not to the extent they must here.

The worst part of deals like NAFTA and TPP is the threat they represent to our national sovereignty. Our Constitution delegates all legislative power to Congress. That means it prohibits legislative power to the other two branches. Many have argued our regulatory agencies are unconstitutional because they represent the executive legislating. Emperor Soetoro made that somewhat moot when he started legislating himself, with his pen and phone.

But NAFTA, TPP, and similar "free trade" deals do even worse than that. They delegate legislative power away from our elected government completely, bestowing it upon unelected, international regulatory boards. That was one of the key issues with Brexit. The Europeans were promised the European Union would not undermine their sovereignty. That promise was broken.

By the time the Brits voted to get out of the European Union, Brussels was regulating everything from medicine and housing to what's on their fruit juice labels.[5] As Tory MP Peter Bone said: "We cannot do anything about this legislation. We cannot amend it, we are powerless to stop it. It is fundamentally undemocratic."[6]

NAFTA and TPP have all the same, undemocratic, internationalist mechanisms built in. They give everybody what they want. The socialists get an international, redistributive, regulatory state with no national borders or local sovereignty. It's another step on the road for them to Marx's international communist utopia.

The multinational corporations benefit because they can increasingly ignore the rights and prerogatives of people in any particular nation and just lobby the international regulatory bodies to get what they want. That's a lot less expensive and a lot less complicated for them. With NAFTA, TPP, and the European Union, they only have to lobby three governments instead of 190.

That's where the globalists were taking us. There was just one problem. The little people are smarter than the globalists figured. First with Brexit and then Trump's electoral victory, the little people stood up and said they wanted their countries back. And there are more shots heard round the world coming. Marine Le Pen is now the front-runner in France.[7] Even the socialist Justin Trudeau in Canada faces the threat of a nationalist backlash.[8]

The smug elites like to paint the nationalists as parochial rubes who don't know what is good for them. They call us "populists" and even imply we're against free markets. That's a lie. Free markets don't involve huge corporations getting advantages over their competition from international regulatory bodies that override national sovereignty. A true free market protects property rights and freedom of entry into the market for everyone.

The TPP deal was NAFTA on steroids, because it involved twelve new countries to which the multinationals can export U.S. jobs. If you think competing with Mexico is tough on U.S. jobs, just wait until it's Malaysia. Even Bangladesh has expressed an interest. Maybe Apple will move there and pay people in food to build iPhones.

TPP also brought with it the same assaults on national sovereignty as NAFTA and the EU brought to North Americans and Europeans, respectively. It was just another piece of the global socialist puzzle.

The Marxist in Chief pushed hard for this deal. He signed it last February but it was never passed by Congress. Even the Turkey Gobbler was too afraid to push it through the Senate in a lame-duck session[9] and Obama gave up on pursuing it.

But that doesn't mean it wouldn't have been back if Trump hadn't killed it on his first business day in office. Remember, the Republicans were overwhelmingly in favor of it just a year ago and as soon as their fear of the voters wears off, they'll surely start thinking about their corporate donors again.

Trump's economic plan takes a flamethrower to the international socialist-corporatist takeover. This isn't anti-capitalist; it's pro-capitalist. While he wants to get tougher on trade, he recognizes American corporations are not evil in and of themselves. That's why he wants to eliminate as much unnecessary regulation as he can. He's not a socialist Democrat who wants to use regulation as an excuse to kill all for-profit businesses as enemies of Gaia.

Neither is he a typical Republican who will sell out American workers to the multinationals and let them maximize profits by manufacturing in destitute countries with rock-bottom wage rates and no regulation at all. He's looking to provide an environment that is fair to American workers, fair to American corporations, and responsible on safety and the environment. It's not Republican or Democrat. It's America First.

Trump has said repeatedly what I've been saying for decades: If you don't have borders, you don't have a country. That also applies to sovereignty over the legislative process. If an unelected, international regulatory board is making your laws, instead of your own, elected representatives, you don't have a country, either.

Trump promised he would pull out of TPP on "Day One,"[10] And he did. The Monday following his inauguration, he wrote an executive order withdrawing the United States from the deal.[11] He also placed a hiring freeze on some federal workers and defunded international groups that perform abortions.[12]

That promise was crucial and Trump came through with flying colors, unlike the RINOs in Congress who stabbed us in the back repeatedly over the past four years. Trump had to follow through on trade and immigration or we elected him for nothing. I said, "Don't expect to get one hundred percent of what he promised; expect to get fifty percent, or at least more than we've been getting." This and withdrawal from or renegotiation of NAFTA were the people's "red lines." On January 23, we won half that battle.

TAXATION AND REGULATION WITH SELLOUT REPRESENTATION

Just like the rigged trade deals, Washington and corporate America have completely rigged our tax code. The United States has the third-highest statutory tax rate in the world at 38.92 percent. Only the United Arab Emirates and Puerto Rico are higher. But the corporations don't pay that rate. They pay an "effective tax rate" of about 23 percent.[13] A lot of the disparity comes from legitimate business expense deductions. But not all of it.

Here is the kicker. Even though the statutory U.S. corporate tax rates are about ten percentage points higher than the average rates for the other thirty-three developed countries in the Organisation for Economic Co-operation and Development (OECD), U.S. effective corporate tax rates are about the same as the average among those countries. That means the U.S. corporations are finding a way to reduce their headline tax rate far more than the rest of the developed world.

Does that mean U.S. companies have much higher business expenses? To some degree, yes. A lot of those welfare utopias in Europe have much freer markets in terms of regulation.[14] They have higher taxes, when you include value-added taxes (VAT) and personal income taxes combined, and they pay out more generous welfare benefits, but they have less regulation in many areas. Europe is moving away from socialism in this regard. Regulations have a cost and U.S. companies must absorb those costs just to do business.

But higher regulatory costs aren't the whole story. The other component in that huge disparity is loopholes. The U.S. tax code is riddled with loopholes to allow special interests to avoid or lower taxes under very specific circumstances. What you must understand about this system is it's very anticompetitive.

Corporations don't pay huge sums to lobbyists to help even the playing field for them and all their competitors. They pay lobbyists to get them an advantage over their competitors. This is why the tax code is more than seventy thousand pages long.[15] It's rigged.

Let me give you the *reductio ad absurdum* example to make my point. Suppose I taxed every company at 100 percent of gross revenues, except one. For that one business, taxes were 15 percent. Obviously, that one business with the 15 percent tax rate would be the only one that could stay open. It would have a pure monopoly on all business, a 100 percent market share.

Well, our tax code operates on the same principle, albeit to a less absurd extreme. We start out at a ridiculously high tax rate that no business could pay and remain competitive. Then the corporations that can afford it send an army of lobbyists to Washington to carve out exceptions for themselves. We call those exceptions "loopholes," because they are a way to wiggle out of the taxes the law says the corporation owes. While they're at it, each firm lobbies for loopholes that give it a leg up on its competitors.

Are you starting to see how the game works? First, only corporations that can afford lobbyists are even in the game. That gives the biggest and most-connected companies an immediate advantage over their smaller competitors. But let me let you in on a secret. The big multinationals' most dangerous competition isn't their peers or even their smaller competitors. It's the business that doesn't exist yet.

The Larry Ellisons and Tim Cooks of the world wanted a free market when they were on the outside, trying to break into the business world with new ideas. But now that they're on top, they seem to want to rig the game against their younger counterparts wherever they can.

The tech giants came into the business world in the 1980s and 1990s and disrupted everything. They put old, established companies out of business, but they created millions of new jobs that never existed before. And the economy grew, just as it did when the automobile industry put all the blacksmiths out of business.

What new businesses ready to do the same thing are out there now, unable to create new, higher-paying jobs, partially because of our rigged tax code? We don't know. We won't know until we get rid of this corrupt system and let new businesses compete on an even playing field.

The regulatory structure is basically a mirror image of the tax code in this respect. Liberals are always pushing for more regulation on businesses, while at the same time complaining there is too much consolidation, making the giant corporations even bigger. They don't understand that the first problem causes the second.

Just like high taxes they can't afford to lobby their way around, many new businesses can't afford the cost of compliance with our gargantuan regulatory state. An Exxon or an Apple has the economies of scale to hire a floor full of lawyers; but the Steve Jobs or Jeff Bezos of tomorrow does not.

That's why established corporations always end up supporting new regulations in the end. They may complain when they're first proposed, but that's just maneuvering for position on their part. In the end, they know they'll help write the regulations, which they'll lace with all kinds of favors for themselves. And the costlier compliance becomes, the more protected they are from new or smaller competitors.

This is what Bernie Sanders' misguided supporters don't understand. More regulation protects big business and the 1 percent. Cutting regulation allows the little guys they care about to compete.

Don't misunderstand me. Like Trump, I don't think corporations are evil in and of themselves. I'm not a 1930s street corner communist like Bernie. It's the game that's rigged. Just as Trump tried to tell the other Marxist Hillary

Clinton during one of the debates: businessmen play by the rules Washington makes. They have a responsibility to their shareholders to maximize profits within those rules. And faced with a 38 percent tax rate and a *Federal Register* full of regulations with more pages than even the tax code, this is the only way to survive.

This all starts with the liberals, for whom no tax is too high and no amount of regulation too burdensome. Liberals say they want high taxes to help the poor and heavy regulation to protect workers and the environment. But what they really want is to attack free enterprise and private property everywhere they can. Taxes and regulation are weapons in their Marxist arsenal.

Don't forget that liberals once had personal income taxes as high as 91 percent[16] and industry was once even more regulated than it is now. They created the environment that corrupted the business world. It's just got to the point where big corporations don't really have any other choice than to play the rigged game by its corrupt rules.

All you'll hear from the liberals about Donald Trump's tax plan[17] is that it benefits the rich. But what it actually does is rip out the rigging I've just described. First, it lowers the headline rate to 15 percent, which is even lower than America's competitors. But just as important, it eliminates a huge portion of the seventy thousand pages of loopholes written into the tax code for special interests. Taking away favors for big business makes the system more capitalist, not less. It allows small businesses to compete on a more even playing field.

That's why you can expect stiff resistance from many Republicans on it, too. They'll be all for lowering the headline tax rate to 15 percent, but they'll want their friends in big business to keep all their special favors. Every loophole in those seventy thousand pages of tax code was put there by a lobbyist who bought off a congressman, a lot of them Republicans. They're not going to give them up without a fight.

The rigged tax code is just another form of slime in the swamp and Republicans will call Trump a closet liberal for wanting to drain that particular slime out of it. Remember when Trump called out hedge fund managers on their own little loophole?[18] Suddenly they sounded like liberals, attacking Trump for not giving enough to charity. Some of them openly endorsed Hillary Clinton.[19]

What does Trump's charitable donations have to do with hedge fund managers being allowed to pay the capital gains rate instead of the income tax rate the rest of them pay? Nothing. They just don't want to give up their government favors. RINOs call Trump a "populist" and imply he's liberal or even socialist for attacking this loophole, but that's the opposite of the truth. Eliminating that loophole is making the system more capitalist, because it eliminates an artificial advantage the hedge fund managers have over other investment professionals.

I believe we need taxation, but it has to be realistic. The maximum federal tax, which should be a flat tax, in my opinion, should be 20 percent. Everybody should pay 20 percent of their income to the federal government, including those on government pensions and disability. Hedge fund managers and those receiving dividend income should also pay 20 percent. There isn't anything substantively different about dividend income from wages or salaries. It's just that the people who receive large dividend incomes have always had the connections to have their taxes lowered, while everyone else pays through the nose.

One tax we don't need is the so-called death tax. Readers of my last two books may remember that Russia and China have no inheritance taxes. We're told Russia is a dictatorship. We're told China is a communist country. Well, neither the Russians nor the Chinese pay an inheritance tax. Meanwhile, here in criminal America, Comrade Barack Hussein raised the so-called death tax surreptitiously through Treasury Department regulations after Congress had lowered it during the George W. Bush years.[20]

It's not surprising our communist former president sought to raise the inheritance tax. "Abolition of all rights of inheritance" is the third of Karl Marx's Ten Planks of *The Communist Manifesto*.[21] Allowing people to pass to their children the wealth they've accumulated from a lifetime of hard work helps build a thriving, wealthy, self-sufficient populace over time. There isn't much opportunity for the envy-peddling socialists in an affluent, upwardly mobile society.

I want Donald Trump to eliminate the inheritance tax completely and I'll tell you why. Let's say you work all your life and build a family business. Or perhaps you have a family farm and you want to give it to your daughter. If your farm is appraised above a certain value, your daughter will be driven off her own farm because she'd have to pay the criminals in the government up to 40 percent of its value in order to keep the inheritance. She'd have to sell the farm to afford the farm, which is obviously self-defeating. I'm going to lobby very hard for elimination of this tax during the Trump administration.

EDDIE NEEDS A FAIR MINIMUM WAGE

While I support vastly reducing regulations in general, I am concerned about the new secretary of labor, fast-food CEO Andrew Puzder. He's for abolishing all regulations, including the minimum wage. He believes getting rid of the minimum wages will create jobs.

I have a different opinion on this than he and many other conservatives. It's easy to say, "I'm against a minimum wage" in principle, letting the market decide the price of labor. That's easy to say when you're a millionaire talk show host. But if you're actually working for minimum wage, would you like to see it go down and argue that it's free-market capitalism? Do academic concepts pay your light bill or put food on your table?

Anyone who takes a purely academic view on this should try working for minimum wage first and see if they still cling so hard to their dogmatic theories. I was poor when I was young and I worked several minimum-wage jobs. I certainly didn't like the pay. I would have liked to have made what the owner made, which isn't as much as most people think. Owners of the kinds of small businesses I worked for weren't millionaires, either, whether it was a pharmacy or luncheonette or similar business.

I took the jobs because I was glad to get them and learned what one benefit of minimum wage is: to motivate you to want to make more money. You get to the point where you say to yourself, "I can't stand this minimum-wage job," and you struggle to get a job where you can earn more. In order to do that, you have to acquire more valuable skills, so employers can afford to pay you more money. It motivates you to want to pull yourself up from the bottom of the labor scale. It's that simple.

So, the market works even with a minimum wage in place. If you're going to be dogmatic about the market, where is the limit? Would you like to see child labor reintroduced? Shall we have children working in factories around the clock, working for a dollar an hour?

There has to be some bottom to the labor cost. We can't just let it be driven into the ground. We can see what the thieves in Silicon Valley are doing, throwing American workers out of jobs to bring in people from India to work for less. Is that what you want going on across America?

We need to be very careful with academic theories. Conservatives can be just as detached from reality as liberals on a few of these points. Unless you've worked for minimum wage yourself, you don't understand what I'm talking about. If you were born into a family that took care of you from birth until you graduated from graduate school or medical school or law school, you frankly don't know what you're talking about when discussing the minimum wage.

You need to have worked a minimum-wage job, to have ridden the bus in the slush to two jobs and then gone to school when you weren't working to know what I'm talking about. You had to have tried to raise a family while working two jobs and sleeping five hours a night before you can make an informed decision on the minimum wage.

We already threw Eddie under the bus by being dogmatic about academic free-trade theories, without taking into account how these trade deals with destitute countries would affect him. Now Trump has to try to go back and renegotiate those trade deals to be more equitable to the people in this country. We certainly don't want to throw away everything we gain on trade by allowing corporations to drive wages down to what they're paying people in Malaysia.

INFRASTRUCTURE

We are going to see something in the Trump administration that many of you are going to gag on: a trillion dollars in infrastructure spending. Many will say "Oh, no! You can't do that! It's going to blow out the budget, expand the deficit, blah, blah, blah . . . "

I want to say, "Wait a minute. Slow down." There are different types of government spending. Even many conservatives don't understand that not all expenditures are equal. If you spend a trillion dollars on welfare, by and large it's money lost. It's true the money goes into the economy, to a certain extent, but it doesn't create anything. A lot of it is sent overseas. It's kind of a negative form of government spending.

Of all the money Obama ripped off to give his "investors," meaning his crony capitalist supporters, has anyone seen a single road, a single bridge, or a single tunnel? No, because there virtually weren't any built.

Franklin Delano Roosevelt, who was a socialist, no question about that, created the Works Progress Administration (WPA) under his "New Deal." It affected my family long before I was born. My father was poor. He was one of tens of millions of unemployed Americans and an immigrant. He got a government job under Roosevelt's program. He was a chauffeur for a local assemblyman.

I don't even know how he got the job and he's been dead many years now, so I can't ask him. He wasn't a political guy. I do remember him telling me about driving an assemblyman around Saratoga Springs, New York. He was able to put food on the table because of it.

Today, I drive through tunnels here in San Francisco and see the amazing tile work. I see LaGuardia Airport in New York and the Ronald Reagan National Washington Airport in Washington, D.C. I see the Florida Keys Overseas Highway, the Bonneville Dam on the Columbia River, and the Upper Mississippi locks and dams. These were all built by the federal government. These are all part of the infrastructure that made America great.

Donald Trump is a builder and he's promised to rebuild our infrastructure. We know our bridges and roads are a disaster and our airports worse than those in Third World countries. They're not going to rebuild themselves.

The immediate, knee-jerk reaction from the knee-jerkers is going to be, "Oh! You can't do this! It's new debt! No deficit spending! Government can never, under any situation, do anything right!"

Let me tell you something. There are two types of spending. According to a study by Wilbur Ross,[22] if you spend $1 trillion rebuilding infrastructure, you'll add $2 trillion to the economy. In other words, the $1 trillion invested would generate an additional $1 trillion return on investment (ROI).

Obama never studied ROI in Marxism 101. He was too busy learning the wonderful benefits of marching and destroying.

Trump will be attacked from the right and the left on his infrastructure plan, but it's going to create good-paying, productive jobs. I'm not talking about Walmart greeter jobs, where you can say hello to people coming to buy cheap garbage made by the people in China your former employer shipped your old job to. I'm talking about jobs making things like we used to in this country before the Republicrats sold us out.

THE FORGOTTEN MAN

Like Roosevelt, Trump referred many times during his campaign to "the forgotten men and women." Trump was talking about those millions of hardworking Americans who have lost their jobs and can't find a new one thanks to the wrecked economy, compliments of the sellout Republicans and Marxist Democrats.

You may be familiar with Roosevelt's speeches about the "forgotten man," but I'll bet you don't know where he got that idea. Roosevelt was actually borrowing from a famous writer of the nineteenth and early twentieth centuries named William Graham Sumner. Only, Roosevelt got it wrong, perhaps intentionally. Roosevelt's forgotten man was anyone unemployed or in need, for any reason. He engaged in the usual liberal class warfare and made the forgotten man anyone who was poor, while blaming it all on those evil rich people who employ everyone.

Roosevelt evoked his forgotten man to win support not only for tax-funded infrastructure programs, but for all sorts of welfare programs as well. As I said, Roosevelt was a socialist. But Sumner wasn't referring to the needy in his essay. For Sumner, the forgotten man was the taxpayer, the man who pays for all the politicians' programs. He wrote about how, when X is suffering, A & B always get together to pass laws forcing C to help X. C was Sumner's forgotten man. He called him "the victim of the reformer, social speculator and philanthropist."[23]

The problem with Republicans and Democrats is they are so bought and sold by special interests they are compelled to take one side or the other. They are either on the side of Roosevelt's forgotten man or Sumner's, the poor and middle class or the rich. It is beyond their comprehension—and against their interests—to consider taking both sides.

Donald Trump's infrastructure does just that. It sides with the forgotten men and women who are out of work and the taxpayer. Unlike Roosevelt's infrastructure spending, Trump's plan will be, for the most part, privately funded and built. Only $167 billion of the $1 trillion over ten years will be guaranteed by the government, in what his plan calls an "equity cushion." To incentivize the rest, he plans on granting tax breaks to investors in infrastructure equaling 82 percent of the equity amount.

In other words, Trump's plan will benefit forgotten men, the unemployed man or woman, and the taxpayer. You can do that when specials interests for one side or the other don't own you body and soul. In fact, taxpayers won't be harmed at all by Trump's plan because the income taxes from new jobs and profits for the contractors will cover the government portion of the investment, with private investors taking the risk on the rest.

It's a win-win for both forgotten groups, but it is already under attack by jackals from the left and right. Of course, you know what the liberals are going to say. Bernie Sanders says it's just a "corporate giveaway."[24] What a surprise. That academic crank Paul Krugman at the *New York Times* says it's just another scam because the government isn't doing the spending.[25]

What could we expect from either of these avowed socialists? Krugman won a Nobel Prize in economics from the same people who gave Obama a peace prize. He's called for going back to a 91 percent top income tax rate and basically supported everything Obama has done to lay waste to our economy and everything Hillary Clinton wanted to do to make it worse.

It always galls me when liberals talk about "tax cuts for the rich." Who do they think pays most of the taxes? You can't cut taxes for people who don't pay taxes. How do you cut zero?

You can expect more of the same from all the usual suspects on the left. Anything with a private component is off the table for the Marxists, no matter how much it might help those middle-class working people they claim to care so much about. Republicans want to privatize everything and Democrats want to socialize everything. The Democrats won't even listen to a suggestion to give the private sector a crack at this. Neither will a lot of Republicans. This despite everyone acknowledging the government has failed!

TURNPIKES

Long forgotten down the memory hole is America's former, private road system. I'll bet you didn't know that for the first eighty or so years after the Constitution was ratified, most roads and infrastructure were built just as Donald Trump is suggesting they be built now: by private companies investing their own funds and running them for profit.[26]

Anyone who has driven in the Northeast has traveled on a "turnpike." But I'll bet not one in a thousand knows what the word *turnpike* means. *Pike* is another word for pole and the roads are called turnpikes because, when they were first built, they were all toll roads run by private companies. They'd have a long pole, a pike, across the road and when you paid the toll, they'd turn the pike to open the road and let you pass. It's similar to the turnstiles at modern subway systems. You pay the fee and the turnstile rotates to let you through.

Just to be clear, I'm not talking about today's system where the money for the road is collected in taxes and the government hires and pays a contractor to complete the road in the longest time and at the greatest expense possible. I'm talking about private investors funding the road themselves and taking the risk that the revenue generated will provide a return on their investment. That's what Trump is suggesting. That's how roads were built in this country until the Republicans first gained power after the Civil War.[27]

Government infrastructure was originally a basic plank of the Republican Party. They had wanted the government to take over roads and infrastructure for generations, when many of the founders of the party were Whigs. Nobody remembers any of this because all they know about the Republicans in the nineteenth century is that they ended slavery. That they fundamentally changed the role of government in infrastructure is largely forgotten.

It seemed to work for many generations. Eisenhower is remembered for building the Interstate Highway System. FDR's New Deal infrastructure program very much borrowed pages out of the Republican Party playbook. But was it really better than the original, more American idea Trump is revisiting now? Maybe it's worth a try to find out. We know that what we're doing now isn't working.

It's not like this would be some radical, fundamental change. We already have privately owned roads, bridges, and other infrastructure in this country now. We've even allowed foreign companies to own and operate our ports.[28] They're all making profits and providing excellent service while the government infrastructure loses money and is falling apart. What could we possibly have to lose by letting American companies take a crack at this?

The Democrats will fight this tooth and nail. They don't even want health care sold in the private market. They're certainly not going to entertain the idea infrastructure can be, too. Thank goodness Trump's fellow Republicans will come to his defense, right?

Wrong. We know Turkey Gobbler McConnell said the Senate wasn't going to cooperate with Trump on anything, except "maybe" repealing Obamacare.[29] Paul "Obama's Beard" Ryan found the suggestion knee-slapping funny.[30] They are the gatekeepers for the sellouts in Congress. It's almost as important to get them out of the way as it was to defeat Hillary Clinton. What good is having a nationalist executive if Congress won't give him anything but liberal-globalist policies to execute?

Half the problem is that many Republicans don't even seem to know what Trump is suggesting. They haven't read his policy paper, so they're talking about his infrastructure plan as if it's the same old Roosevelt-style tax-and-spend plan Hillary Clinton was proposing. Democratic congressmen are trained like parrots to yell "racist!" no matter what a Republican says and Republicans are trained to yell "Deficit spending!" no matter what a Democrat proposes.

So, here we have a Republican who is not like any Republican or Democrat we've elected in generations and he's thinking of the country first and his party second. But without even reading his revenue-neutral plan, Republican congressmen just yell "Deficits!" when they hear the word *infrastructure*.

They are a lot of mindless vermin dwelling in the slime of the swamp.

Anyone who has listened to my show, *The Savage Nation,* or read any of my previous books knows I am not just a Republican parrot, squawking "Privatize it!" with the rest of the flock whenever the Republicans want to hook up one of their corporate donors. Privatization certainly can have a downside in some situations.

Just ask the townspeople of St. George, off the Bering Sea near Alaska. The experiment with privatizing the ocean has cut them out of their birthright to fish their own waters.[31] And it hasn't necessarily solved the problem of extinctions due to overfishing, even if the pedantic think tankers who dreamed it up thought it looked good on paper. There may be a private solution to overfishing; there may need to be a government solution. Granting property rights to the ocean is unexplored territory and true conservatives should proceed with caution, respecting the long-established local rights that should be the starting point for any new policy.

Private roads and infrastructure, on the other hand, is not unexplored territory. It is the original, American approach. It was very successful. We've also had successful government infrastructure programs, just not under Comrade Barry. He managed to spend almost a trillion dollars and build virtually nothing. His projects were "shovel ready," all right, but not the way he meant it.

Thanks to that—sixteen years wasting trillions in the Middle East and eight years under a food stamp president who doubled America's debt—we're not in the same position to undertake a large government spending project as we were in previous generations.

Despite the Great Depression, even Roosevelt didn't have the kind of debt crisis looming over him that we face today. Eisenhower was in an even better position when he built the Interstate Highway System Trump has been dealt a country with crumbling infrastructure and a debt time bomb he must consider before borrowing a trillion dollars to build anything. His largely private approach may be the only way to get the job done. And unlike private oceans, we have long precedent for private infrastructure.

AN AMERICA-FIRST ECONOMY

For eight long years, we've heard nothing from Emperor Barry and the Democrats but Marxist rhetoric on the economy. We've heard that America's most successful businesses "didn't build that." We've heard opposing Obama's socialist health care law is racist and health care prices are high only because of greedy capitalists.

We've heard that the only way to create new jobs is to completely socialize higher education, as if making everyone but the consumers pay for college is somehow going to bestow more marketable skills on a generation of whiny losers who can't get a job because they haven't learned anything but global warming and women's studies.

Despite sending Republicans to Congress in 2012 and 2014 and giving them a majority in both houses, we saw no improvement. Republicans either went along with Obama on issues that benefited their donors or did nothing. Had it not been for Trump's victory and the clear message it sent—that the people were reaching for their pitchforks—they would have approved TPP in the lame duck session. Republicans wanted that crony deal for international, socialist central planning even more than the Democrats.

Trump's war for an America-first economy faces opposition in both parties. Prepare for a propaganda war from the left about how he's a greedy capitalist trying to enrich himself and his friends and a propaganda war from the right on how he's a populist, protectionist demagogue standing in the way of free trade and economic growth.

As with everything else, don't forget to follow the money. Every time you see some "expert" coming on television to opine on why Trump's economic plan is bad, do a search of his or her name and see who's funding him or her. Virtually always, you'll find some special interest that doesn't have your best interests in mind.

What we're fighting for is true capitalism, where new competitors aren't blocked from entering the market, where Wall Street suffers losses when it makes bad investments and foreign workers aren't given artificial advantages over American workers by their own government. Expect privileged elites from both parties to fight it to the end.

SAVAGE SOLUTIONS

★ Recognize the health care system was broken before Obamacare and why.

★ Fix the crony capitalist FDA.

★ Mandate insurance availability for individuals across state lines.

★ Raise the eligibility age of Medicare.

★ Mandate copays for Medicare and Medicaid.

CHAPTER THREE

TRUMP'S WAR TO REPEAL OBAMACARE

Republicans in the House of Representatives have been repealing Obamacare for six years, when it didn't matter. Knowing it was merely a symbolic vote, since Obama was still in the White House and Democrats held a majority in the Senate, even the RINOs took the opportunity to show what tough conservatives they were for their long-suffering constituents. They voted six times to repeal the law in its entirety, with almost fifty other votes to repeal or delay parts of its provisions.[1]

But now that the vote is no longer symbolic, repealing this monstrosity seems to have become a lot more complicated. The first proposal the RINOs came up with was a budget bill that included repealing Obamacare and . . . $9 trillion in new debt over the next ten years.[2] Right out of George W. Bush's playbook, the Republicans were ready to add as much to the national debt as Obama has over his eight-year term. And it only took them three days.

A few congressmen did push back. Senator Rand Paul actually voted against the Senate bill to repeal, saying, "There is no reason we cannot repeal Obamacare and pass a balanced budget at the same time."[3] Paul may be more libertarian than conservative, but at least he's doing what he believes is right. He came up with a plan to replace Obamacare that he said had Trump's support at the time.[4]

Paul's plan is what you would expect from a very libertarian Republican. It depends solely on letting the market work, including letting people buy insurance across state lines, eliminating mandates forcing people to buy coverage they don't need, taking limits off health savings accounts (HSAs), and allowing small businesses and individuals to join together to form larger groups.[5] These are all good ideas. The question is, are they enough to satisfy the electorate so they don't elect another socialist to do something worse in the future?

A few days later, Trump told the *Washington Post* he had a plan to replace Obamacare that would cover everybody. "We're going to have insurance for everybody. There was a philosophy in some circles that if you can't pay for it, you don't get it. That's not going to happen with us," he said.[6] As of this writing, we had not heard details of Trump's plan, but you can see that it sounds a lot more like Obamacare than Paul's.

Clearly, the Republicans are all over the map on how to replace Obama's socialist program. You have very market-oriented, libertarian proposals on one hand and Trump sounding very much like the Trump who told Larry King in 1999, "I'm very liberal when it comes to health care."[7] What are the Republicans going to propose and what should those who elected Trump support?

I think you know where I'm going on this issue. As I said in the first chapter, the otherwise good conservatives in the Trump administration, *including Trump himself*, have to fight their own progressive biases. Let's face it, Trump has always had an instinct that led him to support government health care.

I believe the worldview that says, "This is really important, so the government has to pay for it," is wrong. I believe exactly the opposite. The more important something is, the less you want government involved. Imagine if the government were the "single payer" for food. We'd all starve. Like anything else, the free market does a better job delivering health care than the government.

That's a theory I agree with, but you know how much stock I put in theories when it comes to solving problems in the real world. We don't live in an Ayn Rand novel. We must recognize there were problems with health care even before Comrade Barry foisted his socialist plan on us. It was dissatisfaction with the system before 2009 that allowed the socialists to get support for their disastrous program.

So, any replacement plan the Republicans come up with must address the problems that led to Obamacare. That's number one. They can't just repeal the law and let those problems return or the Democrats will be back and the next time they attain power it will be single-payer. The plan must create the conditions where everyone has a reasonable opportunity to purchase coverage that will keep an unavoidable serious injury or medical condition from bankrupting them.

Just as important, the replacement must not raise the national debt, which is a crisis in and of itself. Only the RINOs would believe it's okay to add $10 trillion more in debt while repealing a program written and passed solely by tax-and-spend Democrats. What use is getting rid of an entitlement that threatens to bankrupt us and replacing it with bankruptcy itself? Even Trump's statement about "covering everybody" has me worried.

WHY IS HEALTH CARE SO EXPENSIVE?

To solve any problem, you must understand what caused it. We have to understand what caused the problems with health care costs before Obamacare. The punditry tries to make this a lot more complicated than it is. There is some nuance to the health care costs, but only in the fine details. We're concerned here with only one question: Why do health care prices behave so much differently than the prices of most other products or services? Why do they rise so sharply, even adjusted for inflation, when the prices of most other goods fall?

We know the prices of goods and services are determined by supply and demand. Health care is no different. The greater the supply of anything, the lower its price, other factors being equal. The higher the demand, the higher the price. We learned that the first day in economics class, in my day.

Our rigged health care system has all sorts of artificial forces skewing both supply and demand. Most of this is government interference, augmented by the usual crony capitalist rent seeking I talked about in my previous chapter, on economics. Simply put, those forces artificially increase demand and artificially limit supply to an exponentially greater degree than in most other industries. The result is wildly disproportionate increases in price for health care goods and services compared to most other industries.

You might be inclined to think demand for health care "is what it is." After all, nobody *wants* to go to the doctor or the hospital. When they get sick or injured, they need to go. That's true. But demand isn't just the desire or willingness to buy a product at a certain price point. It's also the *ability* to buy that product at that price point. A teenage cashier at a fast-food restaurant making minimum wage might want a Lamborghini. But no economist would count that person as demand for a Lamborghini because the cashier doesn't have the ability to buy one at the current market price.

The trillions of dollars the federal and state governments spend on health care entitlement programs artificially and significantly increase demand. The subsidies create a much larger pool of money available for health care spending than would exist naturally. That puts tremendous upward pressure on price that does not exist for other goods and services.

In 2015, Medicare and Medicaid alone accounted for almost 40 percent of all health care spending in the United States.[8] Total health care spending was $3.2 trillion. That means those two programs alone redirected more than a trillion dollars away from taxpayers toward paying the health care expenses of other people.

Let me ask you something. If the government suddenly

decided to spend a trillion dollars per year on cars, would the price of cars go up or down? You don't have to be an economist to figure that one out.

That doesn't mean Michael Savage believes some people should just go without health care. On the contrary, I believe most health care providers are grossly overpaid. Because they have no incentive to deliver their products at a price most of their customers can afford, they don't innovate. Yes, technology in medicine has advanced enormously, but the business model of running a medical practice has not.

That doesn't necessarily mean the doctors themselves should be paid like lower-skilled workers. The physician's salary is just one expense among many in delivering health care services to patients. It's the average medical practice as a whole that is grossly inefficient.

As just one example, think about the last time you went for a doctor's appointment. They asked you for your insurance identification number when making the appointment on the phone. Then they ask you to write it down again when you get there. What are they going to do with that paper form? Is someone going to key it into their system, even though they already captured it before even granting you the appointment? Every other business in the world captures unique information once and stores it in only one place in their database. That way, if there is an error, it only has to be corrected in one place. That's data management 101.

So, you've already encountered gross inefficiency by the time you arrive in the waiting room, before you've even seen the nurse. That's just the tip of the iceberg. My point is medical practices, hospitals, and other care providers have no incentive to control costs because in an environment where health care is considered a "right," demand is unlimited. And if demand is unlimited, all other things being equal, the price will go up indefinitely, until demand becomes limited.

When Medicare and Medicaid go bankrupt, demand will suddenly be limited. The spigot will be turned off and health care providers will have to find ways to deliver high-quality care at lower prices or they will go out of business. That doesn't mean there will be no more doctors or hospitals. They were around for thousands of years before Lyndon Johnson and they will be around for a long time after his disastrous programs are forgotten.

Does that mean I'm saying Trump should try to abolish Medicare and Medicaid? No. The political climate would not allow it. But we do need to understand they are an integral part of why health care is so expensive. When you significantly increase demand, price significantly increases. It's not rocket science.

One thing Trump can try to get through Congress is raising the eligibility age for Medicare to at least decrease the program's bleeding somewhat. If we raised the eligibility age for Medicare by two years and put a $20 co-pay on physician visits, we could save hundreds of billions of dollars every year on this program.

It's just more simple economics. If you give a person unlimited health care for any specialty and an unlimited amount of visits, tell them it's their right, their duty, an *entitlement*, etc., then of course they're going to go to the doctor a lot more often. It's not uncommon for retired people to have three or four physician visits every week. Do some of them need that many? Yes, but I'd be willing to wager the number of visits would go down significantly with just a $20 co-pay, without affecting health care outcomes negatively at all.

While increasing demand on one hand, the government also artificially and significantly limits supply through its regulatory state. This includes overly burdensome medical licensing requirements, regulations on the way hospitals and practices are run, and the U.S. Food and Drug Administration (FDA). All the above are just like the regulations on other businesses I talked about in the economics chapter. They purport to protect public safety but in reality are a hodgepodge of protections for corporate interests against competition.

Let's look at the FDA, just as an example. What does the FDA do? In theory, it protects the public from unsafe or ineffective drugs. In practice, it grossly limits the supply of drugs due to a combination of government incompetence, corruption, and politicized science. All the familiar aspects of crony capitalism I previously discussed are present and on steroids when it comes to the FDA.

You may remember the scandal last year over the EpiPen. The epinephrine injection device cost about $93 in 2007, when the company that makes it was acquired. In the ensuing nine years, the cost went from under $100 to over $600.[9] There was a lot of grandstanding by politicians and media about evil Mylan, the company that acquired Merck's generic drug unit, which included the EpiPen. But very few people asked the key question: Why was there no competition for EpiPen?

Well, there is only one way to enter the drug market in this country and that's through the FDA. And lo and behold, a number of products that would have offered direct competition to the EpiPen were kept off the market by this abominable agency.[10] If Mylan had even two or three other competitors, do you think they would have been able to raise the price of the EpiPen more than 540 percent in nine years? Of course not.

The problem is most people believe the EpiPen example is the outlier rather than the norm. It's not. As of last July, the FDA had more than 4,000 generic drugs awaiting approval. That's compared to just 24 on the European Medicines Agency's waiting list! The EMA is Europe's version of the FDA.[11] How could Europe possibly be so much better at this than the United States?

The FDA claims it's just a matter of manpower. Every time a government agency fails, it wants more funding. Well, I have news for you. The EMA's annual budget is €322.1 million,[12] which is a little over $342 million in U.S. dollars. By comparison, the FDA's annual budget was $4.9 billion in fiscal year 2016.[13] That means the FDA spent 14 times more money to have a drug waiting list 168 times the size of Europe's!

Even the government isn't that inefficient. To produce results that bad, some of it must be intentional. Do you think the pharmaceuticals don't have lobbyists? All over the drug industry, there are artificial monopolies or near monopolies because legitimate competition is waiting years, sometimes decades, for approval by the FDA. If you believe that's all just our saintly government inspectors erring on the side of public safety, you need your head examined. They certainly don't err on the side of public safety when it comes to all the dangerous drugs they allow to flood the markets.

They release tons of OxyContin and other dangerous opioids without any consideration of what it might be doing to the population. Has the FDA erred on the side of public safety when it comes to this problem? Of course not. There's too much lobbyist money behind those drugs. That's why Trump's appointee to run the FDA is so important. If he puts another front man for the pharmaceutical companies in that position, all is lost. We hear quite a bit about the so-called Drug War. Well, the real war should be waged against the drug companies which are doing more damage than narcotic drug dealers.

In addition to limiting competition for specific drugs, the FDA is also waging a war against natural supplements and remedies,[14] a subject I happen to know a little about. I have a Ph.D. in nutritional ethnomedicine and can speak as an expert on traditional medicines. Of course, the agency has a cover story about every natural remedy it attacks. There is always some ingredient they claim could be dangerous, although opium apparently doesn't fit into that category, at least when it's sold by one of their multibillion-dollar pharmaceutical multinationals.

It's just another way the government limits the supply of health care. Remember, the competition for a television show isn't just other television shows. The show also competes with movies, concerts, plays, and other forms of entertainment. If there is nothing good on television, a person may even go bowling. It's the same with natural remedies. They are an alternative to drugs a patient may choose if the drug isn't working or the side effects are too adverse.

Again, if you believe the pharmaceutical lobby has nothing to do with this attack on natural supplements, you belong in the think tank all Obama's sorority sisters ended up in after we kicked them out of Washington. The pharmaceutical industry lobbyists spent between $186 million and $273 million *per year* over the past ten years.[15] They didn't spend that money to increase competition and lower drug prices. They did it to get the government to artificially improve their bottom lines, like the lobbies in every other industry.

I could write a whole book on what's wrong with the health care industry. But one of Donald Trump's key campaign slogans says it perfectly. It's rigged. It's rigged for special interests and connected multinational corporations. Combine that with insane liberal ideas about health care being a right and you get the kind of bizarre price behavior we've seen in health care goods and services since long before Obamacare. Any Republican solution must recognize and address these fundamental problems or it will fail.

BREAKING EVEN ON HEALTH CARE SAVINGS IS NOT ENOUGH

As late as September 2015, months after he had announced his candidacy, Donald Trump was still saying he wanted to replace Obamacare with a plan that covered everyone. Asked who would pay for such a plan, he said, "[T]he government's gonna pay for it. But we're going to save so much money on the other side."[16]

I have news for the new president. Breaking even on overall spending by increasing health care and saving money in other places isn't going to cut it. We have a national debt that's doubled under the last two presidents and is shaping up to do so again if the RINOs get their way. Trump is going to have to reduce spending significantly in all areas, including health care. The government is an old dog that is going to have to learn a new trick: spending less than it takes in.

The national debt got virtually no airplay during the presidential campaign, unless you were tuned in to *The Savage Nation*. Right up to the election, I was saying our fight wouldn't be over just because Trump won. And I listed the national debt as one of the major reasons. Trump may not have been the one who put us into this position, but he's going to have to be the one to get us out of it. That's not fair, but who said the presidency was fair?

According to President Obama's 2016 budget report,[17] the federal government paid $229 billion in interest in 2015. That's about 6 percent of the $3.7 trillion the government spent that year. That doesn't sound that ominous, until you consider why the number was that low. The Federal Reserve has kept interest rates artificially low since the financial crisis in 2008. Grandma Yellen has been pursuing the same inflationary policies that created the housing bubble in the first place, in order to prop up Obama's fake recovery.

That's another booby trap Obama left for Trump and, sometime during Trump's presidency, he's going to have a war with the Federal Reserve on his hands to both depoliticize it and narrow its mandate. Trying to achieve "full employment" through the central bank has been a disaster. It should stick to stabilizing the dollar. In any case, nominal interest rates for the ten-year Treasury bond were at or below 2 percent during all of 2015. That made excessive debt manageable for the federal government.

What happens if they return to their historical average of 4–6 percent and overall interest on the debt doubles? Had that happened in 2015, interest alone would have been over $550 billion, making it the second-largest line item on the budget. And as the debt grows larger, even if interest rates remain the same, the annual interest payments continue to grow. And interest rates have nowhere to go but up.

Don't be fooled by what our former Liar in Chief tells you about deficits. He likes to tout the fact that federal deficits were lower for the past four years than they were during his first term. But that's only because he ran them to such insanely high levels during his first term. The deficit was over $1 trillion for each of Obama's first four years in office.[18] *Unprecedented* is not an adequate word for how high they were.

During his second term, even with Republicans in control of the House for all four years and the Senate for two of them, deficits still averaged over $500 billion. Obama likes to use those numbers to say he cut the deficit in half. That's true, but it was his own outrageous deficits that he reduced to merely egregious. His lowest deficit is still higher than in any year during the Bush administration, although in fairness, Bush's TARP bailout contributed to the deficits during Obama's first year in office.

But don't get confused when politicians trumpet a reduction in the *deficit*. The debt and the deficit are two different things. The deficit is merely the difference between the amount of money the government spent and the amount it collected in taxes and other revenue in a given year. The *debt* is the total amount the federal government owes at any given time.

So, even if the government reduces the deficit by 90 percent, it is still adding to the national debt, because it is still paying out more than it takes in and borrowing the difference. The government has to run a surplus, meaning it takes in more revenue than it spends, in order to reduce the debt.

Trump has to do something the federal government hasn't done since the first year of this century. He's going to have to find a way to cut spending below what the government collects in revenue. His directive to cut "some departments" as much as 10 percent and the federal workforce by 20 percent[19] is a step in the right direction. But just to illustrate how deep the hole Trump's predecessors have dug is, let's apply those numbers to the 2015 budget we looked at before.

During fiscal year 2015, the government spent $3.75 trillion and ran a $583 billion deficit.[20] Assuming Trump cut all spending by 10 percent that year, instead of just some departments, that would have meant the government spent $375 billion less but it would not have eliminated the entire $583 billion deficit.

It would still have added $208 billion to the national debt. Do you see what we're up against?

Don't misunderstand me. I applaud Trump for even suggesting real cuts. Presidents normally abuse the English language by calling a reduction in projected spending increases a cut. In other words, if spending were projected to go up $15 billion the next year for a particular program and it only went up $10 billion, in Washington-speak that's a $5 billion cut, even though the program spent $10 billion more than it did the year before. That kind of logic is what got us into this mess.

But with a $20 trillion total debt, we can't afford to play those games anymore. The Coalition for Fiscal and National Security, chaired by retired Navy Admiral Mike Mullen, called the national debt "the single greatest threat to our national security."[21] Why? Because the very realistic combination of higher interest rates and a larger debt courtesy of continuing deficits could easily push annual interest over $1 trillion in a very short time. The more money the federal government must spend paying interest, the less it has to spend on security.

The U.S. Government Accountability Office said the current federal spending trends are unsustainable. If spending patterns don't change, they say the national debt "could expand to three times gross domestic product by 2090."[22] I believe it could grow much faster. Let's not forget the government always predicts higher economic growth and lower spending increases in its projections. That's why even well-meaning government accountability departments are usually wrong.

Trump is going to have to find a way to cut entitlement spending as well as the departments he's already targeting to bring spending below revenue. And whatever he replaces Obamacare with must be spending neutral at the very least. He's going to have to overcome resistance from liberals, neocons, RINOs, and his own liberal instincts on health care to do so.

A REALISTIC PLAN TO REPLACE OBAMACARE

Despite everything I've just written, we still have political reality to deal with. Any president doing 100 percent of what really needs to be done in Washington would never get reelected. He'd be lucky to make it out of his first term without being impeached on some trumped-up charge, no pun intended. And the reality is that if people who have come to depend upon subsidized insurance through Obamacare are left without insurance again, they will likely vote against Trump in the next election. Obama has bought enough votes with his welfare program to make a Republican victory almost impossible without them.

But there are things Trump can do without paying too high a political price while at least improving the government's fiscal position. I have recommendations that both address the fundamental reasons health care prices behave the way they do and recognize the political and humanitarian reasons we can't leave people without a reasonable way to obtain the care they need.

First, he has to appoint an adversarial commissioner of food and drugs. By "adversarial," I do not mean a Bernie Sanders clone who hates all for-profit industries. I mean someone who is not merely a front man for the established multinationals who already control the industry. We need someone who will slash regulations put in place to protect established corporations from competition, but will bolster those which actually protect public safety. If anti-business Europe can get its backlog of generic drugs waiting for approval down to 24, then certainly the FDA can get its backlog down under 1,000 without jeopardizing public health and safety.

More generic competition on the market will naturally bring down drug prices, which are a significant component of overall health care costs. And with an FDA commissioner honestly working for public health, instead of his connected friends, we can expect the war on natural supplements to end, further reducing spending.

The long-discussed federal mandate to the states to allow individuals to buy health insurance over state lines is a good idea. It would be one of the few times since 1913 the federal government actually exercised the power delegated in the Commerce Clause properly. The clause was put into the Constitution to prevent states from charging tariffs on goods crossing their borders. It was about free trade within the United States.

Right now, health insurers get protection from competition from their state governments the same way pharmaceutical companies get protection from the FDA. Let's let them compete in a freer market, just like they say they want to. When consumers have access to insurance companies in all fifty states—and insurers have access to customers in all fifty states—prices are naturally going to come down.

Third, we need to raise the eligibility age for Medicare to seventy years of age. When Medicare was created in the mid-1960s, average life expectancy was under seventy.[23] Today it's almost eighty.[24] That has naturally raised demand for government-subsidized services. On top of that, the ratio of people paying into the system versus those collecting benefits has been cut in half. In 1965, 4.5 working people paid into the system for every one drawing benefits. By 2012, it was only 2.3 people paying in.[25] As the baby boomer generation continues to retire, that ratio will keep decreasing for a while.

To deny the eligibility age needs to be raised is to deny reality. A seventy-year-old today is likely to be far healthier and able to work than a sixty-five-year-old was in 1965. By raising the eligibility age, it won't just help make Medicare solvent; it will decrease artificial demand for health care services in general, which will lower prices. If that's too academic for you, let me put it another way. It will slow down the gravy train for doctors, hospitals, and drug companies and force them to offer more competitive prices to attract customers who aren't on the dole!

Co-pays for Medicare and Medicaid benefits will do the same thing. The amount of money collected in co-pays, especially for Medicaid benefits, won't be the game changer. It is the effect on behavior that will make a difference. When something is absolutely free, consumers place no value on it. They don't consider whether they truly need to utilize a service before doing so.

Even a $5 co-pay for a low-income Medicaid beneficiary will prompt some consideration before deciding to utilize a service for a minor ailment that might be self-treated. Like I said in the last chapter, I've worked for minimum wage. I know how it is.

The costs for Medicaid are shared fifty-fifty between the federal governments and the states. The federal government already allows states to charge a co-pay, within federally mandated limits.[26] I say the mandate should be that co-pays are required with federally mandated minimums, with the states free to designate higher co-pays based on their own demographic and utilization data.

These are just a few suggestions that are politically difficult, but not impossible, and would make a measurable difference in the cost of health care. Notice I did not say anything about getting rid of safety nets for the truly poor and disadvantaged. In a perfect free-market world, I'd say abolish them. But for political and humanitarian reasons, I think it's a waste of time to talk about them in terms of what Trump should try to accomplish in replacing Obamacare.

Whatever additional measures Trump and the Republicans do come up with, they must accomplish what my suggestions here accomplish. They must address the fundamental problems with the health care market before Obamacare was even passed: artificially high demand and artificially low supply. And they must recognize the political reality that going back to that status quo is going to result in the Democrats regaining power with an even stronger mandate for single-payer. Leave the conservative theorizing in the think tank and make sure you get this right for the Eddies out there who need a break.

SAVAGE SOLUTIONS

★ World War III is being waged by undocumented, unvetted immigrants. Start fighting back!

★ Purge our shores of enemy combatants and limit World War III to Europe.

★ Build the border wall now.

★ Fire the bleeding hearts at CDC and restore sensible public health protocols.

★ Abolish sanctuary cities and deport the illegal vermin who are killing our citizens.

CHAPTER FOUR

TRUMP'S WAR FOR OUR BORDERS

THE NEW WORLD WAR

Once again, the world is at war. Europe is again bathed in blood thanks to the radical Islamist terrorism that found little resistance under Barack Hussein Obama here in America. He kept right on releasing drug dealers from prison, flooding America with illegal immigrants invited in across our southern border, and planting seedbeds of mayhem all over our nation with his insane refugee program.

And, of course, he commuted the sentence of that all-around rat, Chelsea Manning, who was an Army intelligence officer convicted of stealing and disseminating 750,000 pages of documents and leaking them to WikiLeaks. Forget that this put our own military and intelligence personnel at risk. She had attempted suicide because she was a transgender woman incarcerated at a male military prison, so Obama commuted her sentence.[1]

Meanwhile, the psychotic, blood-crazed madwoman Angela Merkel is invading her own nation with murderers, rapists, and thieves. She is a reverse Hitler. Hitler invaded neighboring countries to ethnically cleanse them and impose German culture upon them. Merkel is invading her own country with hordes of Muslims from countries replete with radical Islamic terrorism to ethnically alter her own country, destroy German culture, and replace it with chaos.

The Germans released the truck killer, Anis Amri, from prison. Merkel said "we don't know if he did it." A thousand people may have seen him do it, but his DNA was not in the truck. So they let him go.[2]

On the day of the attack, I told my listeners on *The Savage Nation* to watch for the Germans blaming a right-winger for the attack. It's a classic Stasi trick. It would be just like Merkel's psychotic, socialist police. They released the guy who killed all those people, even after ISIS had taken responsibility and everyone else knew who did it. Why?

I believe Merkel let him go to save her skin. She was up for reelection and her immigration policies were almost universally hated by the German people. If the terror attack were tied to the radical Islamist who actually perpetrated it, it would have been the end of Merkel. The new leadership may just have thrown her in jail for what she did to her country.

But remember Merkel's background. She is an insider from the old, Eastern European bloc and is a communist through and through. So she took her entire security apparatus, which is extremely powerful, and ran a standard old Stasi trick. She released the terrorist who perpetrated the attack and created a new truth called "We don't know who did it." Had she been able to, she would have found a convenient right-wing patsy to frame for the attack and turn public opinion back in her own favor.

Fortunately for all of us dedicated to saving Western civilization, her plan was foiled. After being released from custody by the communist Merkel, Amri escaped to the Netherlands and eventually ended up in Milan, where he was shot dead after shooting a policeman.[3]

What we now know about this barbarian shows you just how much wiser the so-called populists were in electing Donald Trump than are the multiculturalist elites who talk down to them. Anis Amri had at least fourteen different aliases[4] he used, among other schemes, to collect large amounts of welfare benefits. It also made him harder to find once authorities began looking for him.

Amri is a textbook example of the danger Barry O's refugee program, which would have been expanded under Hillary Clinton, posed to America. This was one man who became fourteen different killers, bleeding Germany of welfare benefits while pledging allegiance to ISIS and plotting mayhem against the very people who took him in.

I was especially struck by what Amri's mother said when asked for comment. "I am in shock after hearing the news in the media," she said. "My son is completely removed from religion. He used to drink alcohol."[5]

He wasn't religious but he pledged allegiance to ISIS. That confirms what I've been saying for years. Radical Islam is a violent political movement masquerading as a religion. And until the needed reformation that even moderate Muslims are calling for takes place, radical Islam *is* Islam.

A few days after the Christmas attack, the Russian ambassador to Turkey was shot in the back on live television by an Islamofascist yelling "Allahu Ahkbar!" But that's not all he shouted. You didn't hear the rest of the killer's message in the liberal media, but I had the translation for my listeners the next day. He went on to say, "We are those who have given a pledge of allegiance to Muhammad that we will carry on jihad."[6] That may offend Anderson Cooper, but that's what the man said. He was acting in the tradition of jihad that goes right back to Muhammad himself. Who do you think was behind the ambassador's murder? Do you think it was just a deranged Turkish cop? I don't. Who do you think it was who drove the truck into the crowd in Germany?

With blood all over the streets of Germany, where are the German men? I see people who look like German men. They talk like German men. But where are the German fighters who were as tough as any in the world? What happened to them?

I'll tell you what happened. They were beaten to death by the radical feminist, socialist left. That's just what would have happened in this country if God had not intervened and given us Donald Trump.

Trump's election has ushered in a "new world order," but not the one the radical feminist socialists thought they had locked up with Hillary Clinton's election.

Yes, I have been critical of some of Trump's appointments, but never of him. I truly believe it was God's hand that saved us from Merkel's twin sister, the evil one, Hillary Clinton. Just remember how lucky we are to have Donald Trump instead of her.

Trump has put one military man after another into all those top positions for a reason. He knows World War III is already under way. It's not a conventional war like World War II. It's a war to save Western civilization from the barbaric, anti-civilization elements in both the radical left and radical Islam.

The enemy doesn't come in uniform, marching next to tanks or flying in fighter jets. They come as refugees and immigrants, appealing to the bleeding hearts of liberals who let them walk into the country without firing a shot and then wait for their moment to strike. How many Anis Amris did Barack Hussein bring into America during his eight-year reign of terror?

But while World War III is different from World War II in the way it's fought, there is one crucial similarity. Just as the United States emerged relatively unscathed from World War II because we kept it away from our shores, so must we keep World War III away from our shores. The Islamofascists have already taken over Europe, just as Hitler had by the time the United States entered World War II. But Hitler never came to America. He was never even able to conquer England, thanks to Winston Churchill and the Battle of Britain. Hitler was kept in Europe and North Africa and eventually defeated there.

Unfortunately, the situation in our present world war is not so cut and dried. England is already greatly compromised by the same kinds of insane immigration policies the rest of

Europe has enacted. Even the United States has pockets of Islamofascist sleeper cells waiting to strike. But we haven't been overrun the way Germany has, at least not yet.

The terror you are seeing there would be visiting us here if not for Trump winning. Now Trump must stand firm against the liberals and the RINOs, both of whom have demonstrated their commitment to erasing the borders of the United States of America.

While we may be fighting a new kind of war, the precedent for ruling elites to attack the borders, language, and culture of the populations they rule is thousands of years old. Let me enlighten you on some history you weren't taught in your socialist, multiculturalist, environmentalist public school.

ANCIENT MASS POPULATION CHANGES

You may be familiar with the Babylonian exile story in the Old Testament. After Nebuchadnezzar conquered Jerusalem for the Babylonians, he marched most of the population off to the Babylonian homeland. According to the biblical account, the Jews were later allowed to return to Jerusalem and rebuild Solomon's Temple.

What you may not know is that mass deportations like this were fairly routine in the ancient world.[7] It didn't just happen to the Jews; it happened to most conquered peoples. Not only would conquering emperors march the existing population out of the conquered territory, but they would march populations from a different conquered territory in. There were many reasons for this, but one is intuitive. By separating conquered peoples from their homelands, they were easier to control.

Not only are people with long ties to the land they reside on more willing to defend it against enemies; they are more resistant to centralized control by a distant capital. They build up long-standing legal and cultural traditions that form the basis for local self-government.

This is the argument Thomas Jefferson made in his *Summary View of the Rights of British America* against taxation and legislation by the British Parliament. He didn't merely say the colonists rejected Parliament's legislation because the colonies weren't represented. He also said they didn't want to be represented in Parliament; that, in fact, they could *never* be represented in Parliament. That's because their long-standing tradition of legislation by their own local assemblies was the basis of their liberty.

Only a blind man could fail to see the parallel to what governments all over the West are doing now and what ancient conquering emperors did. By importing mass populations from alien, hostile cultures and deliberately planting them throughout their countries, Western nations are fundamentally changing the existing populations. Allowed to continue, the populations of Europe and the United States will no longer be the same peoples who have existed there for hundreds or thousands of years and who built long-standing traditions of liberty and local self-government.

This has nothing to do with race. It has to do with culture. In Government Zero, I told you about "Little Mogadishu" in Minnesota. That population has no long-standing tradition of local self-government or individual liberty. These refugees from an alien culture, whose offspring will be American citizens, hold beliefs that conflict with the long-standing local traditions that form the basis of local self-government for the rest of Minnesota. If the process that brought them there continues, at some point the culture and traditions of the former population disappears. With them goes their liberty.

It's always a tough call, determining whether the liberal elites who enact these policies are attacking America and the West deliberately or are just too detached from reality in their ivory towers to see how disastrous their policies are. But regardless of whether it is deliberate or not, the result is the same. The populations and culture of the West are being artificially and fundamentally changed. It seems awfully coincidental that the new populations would be less likely to resist the borderless, globalist new world order where international boards of unelected bureaucrats regulate the political and economic lives of everyone on the planet.

BUILD THE WALL

Trump drew millions of new supporters to massive rallies during his presidential campaign. They recognized in him someone who would finally fight for the American people on trade, religious freedom, infrastructure, and jobs. But they didn't chant "Build that bridge!" or "Cut those taxes!" at his rallies. They recognized the first and most important reason they were voting for Trump. They chanted, "Build a wall!"[8]

It's no accident that the one thing the people want most,

that is most in their interest, is the Trump policy facing the most resistance from the Establishment. Since the day Trump announced his candidacy, Democrats and most Republicans have opposed the will of the people on Trump's Wall. The elites know regaining control of the borders is the first step to ending their corrupt regime.

As I said in the opening chapter of this book, one of the things Trump must fight is the temptation to backpedal, to go along to get along. Immediately after the election, he was starting to say it might be a fence in places,[9] while the RINOs quickly jumped in saying, "It's not realistic."[10] Trump was already feeling the pressure and his first instinct was to compromise. That's the businessman in him doing what he's done all his life to get things done in the business world.

I have no confirmation of this, but I believe the Trump team heard me say on my show, *The Savage Nation,* what tens of millions of Trump voters were thinking when they heard this. No! This is nonnegotiable. The wall must be built and it must be a wall. Not a fence. Not electronic security. Not some strongly worded signs. We elected Trump to build a wall.

By the time of his first trade victory, the Carrier deal, Trump was already recommitting himself. "Trust me, we're going to build a wall,"[11] he told Carrier employees, like a boxer recovering after being momentarily shaken by a hard blow from his opponent. The blow was the all-out assault by the media, the Democrats, the RINOs, and every other corrupt interest bent on denuding Trump's agenda, if they couldn't stop him from being elected.

Perhaps he was a little surprised he won and was unprepared for so quick and vicious an attack. He wavered, but then he steadied himself. I think we're going to see his resolve tested like this over and over again, no more so than on the crucial issue of immigration.

By early January, Trump was again running downhill with his plan to build the wall. On January 4, Reuters reported[12] the Trump team was reviewing documents requested a month earlier from the Department of Homeland Security on "all assets available for border wall and barrier construction." Trump knew this was priority number one and he was committed to taking office with a plan already under way.

But the Establishment wasn't finished trying to undermine him even before he took office. Just two days later they tried to characterize Trump's request for congressional appropriations for the wall as breaking a campaign promise.[13] Trump had repeatedly promised Mexico would pay for the wall, not American taxpayers. Supposedly he was breaking that promise by asking Congress to set aside the funds.

It was a shallow, transparent lie that Trump didn't have much trouble exploding. In another of his devastating tweets, Trump thundered, "The dishonest media does not report that any money spent on building the Great Wall (for sake of speed), will be paid back by Mexico later!"[14] Obviously, Trump was referring to his negotiations with Mexico over trade.

Representative Chris Collins (R-NY), Trump's congressional liaison, confirmed as much the same day. Mexico exports more than $300 billion in products to the United States.[15] Their economy depends upon that trade continuing, although under Trump it's going to be much more equitable. When Trump starts the NAFTA exit clock ticking, they'll pay.

Personally, I don't care who pays for the wall, as long as it gets built. We're not talking about a monumental expense, relatively speaking. Trump estimated the cost at $10 billion to $12 billion. The highest number I've seen is $38 billion.[16] Even if that unsubstantiated highest estimate were the final cost, it's 1 percent of what the federal government spends now, mostly on boondoggles that harm us more than they help us.

I'm a fiscal hawk and I recognize the national debt is almost as dangerous to us as open borders. But even $38 billion is a rounding error in a $4 trillion budget. As long as Trump keeps his promise to build the wall, I don't mind paying for it. It would be the first time in a long time the taxes we pay were actually employed for our benefit.

Fabricating a controversy over this is just more smoke being blown by the Establishment to try to derail the wall. It's up to you and me to see through the smoke and stand behind Trump on this. The wall must be built and the borders secured.

THE DREAM IS OVER

In addition to all documents related to border wall construction, Trump also asked Homeland Security for "copies of every executive order and directive sent to immigration agents since Obama took office in 2009."[17] That includes the infamous 2012 executive order granting temporary clemency to children brought here by illegal immigrants.

Trump has promised to handle that situation humanely, but it must be addressed. Barry O seriously undermined the rule of law by signing that executive order, using his "pen and phone" to stab his own countrymen in the back. And he appealed to the same bleeding-heart liberal sensibilities in undermining American borders as Merkel did in undermining Germany's. Yes, many of these young people didn't have much choice when their parents brought them into the country illegally, but we've seen the results of supporting policies with one's heart instead of one's head.

By "with one's heart" I mean the millions of liberals who support "open borders," not the evil-minded politicians like Obama, Merkel, and Clinton who intentionally invade their own countries.

While there is at least room for a discussion on how to handle the DREAMers compassionately, the hundreds of thousands of illegal immigrants in our prisons or some other form of custody is a no-brainer. They have to go, day one, or as close to it as is reasonably possible.

For eight long years we've watched U.S. Immigration and Customs Enforcement (ICE) and the U.S. Border Control arrest—and then release—illegal aliens who have committed serious crimes in the United States. In 2015 alone, ICE released almost 20,000 criminal illegal aliens, including 208 convicted of murder and more than 900 convicted of sex crimes.[18] Over 12,000 more were convicted for drunk driving.

If you think that last statistic is less onerous, think again. Just last October, illegal alien Edwin Elvir-Palma killed

Margarito Nava-Luna while driving drunk and harassing a female driver in another car.[19] As you can probably tell by the names, both men were of the same general ethnicity. This is not a racial problem. It's an immigration problem. Nava-Luna was described as a hardworking family man whose partner and three children are now struggling financially.

It was by no means an isolated incident. Fatalities caused by drunk-driving illegal aliens were a routine occurrence in Obama's Third World America.[20] I suppose it was easy for him to dismiss these incidents when presented as statistics. They are probably "collateral damage" in his war to "transform" America. A few more traffic fatalities was just the price he was willing to pay for a multiculturalist, socialist "paradise."

But I don't know how any human being could have ignored the heartfelt testimony of a mother whose twenty-one-year-old daughter was killed by an illegal alien driving drunk on a Nebraska road.[21] The victim, Sarah Root, had just graduated from Bellevue University with a 4.0 GPA and was planning on pursuing a master's degree. She was one of our best and brightest, taken away from her family and her nation by someone who should not have even been here in the first place.

Root's mother spoke for all of us when she said she is not against immigration. Root's grandmother was a legal immigrant, as were my own parents. "It's the illegal immigrants that are already breaking the law once they come over here and they continue to break our laws," said Root's mother.[22]

It's just common sense. Anyone here illegally has demonstrated a willingness to break the law. Are some of them in desperate circumstances? Certainly. Some armed robbers are in desperate circumstances, but we don't look the other way when they rob someone. That doesn't mean that every illegal alien will go on to commit other crimes, but a much higher percentage of them do. If we could have fewer tragedies like Sarah Root's just by enforcing existing immigration laws, how could anyone argue not to do so?

Even if you're not killed by an illegal alien, just having 11 million of them driving on our roads represents a liability. Traffic accidents are a fact of life, which is why every state requires drivers to carry liability insurance for their automobiles as a condition of issuing a license. But if you're hit by an illegal alien, you're out of luck getting damages or medical care covered, even if the accident is not your fault.

The ivory tower elites in Washington don't have to worry about such mundane issues as losing your only transportation to work and having no way to pay to replace it or having a skilled-labor job that doesn't pay you when you're injured. Those are the kinds of concerns Eddie has to worry about. In his world, the real world, even a simple car accident can mean financial ruin if the party at fault can't make the plaintiff whole.

DISEASE IMPORTS STILL ON THE RISE

Longtime listeners of my show, *The Savage Nation,* know I've been talking and writing about the dangers of disease and epidemics posed by illegal immigration. My 2015 book, *Government Zero,* had an entire section called "Importing Disease," but I've been writing about this subject since 1981. I wrote a book that year called *Immigrants and Epidemics* but could not persuade a publisher to publish it at the time, even though all my previous books had sold. That's how pervasive "political correctness" already was.

Importing new or previously eradicated diseases was just more collateral damage for Emperor Barry in his quest to transform America. Breaking just about every public health principle known to man, Barry O first let people from high-risk countries walk into America without adequate screening and then sent them all over the United States, making their diseases impossible to contain.

We've seen outbreaks of EV-D68, hand-foot-and-mouth disease, Chagas disease, all foreign to this country or previously eradicated, thanks to Obama's immigration policies. Particularly disturbing is the resurgence of tuberculosis, which continues to rise. In the latest reports from the U.S. Centers for Disease Control and Prevention (CDC), 1,565 refugees have been diagnosed with tuberculosis alone since 2012.[23] That doesn't even count 2016 data, which is not available yet.

Measles, whooping cough, mumps, scarlet fever, and even bubonic plague are all making a comeback[24] in our formerly First World nation, thanks to Obama's immigration policies. Can you believe twenty-first-century Americans have to worry about bubonic plague? Well, there were sixteen cases in the United States last year. Four of the patients died.[25]

Welcome back to the Middle Ages, folks. That's where a government with the mental disorder called liberalism has taken us. They've empowered the ninth-century throwbacks ISIS to take over the Middle East and invade Europe, so people can be murdered and raped Middle Ages-style by barbarians, based on a thousand-year-old murder cult. And they've undone the greatest public health achievement in human history by allowing previously eradicated, Middle Ages diseases to regain a foothold in the twenty-first-century First World.

More of both were scheduled to arrive in this country starting January 20, when Hillary Clinton was supposed to take office to oversee the "transformation" progressives had planned for America. In addition to war with Russia, free college, more welfare, and higher taxes, Hatchet Hillary planned on expanding Obama's disastrous refugee program and signing into law whatever amnesty for illegals bill the liberals and RINOs in Congress finally came up with.

Obviously, immigration was a centerpiece of Donald Trump's campaign. It's the number one reason he won. But the danger from importing diseases the population is not equipped to handle is one that rarely gets the attention it deserves. As a trained epidemiologist, I am particularly interested in this issue. But most presidential candidates don't go near it. Up until now, it's been yet another politically incorrect third rail.

I had Donald Trump on my show back in July[26] and he said even his people had told him not to talk about this. Donald Trump, the Grim Reaper for Political Correctness, had actually been told to avoid the subject of diseased immigrants while campaigning. Of course, Trump didn't heed the campaign advice. He talked about it and was roundly excoriated by all the usual liberal suspects in the media. As we now know, that only made him more popular with the voters.

It is imperative that Trump's administration clean house at the National Institutes of Health (NIH) and CDC. We need to restore the commonsense public health policies that helped us eradicate all of these diseases in the first place. It's not rocket science.

First, we know exactly where the diseases are coming from. According to the CDC, 66 percent of all U.S. tuberculosis cases occurred in foreign-born individuals, the majority from seven countries.[27] I'll bet you can't guess the name of the very first country on the list. Or maybe you can. It's Mexico.

That's one more reason for a big, beautiful wall. Do you think not allowing hundreds of thousands of people from the number one exporter of tuberculosis to just walk into the country without so much as an ID check, much less a medical screening, might be a good idea? Is it now beginning to become clear just how completely the open borders crowd in D.C., Democrats and Republicans, have sold us out?

The Democrats want multiculturalism, the Republicans cheap labor. Both have been willing to let a previously eradicated, fatal disease regain its foothold in the United States to serve their own ends.

The CDC is part of an international association known as the "Stop TB Partnership." That organization's website lists the "countries with the highest burden of TB, TB and HIV co-infection (TB/HIV) and multi-drug-resistant TB (MDR-TB)."[28] There are thirty of them and they read like a list of every country from where Obama either imported refugees or invited in sick illegal immigrants.

So, if we know where most of the diseases are coming from, we should institute a policy to screen individuals traveling from those countries into the United States. Public Health 101: Don't let the disease in.

But no screening program is ever going to be perfect, so the next logical step is to contain the disease geographically. It's just common sense. When a family member has a cold, what do you naturally do? You try to avoid contact with that person for a few days, until they are no longer contagious. People even quarantine themselves to a certain extent. Have you ever had a friend decline to shake your hand or embrace you because they are sick and don't want to pass the infection on to you? That's a good friend. It's the right thing to do.

That said, doesn't it stand to reason we should exercise at least the same precautions, possibly even a few more stringent ones, for someone with *tuberculosis or bubonic plague*? What about travelers arriving in the United States from high-burden countries for those diseases? Is it not the responsibility of our government to ensure they are not admitting people infected with these deadly diseases?

I wrote another whole book on this subject last year. It is an ebook called *Diseases Without Borders*. Not only does it go into much more detail on the threat posed by immigration from countries with high infection rates for deadly diseases, but it provides a host of information on using diet, proper hygiene techniques, and other simple steps to supercharge your immune system and protect yourself against the threat to your health millions of immigrants and visitors from high-risk countries represent.

There is a chapter in that book called "The Case for Quarantine," in which I exposed the ineffectiveness of "self-quarantine" policies, reviewed the history of quarantine in this country, and made the case for why we need to bring back this common-sense response to the presence of potentially pandemic diseases. I'll give you the short version here: We've done it before and it worked. We need to do it again when dealing with travelers coming from countries with live epidemics or higher-than-normal infection rates of deadly diseases.

I don't need to tell you that this is precisely the opposite of what has been going on under the Community Organizer for the past eight years. Instead of screening immigrants and visitors, we've let them walk right in. We've even subsidized their travel here from high-infection-rate countries under Obama's refugee program. Then, as if that weren't bad enough, Obama shipped them to every corner of the nation, as if trying to start an epidemic. That's what happens when political ideology takes precedence over public health. Not only has the government abandoned basic public health protocols; it's abandoned science itself, something I talk about in more detail in another chapter.

Trump is going to have to turn this around, no matter how many people have to be fired and how many politically correct taboos have to be shattered. He's going to be resisted by every progressive, socialist, and RINO in Washington, who all have vested interests in keeping the immigrant spigot wide open.

HOW ABOUT SANCTUARY FOR U.S. CITIZENS?

The plot to invade America with hordes of foreigners from alien cultures, just like Merkel has done to Germany, doesn't end with the federal government. Virtually every liberal government official in the country is in on it, including the mayors of so-called sanctuary cities.

I've been talking and writing about sanctuary cities for years, but in case you're late to the party, sanctuary cities are called sanctuaries because, in one way or another, they refuse to cooperate with the federal government on enforcing immigration. Often, they instruct police and even employees dispensing welfare benefits not to inquire about a person's immigration status or require proof of citizenship.

At least thirty-seven of these cities have declared their intent to resist Donald Trump's promise to cut off federal funding to sanctuary cities that persist in these policies.[29] And you'll never believe how they're attempting to justify this virtual treason: with states' rights. "It's about federalism. It's about separation of powers," said Bill Ong Hing, a law professor at the University of San Francisco and the founder of the Immigrant Legal Resource Center.[30]

Can you believe this? I thought states' rights was an argument only made by racist right-wingers who wanted to bring back slavery. Doesn't this mean that the Immigrant Legal Resource Center is a "neo-Confederate," racist organization? Why hasn't the Southern Poverty Law Center put it on its hate group list?

It would be funny if it weren't so dangerous. Can you imagine any liberal citing the Tenth Amendment after supporting the dictator who nationalized the health insurance industry and ran roughshod over states' authority to regulate their own energy industries with his Clean Power Plan, not to mention the Supreme Court's nationalization of marriage in its same-sex-marriage decision? Such a person should be laughed out of the room, but he won't be. Instead, he's held up as a constitutional scholar making a serious argument about states' rights.

Trump is going to have a battle on his hands with this issue. The liberal media will repeat arguments like the law professor's as if they're reasonable and then jump all over Trump for breaking his promise to support local police if he cuts off funding to sanctuary cities. Trump will be in a tough spot and may have to back off his threat to cut off funding. We already have chaos in several major cities. Can you imagine if there were even fewer police on the streets?

Speaking of cities in chaos, the mayor of the murder capital of the United States, Mayor Rahm Emanuel of Chicago, met with Trump last December. We don't know all the details of that conversation, but Emanuel spun it that he had "stood up to Trump on immigration, arguing for the continued protection of young immigrants."[31] The Trump team didn't say much about the meeting, so we're left mostly with Emanuel's version.

I haven't been completely happy about some of the meetings Trump had in his tower before the inauguration. But this one didn't bother me. It was more of a curiosity. Here you have the consummate liberal who, after resigning as Obama's chief of staff, became the mayor of a city with some of the strictest gun control laws in the nation and a policy of not complying with immigration laws.

Do you think it's an accident that the same city had a record-setting 3,550 shooting incidents and 762 murders in 2016?[32] Rahm Emanuel is the man who seems to have been the self-appointed spokesman for rest of the liberal mayors who have run their cities into the ground, not only with disastrous gun and immigration policies, but with a host of other liberal stupidity. He provided quite a contrast to Trump, who stands up for gun rights, borders, and law and order.

The meeting reminded me of old-time kings or generals meeting for a parley before a major battle to discuss terms. Often there was a ritualistic attempt to avoid the conflict, but both sides usually knew it was unavoidable. They would politely bid each other farewell and return to their armies to prepare for war.

That's just what happened in Trump Tower last December when Emanuel met with Trump. Now Trump's War for Our Borders is officially under way. The opposing generals in the form of mayors of sanctuary cities are like rebellious dukes who must be brought to heel by the people's legitimate sovereign.

If you don't have borders, you don't have a country. You've heard Donald Trump say that during his presidential campaign and me say it for decades. Well, you can't have borders if dozens of cities act as if they don't exist. Trump is going to have to find some way to abolish sanctuary cities, regardless of the political consequences.

SAVAGE SOLUTIONS

★ Kill Common Core at the state level.

★ Restore civics classes at
the local level.

★ Abolish the Department
of Education.

★ Use the bully pulpit to
preach Americanism.

CHAPTER FIVE
TRUMP'S CULTURE WARS

No one's talking about the culture. There's almost no mention of cultural topics or issues. Have you heard anyone, even in the Trump administration, talk about pornography or the drug epidemic? I haven't heard it.

We heard about the drug epidemic during the campaign. That came up for a little while when he was in New Hampshire, because they're suffering greatly from epidemic overuse of OxyContin, due to the evil people in the Oxy business, the drug manufacturers, some of whom should be in prison for life.

You talk about the swamp. We know about the swamp of corruption in Washington. That's a given. How about the social chaos that we experienced after almost a decade of the swamp creature in the White House?

We don't want the same radical, political leadership that caters to pornographers, drug dealers, perverts, illegal immigrant felons, and foreign competitors. Nor do we want another administration that disdains church, family, fathers, mothers, children, and decency.

It seems to me that in America, Justice is not only blindfolded, she has been castigated altogether. It is a perverted masquerade where the rich are innocent even when proven guilty, and average Americans are guilty, with no money to prove their innocence.

Their rights are mocked and their values the brunt of filthy humor.

When this kind of disease appears on earth, nature usually follows with its opposite. When the world order collapses this way, what usually happens? What inevitably follows this kind of decadence?

Simply, that at some point, anarchy and social decay are followed by tyranny and oppression, as they were in Weimar Germany. But unlike in Weimar, we pride ourselves that we have a good economy and delude ourselves it can't happen here.

I can give you one example after another.

Unlike any president in history, Obama pushed hatred, envy, and suspicion wherever he went, while feigning compassion and understanding. But behind the smiles, the finger wagging and the promises, there was only arrogance, corruption, and deceit.

Need we follow? Wasn't one Weimar enough?

The left likes to portray Trump as a dictator because he says he wants to restore law and order to a society laid waste by eight years of allowing left-wing brownshirts and Islamist sleeper cells to run amok. To the left, everyone who isn't a progressive is a dictator. But my real concern is not that Trump will be too authoritarian, but that he won't do enough to restore American culture while governing. Yes, you need borders, you need security, and you need a booming economy. But all those are simply support for the thing a society exists for: its culture.

WHAT IS CULTURE?

For more than twenty-five years, the theme of my show, *The Savage Nation,* has been "Borders, Language, Culture." That's because everything that makes America what it is can be reduced to those three words.

A lot of pundits and think tankers will tell you the U.S. Constitution or its first Ten Amendments, the Bill of Rights, is what makes America what it is. They're not completely wrong. Those documents and the ideas they contain are monumentally important. But they aren't fundamentally definitive. As I wrote in my last book, *Scorched Earth,* the Constitution is the result of our borders, language, and culture, not the other way around.

I know that sounds like sacrilege, but it's true. This is one of those subjects upon which conservatives can become as pedantic and utopian as liberals. They believe the Constitution was inspired by God Almighty and everything in it is sacred scripture.

Everyone seems to forget how much compromise was necessary just to draft the document. Once it was drafted, a large part of the country wanted nothing to do with it. They

called themselves Anti-Federalists. Rhode Island didn't rat-
ify this divinely inspired document until 1790. It was one of
many states that wouldn't agree to it at all without assurances
it would be amended immediately.

The founders disagreed on how the federal government
should be organized, but they didn't disagree on what its purpose was. If you read what they finally came up with for a pre-
amble, it can all be reduced to this: Preserve and defend our
borders, language, and culture.

I want to talk about culture for a moment, because it's
an important concept. People define it a lot of different ways.
For some, culture is limited to the arts, like music, literature,
painting, sculpture, and dance. Others define it more widely,
to include constitutional and legal institutions.

I see it differently. Culture to me is the character of a given
society *within* its constitutional and legal framework. The laws
are like the walls of a house or a fortress. They don't define
what's inside them. They're built to protect what is inside.

Culture is everything besides legal institutions that makes
societies unique. It's their traditions, their habits, their customs, and their social mores. Culture is the unique way they
celebrate holidays, mourn their dead, decorate their homes,
and dress for special occasions. It's the way they do business
with each other and support each other during times of need.
It is their predominant religious beliefs. And yes, it is their literature, art, and music.

Our Constitution was instrumental in America rising
from a poor, agrarian backwater to the mightiest nation in the

history of the world in just a few decades. The Constitution limited the power of the government and provided the freedom to innovate and explore that wasn't available in most other countries. But without American culture, the Constitution would have been worthless. What good is freedom if you don't use it productively?

Let me tell you what American culture has been for most of our history. Until the 1960s, America was a socially conservative nation based on Judeo-Christian morality, the Protestant work ethic, and love of country. Businessman used to be called "captains of industry" and were revered for their achievements. Working people found long hours and frugality rewarding, knowing that even if they never became millionaires themselves, they were building a better future for their children.

Americans have always loved a party, but sobriety and responsibility were virtues. Licentiousness and excess were frowned upon. The man who allowed drunkenness to impair his ability to provide for his family was called a drunk. The man who wasn't faithful to his wife was called a cad.

As late as the 1950s, Americans overwhelmingly loved their country. They revered the founding fathers as pioneers of the ideas that had built the bountiful society they enjoyed. They sought to emulate wealthy businessmen, rather than excoriate them as "exploiters" of victim workers.

They dutifully attended religious services and thanked God for the blessings they had received. They worked hard and complained little. Complaining about one's circumstances used to be considered a sign of personal weakness. People used to talk about how they were going to improve their own condition, not what somebody else owed them.

Anyone under forty reading this probably thinks I'm talking about another planet. Certainly nothing I've just written describes America today. The wealthy are now vilified, no matter how honestly they earned their money. Licentiousness, drunkenness, and drug use are now revered as "hip," while sobriety and self-control are denigrated as square.

The Protestant work ethic persists out in "flyover country," but in America's urban centers, it's extinct. Rather than starting out at the bottom and working their way up the ladder as they gain skills and experience, America's baristas and burger flippers would rather protest until some politician forces employers to pay them more than they're worth.

THAT'S NOT ENTERTAINMENT

The entertainment industry today is ground zero for the destruction of American culture. Not only do most movies, popular songs, and television shows celebrate licentiousness, irresponsibility, and violence, but they are also a nonstop propaganda vehicle for left-wing ideas.

When a spoiled kid comes out half-naked in front of a stadium full of people and "dances" in a manner that would have gotten her arrested a few decades ago, she's rewarded with record-breaking CD sales. Being a loser drug addict is not only accepted if you're a famous musician; it's admired.

How far we have fallen really hit me when I watched the

American Music Awards last November. It was all on display. Hip-hoppers grabbing their crotches, women dressed like prostitutes, and some of the most horrible "music" I've ever heard in my life. All of that was bad enough. What was infinitely worse was being treated to this true basket of deplorables' political opinions.

What could anyone expect from a bunch of talentless junkies? Did you expect intelligence from them just because they can sing and dance like a bunch of puppets? I didn't.

Of course, we had to hear the political musings of Gigi Hadid, the sum of whose qualifications is that she looks nice in a bathing suit. She attacked Melania Trump and the whole audience cheered.

It was about the same time the racist cast of the play *Hamilton* hauled forth with their lecture to Mike Pence. This was a play whose producers specifically requested "nonwhite" actors for its casting calls. All the white actors in New York who were denied even applying for this job because of their race probably still hated Trump and voted for Hillary.

So, the audience attending this racist production booed Mike Pence, just as the audience at the music awards cheered Gigi for attacking Melania Trump. It's ironic how we're constantly warned about Trump inciting violence or encouraging racial hatred, but only Hillary supporters actually perpetrate violence and racism.

Robert De Niro is another one. He didn't attack any police officers or loot any buildings, but he threatened Trump with violence, saying he'd like to "punch him in the nose." Can you imagine what would happen if Donald Trump said anything like this?

Well, De Niro backed the wrong horse this time around. I wonder if he's still looking for a fight now? I've always admired De Niro as an actor, but I won't even watch reruns of his movies now. He's dead to me.

The entertainment industry's assault on American culture has been wildly successful. An entire generation has grown up hearing nothing but its overt left-wing message and doesn't know any other way to see the world. That's how a 1930s-style street corner communist like Bernie could trot out tired old Marxist tropes and convince so many young people he had "new ideas."

This is nothing new. Entertainers have been potentially subversive elements within society for all human history. You probably won't believe how far back concern over the influence of entertainers goes.

That's why I found it so disturbing that Trump invited Kanye West to his tower during the transition last December. I understand Trump is coming from the entertainment business and has friends there. I understand Trump is a showman; it worked well for him in the primaries and in the general election.

But the elections are over and it's time to govern. Trump is no longer a showman; he's a statesman. He has to start acting like a statesman, which means he may have to distance himself from the people he associated with in the entertainment business.

Eddie didn't elect him to continue Obama's decadence. He elected Trump for a return to American values. It's great that we're going to have a booming economy and a safer America under Trump, but we need our culture back just as badly.

PLATO WARNED US

I started in radio in 1994 and based my show, *The Savage Nation*, on Plato's *Republic*. I had to read that book in high school. That shows you how far we've fallen. I'm sure most high school graduates today have never even heard of Plato. Their liberal faculty couldn't fit him in between "Gender Pronouns 101" and "Introduction to White Privilege." We've gone from Plato's *Republic* to "Donny Has Two Daddies" in just a few short years.

The classics both educate and expand your mind. Twenty-seven hundred years ago, Plato mapped out his plan for an ideal society. In addition to providing a plan for government, Plato wrote about sports, wrote about welfare reform, and invented the field of philosophy.

What may surprise you is what Plato wrote about entertainers. Plato foresaw the lowlife degenerates who would come to dominate the entertainment world. He wrote a whole dialogue on artists and musicians and what they would do to society "if amusements become lawless."

Plato said that music could bring with it a "spirit of license," which at first appears harmless, but eventually penetrates all aspects of society, from "manners and customs" to contracts, laws, and constitutions. By doing so, he wrote, this spirit of license can result in the "overthrow of all rights, private as well as public."

Just think of today's rap stars rubbing their crotches onstage. Is that what Plato was talking about? Certainly such amusement is harmless, isn't it?

Plato recognized that artists always mislead people. They're like a weed. Take a look at the filth on display at the American Music Awards and in the entertainment industry in general. Ask yourself if that has something to do with the wreckage and disorder of our society.

Art has been used to corrupt people since before Plato. And if you thought that when the election results were in the fight would be over, you were wrong. Immediately there were protests in the streets. They were created by community organizers who bused people in to destroy property and create chaos.

And then came the artists and celebrities who chimed in on their shows, on stages, and on Twitter, whining, crying, and agitating for a different result.

Some people say we should just ignore them. They're just a bunch of dumb celebrities. I believe you ignore these dumb artists at your own peril. Art and music have been used for centuries to influence the masses, often leading to the demise of great societies.

Plato saw art and music as powerful and therefore potentially dangerous. We saw last fall what happens when a group of deranged junkies have the power of Hollywood, armies of lawyers and public relations agents behind them and the unquestioning support of the newspapers. You get the corrupt, degenerated society we have now as millions of impressionable young people follow their lead.

Plato thought art and music should be part of educating young people, but he thought it should be controlled to present only what is constructive for society. Largely, art and music have been used to tear down cultures for millennia. Plato saw it in ancient Greece. An argument could be made that artistic subversion helped bring down the Roman Empire.

I am not calling for censorship, but self-control. I don't agree with all of Plato's ideas. Let's not forget he called for a socialist state.

We're seeing what Plato saw right here in America today. Take a look at the degenerates in the music business. You may like the tunes. I listen to music, too, but I also think about the effect it has on people. That's why the left controls the arts. By controlling the arts, they control minds.

FDR knew this way back in the 1930s, when he commissioned twenty thousand artists to help him sell his Soviet New Deal policies. In the last election cycle, artists and musicians were out in full force pushing for Hillary Clinton.

The good news is there are many of us out there still thinking and not letting these artists influence our thoughts. That's a small miracle, considering virtually every song has either an anti-capitalist, anti-police, anti-religion, or pro-immorality theme. Every movie depicts white businessmen as evil, becoming successful only by cheating or murdering people. Occasionally, an entrepreneur is a hero if she is female or a minority.

When the white guy isn't evil, he's the prime dunce of the world, always in need of being instructed like a child by a woman or a minority, preferably both. If it's a romantic comedy, the entire movie revolves around how the leading man must learn how wrong he is about everything and ends with him finally "getting it" by completely abandoning his former worldview and adopting that of his staunchly leftist female lead.

I believe the pervasiveness of these anti-American themes had a role in Trump's victory. You can only throw so much filth and derision at decent people before they've had enough. They felt under attack from every direction, just for being decent, hardworking Americans. When they weren't getting it on the radio, in the movies, and on television, they were getting it straight from the White House. Just look at the lowlifes Obama awarded the Presidential Medal of Freedom. They couldn't do anything about the entertainers, but they sure sent a message to Washington.

"We've had enough."

I'm not suggesting we attack freedom of expression or speech. I'm not a leftist looking to legislate how people think or speak. But we do need a fundamental revolution in education. That's also been firmly under leftist control. Given the hold leftists have over so much of popular culture, education must be decentralized and depoliticized if future generations hope to live in freedom.

TRUMP'S WAR FOR EDUCATION

Many of the people who put Trump in the White House voiced some concerns when Trump appointed Betsy DeVos as secretary of education.[1] I had concerns myself. She had been on the board of the pro-Common Core Foundation for Excellence in Education, led by none other than Jeb Bush of "illegal immigration is an act of love" fame.

I've spoken and written plenty about Common Core. Abolishing it is more important than abolishing Obamacare, because it has the potential to become a federal Ministry of Truth, just like Orwell's. It's mainly being adopted at the state level right now, but those of us who understand it see where it's going. If the federal government adopts it and makes its standards mandatory, the next generation won't have the capacity to understand why they should oppose Obamacare or any other left-wing scheme.

DeVos quickly disavowed the program in emphatic terms. In a tweet, she said, "Many of you are asking about Common Core. To clarify, I am not a supporter—period."[2] She provided a link to her website,[3] where she says all the right things. She is in favor of local control of education and says Common Core is a federalized boondoggle. She admits to having been part of organizations that support the left-wing scheme, but says she has never been a supporter.

Has this always been her position or was she, as some Common Core opponents suggest, in favor of the program early and only later disillusioned by it? Is she only disavowing it now to quell the backlash against her nomination?

All we can do is take her at her word. I have no compelling reason to believe she's insincere, but let's not forget what sincere people have done in the past. Ronald Reagan campaigned on eliminating the Department of Education completely, which wouldn't have been nearly as controversial back when it was only a year old. I believe he was sincere. It grew under his administration.

By the time we put George W. Bush in the White House, with a Republican Congress, Republicans weren't even talking about eliminating the department anymore. They doubled its size.[4]

Don't forget, giving states and local school districts back their control over education isn't going to turn America into a conservative utopia. I don't believe in utopias. There will be some states or local districts where education is skewed even farther left than it is today. There will be some others where it is skewed right. I can live with that. I think every conservative could. That's true diversity and it's always been a part of our federal system.

One of the 40 Actions to Save America in my book *Government Zero* was to reintroduce civics classes to elementary and secondary schools. This is something that can be done on a state-by-state level as long as top-down, uniform standards like Common Core are not allowed to crowd it out. The left doesn't want schoolchildren to know how our federal system is supposed to work. That's because it doesn't allow 99 percent of what they're trying to do.

Trump talked about eliminating the Department of Education or at least "cutting its power and reach" in his campaign book, *Great Again: How to Fix Our Crippled America*. But he also talked about redirecting the department's spending away from public schools and into voucher programs. As DeVos has been an active supporter of school vouchers, the latter plan seems more likely under Trump's administration.

This is a mixed blessing. Assuming DeVos is sincere and remains consistent with her previous support of vouchers, we can expect more American children to be liberated from the leftist brainwashing centers they're sentenced to attend now. They may even be able to use the vouchers to attend religious schools. Every freed mind is certainly a victory.

But here's the rub. It's still a *federal* program. We're still sending our money to Washington and allowing the federal government to decide what is done with it. Today, we may like the way the funds are spent. But what happens if a Bernie Sanders or worse wins the next election? We're right back where we started from, with the power of the federal government over education expanded.

Republicans now have control of the White House and both houses of Congress. There is no reason the Department of Education can't be eliminated completely and authority returned to the states, where it resided for hundreds of years before 1979. That's the only way we can ever really be free of the left's control over education.

This is one of the dangers I've been warning about since before the election. I believe Donald Trump is sincere in trying to restore truth and integrity to education. But do you see how easy it is to backslide once you get to Washington? You have a thousand things coming at you at once, a dishonest media waiting to pounce on your every move, and suddenly merely improving education administration in Washington sounds much easier than trying to eliminate the Department of Education completely. The swamp has sucked you in another few inches.

The other possibility is Trump is simply taking what he thinks he can get in a first term. The left is already spouting its usual lies about policies the Trump administration hasn't even implemented yet. *Slate* was in hysterics over his possible plans for education before he even took office.[5] The teachers' unions attacked the DeVos appointment within an hour of Trump making it.[6]

The left knows any change in course for public education is a potentially fatal blow to it's all-points assault on the minds of the young. What if children started hearing that the founding fathers weren't just racist slave masters who oppressed women and slaughtered Native Americans? What if they started learning that the great nineteenth-century captains of industry were really brilliant innovators, rather than robber barons? Who were they robbing by inventing the telegraph, railroads, electric lights, the automobile, and the airplane? Were average Americans exploited or blessed by cheaper oil, steel, and textiles? The left can't afford to let schoolchildren learn the truth.

HOW ACADEMIA IS POISONING OUR CULTURE

The vehicle and stabbing attack perpetrated at Ohio State University by a homegrown Islamic terrorist last fall provides a perfect example of how academia is poisoning our culture. One of the professors injured by the Muslim said he wouldn't judge the attacker, "out of respect."[7] A Muslim runs people down with his car, jumps out, and yells, "Allahu Akbar!" before stabbing him and he doesn't want to judge him.

I hesitate to even tell you what else this unhinged professor said. Sometimes when you read the statements of deranged people, it actually screws you up. But it's important you realize just how twisted the reasoning of those instructing your children in higher education is. He said, "[B]efore I pass judgment on this young man, I would like to see exactly what the circumstances are and exactly why he took the course of action that he chose to."[8]

He wants to see why Abdul Razak Ali Artan took the course of action he did? ISIS even took credit for the attack, but this professor hasn't figured it out yet. Maybe he should read Artan's Facebook tirade the night before the attack, where he said, "By Allah, we will not let you sleep unless you give peace to the Muslims. Btw, every single Muslim who disapproves of my actions is a sleeper cell, waiting for a signal. I am warning you, Oh America!"[9]

How many times have I told you liberalism is a mental disorder? One of the primary theories of liberalism, going back to the 1970s, is "don't be judgmental." If you criticize anyone who does something crazy, stupid, perverted, or just plain wrong, liberals say to you with a sneer, "Don't be judgmental." Have you ever been told that?

Why is it that liberals claim they don't want to judge anyone? They do. They judge anyone negatively whose politics don't conform with theirs. But anyone who is a communist, a socialist, or a fellow traveler is judged positively by them. So they're hypocritical when they say, "Don't be judgmental." They use that phrase as a weapon to prevent any criticism of leftist thoughts or actions.

So, the college professor didn't want to judge young Abdul, the Somali Muslim refugee, for perpetrating terrible acts of violence against innocent victims, because maybe Abdul had a proper, noble cause, based upon his religious teachings. Certainly, we should restrain our "white privilege" and not jump to conclusions, right?

It gets even better. The diversity officer at Ohio State urged compassion for the attacker.[10] Calling him a "Buckeye" and "a member of our family," Stephanie Clemons Thompson threatened to "unfriend" anyone who posted a picture of the terrorist's dead body to their Facebook timeline, saying they should have compassion for the pain he must have been going through.

She used the hashtags #BlackLivesMatter and #SayHisName at the end of her bizarre Facebook post. Do you remember the progressive-Islamist takeover I talked about in my previous book, *Government Zero*? I was talking about how progressives and radical Islamists were pursuing the same agenda for different ends. It's not a conscious conspiracy, of course, because both groups would exterminate the other if under their power. Rather, they both want to destroy Western civilization and remake it in their own, respective images: a socialist utopia for the progressives and a sharia law theocracy for the Islamofascists.

Do you need any more proof of it than this? Here we had a confirmed terrorist attack by a Somali Muslim yelling "Allahu Akbar!" for which ISIS took credit after the fact, and this progressive diversity officer uses the hashtag #BlackLivesMatter, as if there were some question of police brutality.

Why do we have such a predominance of radical left-wing activists running colleges and universities? If the police officer hadn't shot the terrorist when he did, he would have continued stabbing people, likely killing people instead of only injuring them. How could #BlackLivesMatter possibly apply to this situation? Because for the diversity officer, race trumps sanity. Race trumps everything else in her life. And she is another person shaping the minds of impressionable young people on college campuses today.

What does a diversity officer do, anyway? The KGB in the ex-Soviet Union used to have what they called "political officers" throughout the Soviet Union. They were also on ships in the Navy and in every other area of the military. These political officers ensured that every soldier, sailor, and airman in the Soviet Union was true to *The Communist Manifesto*. They were the equivalent to our "diversity officers" in the United States of America.

This is why Trump was elected, to make sure the future Abdul Razak Ali Artans do not enter our country. He was elected to make sure all the Abduls already here, lying in wait to cut your throat, are ferreted out by the FBI and thrown out of the country. And he was elected to ensure that these diversity Nazis infesting our universities are no longer given positions. They must be purged from the campuses so that students can learn, instead of being intimidated and indoctrinated by them.

The left will fight to the death any threat to its absolute hold over education. We may have to win what battles we can early on and hope to make further advances in a second Trump term, based on the successes of the first. Changing the Department of Education's mission may have to come before shutting it down completely.

THE BULLY PULPIT

President-elect Trump's reaction to the OSU attack was a short-and-sweet post on Twitter: "ISIS is taking credit for the terrible stabbing attack at Ohio State University by a Somali refugee who should not have been in our country."[11]

Not in eight years have we heard a president say so much in so few words, although he was still only president-elect at the time. In one sentence, Trump said what the Islamophile Obama had refused or been unable to say in ten thousand sentences. The attack was an act of Islamic terrorism. The Somali refugee who committed the stabbing attacks should never have been here in the first place.

With that one sentence, Donald Trump destroyed the entire progressive narrative. It was like a sonic boom that didn't just break all the windows, but knocked down the buildings of the emperor's evil city. To paraphrase Orwell, Trump said, "No, war is not peace; ignorance is not strength; freedom is not slavery; and our enemies are not merely 'zealots' attacking some 'folks.'"

Let the enemies of America beware. There is no longer an enabler in the house on Pennsylvania Avenue.

Perhaps the most significant impact a President Trump can have on our disappearing American culture is just to say what he believes directly to the American people. For eight years, we've had a president who took every opportunity to lie to Americans and the world about how terrible America is and has always been. Anyone basing their opinions on Emperor Barry's remarks would think this blessed land was one of Dante's circles of hell, populated only by racists, robber barons, and their oppressed minority victims.

Trump has already shown his support for law enforcement and the military on the campaign trail. And unlike his vicious, elitist opponent, who cursed at security officials for deigning to wish her "Good morning,"[12] Trump praised the Secret Service, even when they had to treat him less than delicately to protect his safety.[13]

What a complete turnaround from what we've been subjected to. How many times has O thrust himself into a local police case to pronounce his disapproval of the way our local law enforcement officers do their jobs? Whenever the leftist media starts one of their Black Lives Matter publicity campaigns about the supposedly racist police shooting an innocent, unarmed black man, His Excellency felt the need to pontificate on the terrible injustice done by evil white cops.

Forget that virtually all of these stories turned out to be lies. Remember "Hands up, don't shoot"? That was a lie and it had terrible consequences for the good people of Ferguson, Missouri, most of whom, by the way, are black. But did we hear the president retract any of his hate speech regarding that or any other false media narrative he decided to weigh in on, after finding out it was all a lie? Or course not. He just had his speechwriters change the names and places in his teleprompter for his next anti-police tirade.

Let me make one thing clear: I don't think the president should say much about most local police matters, except to bestow honors upon hero cops. Policing should for the most part be left to states and local municipalities. You won't find any reference to policing power in the Constitution. Unfortunately, we had a president for eight years who, in addition to being divisive, was also a narcissist. There wasn't a day that went by that we didn't have to hear his imperial pronouncement on something.

That said, you know the media will pounce on any opportunity to try to portray Trump as a throwback dictator, merely for supporting law enforcement against what is, in many communities in this country right now, open rebellion. When George Soros' Black Lives Matter blocks a highway and threatens trapped drivers with violence, you won't hear Donald Trump referring to them as "protesters." Protesters carry signs and chant. They make speeches. They don't endanger lives on the highway or loot neighborhoods. They don't burn down cities.

We've had a president who looked the other way while innocent people were terrorized, property destroyed, and civil society dismembered. Donald Trump made it clear on the campaign trail and during his acceptance speech at the Republican National Convention that those days are over. Under his administration, there will be law and order.

Does that mean he doesn't support the First Amendment? No. Peaceful protest is protected by the First Amendment; violence is not. It's the left that has attacked the First Amendment by initiating violence against anyone they believe doesn't agree with their socialist views. This lawless culture has become so pervasive that violent thugs felt emboldened to beat a man on the street just because they suspected he voted for Donald Trump.[14]

Under attack on our native soil by Islamofascists, their Enabler in Chief told the audience at a counterterrorism conference that "Islam has been woven into the fabric of our country since its founding."[15] He was referring to many of the slaves being Muslim, sold into slavery in Africa by their fellow Muslims. That's how the religion of peace treated prisoners of war in Muslim countries in previous centuries. The Islamofascists in Africa and the Middle East are still living in that century today.

Somehow, here in America we've managed not to make a regular habit of chopping off heads, throwing homosexuals off rooftops, or forcing female children to get married, even though Islam is supposedly woven into our fabric.

Meanwhile, Obama still refused to refer to our enemies as Islamic terrorists or their ideology as radical Islam right up to the day he left office. As you can see, things have changed. The end of political correctness starts at the top and however he may disappoint us on individual issues here or there, Trump has destroyed political correctness, possibly forever. We now have a commander in chief who will at least name our enemy.

If, God forbid, another attack on Jews occurs like the one in Paris back in 2015, you won't hear Donald Trump referring to the victims, murdered because of their religion, as "a bunch of folks," as O did.[16] Obama didn't want to refer to the "folks" as Jews because he wanted to obfuscate who perpetrated the attacks and why they did so. As for the animals in question, they weren't Islamic terrorists, they were "violent zealots."

If someone who had been asleep for twenty years woke up and heard some "violent zealots" had murdered "a bunch of folks" in Paris, would that person have any idea what had occurred that day? Are innocent people well served by obscuring the identity of their enemies and concealing their motivations? Does that make them safer or less safe?

You can expect to hear a President Trump call murderers and rapists what they are and promise decisive action against radical Islamic terrorists at war with civilization itself.

Let's not forget Obama's offensive remarks at Selma, Alabama, when he said it was the slaves who built the White House and the southern economy. You have to give him credit for killing two birds with one stone there. He was able to advance his usual narrative about racist America and his childish, Marxist view that it is workers who provide all the value of production and are merely exploited by capitalists and managers. This during a commemoration of truly oppressed civil rights heroes who were unjustly beaten by police for peacefully protesting injustice.

Back when blacks were really oppressed in this country, they conducted themselves like statesmen in winning their rights. They didn't burn down their own neighborhoods and beat up people who didn't agree with them. That was before Lyndon Johnson's Great Society destroyed the black family, creating generations of fatherless children, many of whom predictably drifted into a life of crime.

For Comrade Barry and the Democrats, it's always 1964. In 2015, he talked as if blacks today suffer the same injustices they did in the Jim Crow South fifty years ago. That these deceptions emanate from the lips of a man with a black father and white mother who was raised by radical leftist, middle-class white grandparents in Hawaii explains his confusion.

What presidents say matters. When Northeastern states were considering secession from the Union following Thomas Jefferson's election, Jefferson said, "We have called by different names brethren of the same principle. We are all Republicans, we are all Federalists."[17] While he didn't eliminate all acrimony between the parties, his speech was lauded by members of both. He may have saved the union with unifying words.

It was a sentiment present in Donald Trump's victory speech on election night, when he said, "I pledge to every citizen of our land that I will be President for all of Americans, and this is so important to me. For those who have chosen not to support me in the past, of which there were a few people, I'm reaching out to you for your guidance and your help so that we can work together and unify our great country."[18]

Can you recall any time O asked anyone for guidance and help, much less his political opponents? Did he ever seek to unify the country as Americans, as Jefferson and Trump both sought to do, upon their respective triumphs? No. From the moment he took office, he sought to divide America by party, by race, by gender, and by sexual preference.

Even when his policies were censured by a devastating midterm defeat, he refused to consider the views of Americans who disagreed with him, continuing to override the will of the people with his "pen and phone."

All of this drives American culture. It is delusional to think the Soros-funded domestic terrorists wrecking our cities haven't noticed the encouragement implicit in every statement coming from the White House. Had Obama supported the police, it may have saved the lives of some of the police murdered by assassins, who were emboldened by Obama's constant hate speech against them. There is a saying, "A fish rots from the head down." The war on police we have lived through for the past eight years began in the rot of the White House and was amplified by the media, resulting in the murder of police across the nation.

Had Trump been president during the riots in Ferguson, based on a false narrative, his statements may have saved cities burned afterward.

Even if we get 50 percent or less of what Trump promised on the campaign trail, his speeches and statements have already changed American culture for the better. And for at least the next four years, there will be a powerful voice in Washington counteracting the deafening din of left-wing noise. The voice of America will again be heard.

SAVAGE SOLUTIONS

★ To beef up the military,
man up the military.

★ Help wounded warriors, not sexually
confused enlistees.

★ It's biology, not misogyny: gender
equality has no place in the armed services.

★ Make the VA more transparent and
accountable via the Accountability First and
Appeals Modernization Act and the Caring
for our Heroes in the 21st Century Act.

CHAPTER SIX

TRUMP'S WAR TO RESTORE THE MILITARY

I haven't minced words about appointments Donald Trump made that I don't agree with. But General James Mattis was one I certainly do agree with. And secretary of defense is an important one. As I said throughout the presidential campaign, it was going to be death under Clinton, life under Trump. That's because Hatchet Hillary is as much a neocon on foreign policy as any Republican and she was already pushing us toward a war with Russia before the election. Trump's call with Putin before even taking office was like turning the dial down on a boiler that was ready to blow.

His selection of Mattis signals two things. Number one, Mattis is a hard-nosed soldier, but not a warmonger, contrary to the sorority's opinion. He told his troops in Iraq, "Engage your brain before you engage your weapon,"[1] and told the Iraqi leaders, "I come in peace. I didn't bring artillery. But I'm pleading with you, with tears in my eyes: If you f**k with me, I'll kill you all."[2]

Both of those statements carry the same message. Mattis seeks peace, if it's attainable, before resorting to war. But if war is necessary, it has to be waged as war, not as a social program. The military has one purpose: to destroy the enemy before the enemy destroys us. Mattis understands this.

The guy in the Defense Department before him, a creature from Harvard, a physicist who has never fired a Daisy BB gun, so denuded the United States military that it's going to take more than Mattis to restore it. Among other things former defense secretary Ashton Carter, Mr. Shaky Voice, put surgery for transsexuals ahead of surgery for battle-injured troops.

Can you imagine there is no punishment for men like this? Can you imagine we live in a nation where a man can come in and gut a Defense Department like this simply for the contracts he can steer to his friends? It's unbelievable to me.

Maybe this will all change now that Donald Trump is president. Mattis is a great appointment for secretary of defense. I will thank Donald Trump personally for that when I see him again.

RESTORING THE PURGED OFFICERS

I wrote about Mattis back in 2014 in my book *Stop the Coming Civil War*. I was raising the red flags about how Obama had purged more than two hundred military officers at the rank of colonel or higher. He had replaced these officers with useless puppets who would go along with his plans to transform the military into a progressive social program.

One of those fired by this Castroite was General James Mattis. And who is James Mattis? He's a great Marine and the former head of the U.S. Central Command, or CENTCOM. In January 2013, Castro's cousin, Fidel Obama, dismissed Mattis for being too hawkish, especially concerning the administration's lenient Iran policy. Mattis understood how dangerous a nuclear-armed Iran would be to our allies and to U.S. interests in the Middle East. And he's not the type to keep his opinion to himself.

Mattis also once said, "There are some a*****es in the world who need to be shot."[3] He tells it like it is, as he sees it, just like I do on my show every day. He's precisely the kind of straight shooter we need between the troops fighting our battles and the politicians doing everything they can to make it harder to win. He's just the kind of true American soldier Obama couldn't tolerate in his sorority. So, Obama purged him.

Mattis actually received a note from one of his own aides letting him know he was being replaced as head of CENT-COM. Not one of the lowlife stooges in the Pentagon or the communist White House was gracious enough to tell him to his face.

I can relate to that. That's what they do to big men. I've seen it happen in my own life, just recently. The sneaks in the night are afraid of men like us and so have underlings do their dirty work for them. But eventually, men like me come back to the surface and the underlings run like the cockroaches they are, once light is shed upon their behavior.

As I noted in my earlier book, *Stop the Coming Civil War,* the sorority also purged two top nuclear commanders, Major General Michael Carey and Vice Admiral Tim Giardina. Both left the armed forces within days of each other based on accusations of misconduct leaked to the media. They didn't even get a trial. The fake, tinfoil warriors and the girls Obama dressed in uniforms did this to them.

They said Carey drank too much one night and tried to get onstage with a Beatles cover band in a Mexican restaurant in Moscow. But do you want to know why he was really fired? Because he was another real soldier who didn't fit the profile in Obama's new, feminist military.

At the time he was fired by the girls in the band, Carey was Commander of the Twentieth Air Force, responsible for all 450 of the Air Force's Minuteman III intercontinental ballistic missiles, located in five U.S. states. Prior to that, he served in both the Iraqi Freedom and Enduring Freedom missions. He had received thirteen military awards and decorations.

This was the man the vermin in Obama's Defense Department, those fakers in uniform, threw out of the military. Carey is an American hero but was relieved of duty for drinking vodka in Russia. Assuming his alleged drinking problem wasn't wildly exaggerated, wasn't it possible to get an officer of this man's credentials any sort of rehabilitation, instead of firing him?

I hope Donald Trump and General James Mattis get together and bring General Michael Carey back next. But now I'll go to the next one. Who else did Obama fire? Most of you have forgotten Tim Giardina, but I haven't. Giardina was a U.S. Naval Academy graduate, a three-star admiral, and former deputy commander and chief of staff of the Pacific Fleet. He's another one relegated to a desk job over spurious charges. This time it was playing poker with counterfeit hundred-dollar chips in a casino in Iowa.

This was another charge never vetted in a court. But his dismissal must have been approved personally by Obama the Sneak himself.

In other words, both of these commanders with outstanding military records and who have risen to the highest ranks of command were dismissed on charges that would likely, in my opinion, have resulted in no more than a slap on the wrist for an enlisted man.

Nor would the secretary of the Air Force, who has never flown an airplane, have had to fear such disproportionate retribution. These dismissals were unprecedented.

There are many other great military men purged by Obama who may be coming back to serve this great nation in place of the turncoat rats Obama has put in, now that honest men are in charge of the military. But Trump is going to need our help every step of the way. Thank God he started at the top, putting Mattis back where he belongs. Let him go after the internal enemies first. That's the only way he'll survive.

Trump and Mattis are going to have to purge the military of the KGB-like operatives that Obama planted in every part of our armed forces. And they should look at every one of the officers purged by Obama, including not only Carey, Giardina, and General Stanley McChrystal, but lower-ranking officers like Lieutenant Commander Wes Modder, whom I wrote of being purged for his Christian beliefs, as well as those ninety-three officers purged from Malmstrom Air Force Base, supposedly for cheating on a test. If the Obama sorority got rid of them, there is a good chance it was for the wrong reasons. Perhaps not in all cases, but they should all be investigated.

TREAT OUR BATTLE-INJURED, NOT SEXUALLY CONFUSED

There are all sorts of political reasons why so many officers were purged from the military under Obama, mostly revolving around their not fitting into Obama's vision of the military as a multicultural, progressive social engineering experiment. A prime example was Ashton Carter's announcement that the Defense Department was going to begin covering sex-change operations deemed "medically necessary" for transgender personnel.[4]

One of the reporters at the press conference apparently couldn't believe his ears. He asked for clarification that Carter really meant sex-change operations. Carter confirmed it.

I've called Carter the creepiest Secretary of Defense in U.S. history and that's in a long line of creepy. But this deep, wobbly, left-wing fanatical plant really takes it to a whole new level. He was handpicked to do the sort of thing he did last June, which was to put the "medical needs" of transgender soldiers ahead of everyone else in the military. So transgender personnel can line up for sexual reorientation surgery while your grandfather or father is rotting in a VA hallway waiting to be treated for bullet wounds or lost limbs.

This lunatic Carter actually justified this as "consistent with military readiness, because our mission—which is defending the country—has to come first."[5] But if a transgender soldier says he wants surgery, he is immediately rendering himself unable to serve! How can that possibly be maintaining military readiness? So there is a red flag around this. It's nonsense, a scam. We've gone from leathernecks to feathernecks under the leadership of this unhinged leftist.

Certainly, the one-tenth of 1 percent of the soldiers Carter said were transgender may have celebrated this decision, along with all the stoners who went to Harvard or New York University. But what about the other 99.9 percent of the soldiers serving at the time? If you are a red-blooded, testosterone-driven American male who enlisted in the U.S. military because you were willing to give your life for your country, you'd be ready to throw up and leave the military.

Just imagine walking into combat knowing that if you're hit, not only will your medical care be delivered in incompetent fashion by a horribly run VA, but you also may have to wait to have your battle wounds treated until after some confused soldier is changed from a man to a woman. It's not just purged leadership and substandard equipment that have weakened our military.

We're often told that when ISIS burns someone alive or throws a homosexual off a rooftop, it isn't Islam. It's just a small percentage of radicals who have hijacked the religion. Well, that reasoning certainly applies to our military. A small group of radicals, appointed by Obama and his sorority in place of purged heroes, has hijacked the once-proud institution called the U.S. Department of Defense.

Let me be clear. I remain a sexual libertarian. I don't want discrimination against gays, lesbians, bisexuals, or transgenders. As Trump said of the murdered innocents in the gay club in Orlando last year, they are all beautiful people. But there is a huge difference between not discriminating against LGBTQ people and integrating them into a macho culture that must remain so to kill the enemy. The military is not a social experiment and it's not about a pair of shoes, a uniform, and a pension, as Obama has tried to make it.

That's why Obama picked Carter and why Carter purged so many real soldiers from his officer corps. You didn't hear one word of protest from the generals about Carter's announcement, even though it came one day after a bombing in Turkey. That's because they were either appointed leftists like Carter himself or too afraid to speak up against him.

Well, we already have good news on this. Before Trump even took office or Mattis was confirmed, the U.S. Department of Veterans Affairs was already indicating it received the message sent by the Savage Nation with Trump's election. Suddenly they don't have the funding for gender reassignment surgery, but "continue to explore regulatory change in the medical benefits package when appropriate funding is available."[6]

Do you understand what that is? It's called reading the handwriting on the wall. As I said, clichés become clichés because they're true. The bureaucrats in Obama's Defense Department knew their days were numbered. Some of them may have wanted to avoid the axe. And they won't be around long if they don't put some distance between themselves and insanity like this once a guy like Mattis takes over. This is the guy who has a plan to kill everyone he meets. He's not going to tolerate nonsense like this for a minute.

RESTORE QUALIFICATIONS STANDARDS IN THE MILITARY

Mattis is going to have to address another aspect of the social engineering experiment—women in the military. From leadership to the front lines, Obama has prioritized gender equality over the safety and effectiveness of our fighting forces. While this thin, smoking snake in the White House was distracting you with the toilet story to make you preoccupied with trans this, trans that, a man in a woman's room, and a woman in a man's room, what he was really doing was dismantling our entire military.

Take General Lori J. Robinson's appointment to lead the North American Aerospace Defense Command and U.S. Northern Command in Colorado.[7] Now, I have nothing against women who have flown in combat rising to the level of general and heading a U.S. war-fighting command. But she's never flown in combat. In fact, she's not a pilot. She's basically . . . an air traffic controller.

But they made her the head of the whole North American Aerospace Defense Command.

Everything with liberals is change, even when it's change for the worse. Obama sought to change the mightiest military in the history of the world into something no military can be. The military is never going to be a gender-equal institution, but Obama and like-minded liberals never gave up trying.

"General Robinson reflects that change as much as anything else," said Maria Carl, retired Air Force colonel. She was another one who never flew a plane but the sorority made into an Air Force colonel.

I'm sure Robinson is a brilliant woman. I'm sure she's a great organizer. But the military is not a school. The military is about fighting the enemy and defeating the enemy, and not about social engineering. But since we had a man who was so intent upon reengineering the entire society from the toilets to the Thunderbirds, he put a woman in charge of this combat command.

Do you think it is appropriate to simply appoint a woman in a combat-control position because she's a woman? How in the world can you approve of a thing like this? Why not put a transgender who can't fly a Piper Cub in charge of the Air Force?

This is just another layer of insanity Trump and Mattis have to confront in order to rebuild our military. As Trump himself said on the campaign trail, it's not all about spending more money. We can improve our military vastly without spending an extra dime by simply stopping this kind of nonsense. Not all progress means going forward. Some improvements require going backward. We need to return to promoting military officers based on their ability to lead troops to victory, not their demographics.

It looks like we won't be drafting women for combat quite yet, either. That was another gift the lefty looney Ashton Carter gave us, when he lifted all restrictions on women serving in the military.[8] This insane liberal actually said, "They'll be allowed to drive tanks, fire mortars, and lead infantry soldiers into combat. They'll be able to serve as Army Rangers and Green Berets, Navy SEALs, Marine Corps infantry, Air Force parajumpers, and everything else that was previously open only to men."

There's only one problem. They can't do it, at least not physically. I hate to break it to any snowflakes who may have picked up this book by accident, but men and women are physically different and not just in their sexual organs. Men are on average physically much stronger than women.[9] And there are aspects of combat that require 100 percent of that strength for the military to be successful.

One might think that would be a deal-breaker for a Defense Department looking to integrate women into combat, but not for the "transformed" left-wing military Obama tried to build. If women couldn't meet the physical standards, they'd just lower the standards so women could meet them. I wish I was making this up, but it's true.[10]

I don't have to tell you that General Mattis finds all of this as idiotic as I do.[11] He's not alone. There are plenty of women in the military who oppose putting women into combat. They are proud to serve, but they understand that while men and women have equal rights, they don't necessarily have equal abilities in all areas. There are some things women are better at than men. Soldiering happens to be one thing men are just more physically equipped for than women are. I'm sorry if you're not happy with that reality. Take it up with God. I'm just the messenger.

Here's another little detail Mattis has brought up that doesn't sit well with the politically correct classes. This may come as a shock, given what we were led to believe by the previous administration's priorities, but most soldiers are not LGBTQ. Believe it or not, the overwhelming majority are heterosexual. And if they're put in the close quarters of combat service, they're likely to do what healthy young men and women usually do. That's not "setting them up for success," as Mattis put it.[12]

I have no objection to women serving in the military. Women have supported our armed forces in one way or another throughout our history. But I do object to jeopardizing the lives of men and women in combat, as well as the success of the mission, just to satisfy some leftist academic's dreams of absolute equality. That's where the military has been going for eight years.

The lunatic Carter was still pushing right up until Trump took office. As late as last December, he wrote, "I am proud to say that the first woman has entered training to become a tactical air control party airman."[13] There was only one problem. The woman he was referring to had left the program the previous July![14] What a perfect ending, if it turns out to be the end. The man whose entire military career was built upon denying reality proudly writes about a female trainee who wasn't even in the program anymore.

RESTRUCTURE MILITARY SPENDING

Whenever I say we need to rebuild the military, people automatically think I'm talking about spending more money. I'm not. We already spend more than the next ten or eleven nations combined on our military. It's not about how much we're spending. It's about how we're spending it and on what. Perhaps what I've told you so far in this chapter has given you a little insight into how wisely we've been spending our dollars over the past eight years. But the spending problem goes back far before Obama.

Spending more on the military doesn't necessarily mean you get a stronger military. Just look at the Air Force One boondoggle. The cost of a typical, commercial Boeing 747 is a little over $350 million.[15] But Boeing gave the federal government a cost estimate of over $3 billion to build two of them for the president to fly in.

Now, I understand the plane built for the president has many features not found in the average commercial airplane. There are all sorts of additional communication and countermeasure functions Air Force One has to have to ensure the president can continue to govern while in the air, not to mention protect him against a potential attack. That doesn't mean the plane has to cost five times as much.

Donald Trump sent a signal before he even took office. He said, "Get the price down or I'm canceling the order," in so many words.[16] The party is over for the contractors who have helped the politicians run up a $20 trillion national debt. This is what you get with a businessman in the White House instead of a community organizer. It's called "vendor management," something every Fortune 500 company does. We can argue about what the government is going to spend money on, but whether you're a Republican or a Democrat, you should have no objection to the government paying a fair price for whatever it does eventually buy.

But of course, the vicious left-wing media couldn't even give him credit for this. What was their answer to his encouraging "tweet" to Boeing? They fact-checked his number.[17] Trump said the cost was $4 billion instead of $3 billion, as if that were somehow important. Even if it were $2 billion it would be too much!

Trump sent his message out one day after Boeing committed to donating $1 million to Trump's inauguration,[18] which demonstrates again that the man can't be bought. You may not agree with everything he says, but you would think that on something like this, the media would put aside their pettiness and recognize someone they may disagree with on many other things for genuinely putting his interests aside to do what's right for his country.

But no, they'd rather fact-check whether his $4 billion figure is accurate or not.

There was a time in this country when Republicans and Democrats put their differences aside and worked together on nonpartisan issues of obvious national importance. Let me tell you something, those times are back. Republicans and a lot of Democrats and independents just worked together to elect Donald Trump, overcoming the Clinton machine, the media, and every rotten special interest, within this nation and without.

And while the media couldn't even take a few minutes off their nonstop propaganda campaign against Trump and the rest of us "deplorables," the people had a much different take on the Boeing tweet. His audience in North Carolina erupted in thunderous applause a few nights later when he flatly said, "I'm not paying $4 billion for an airplane."[19]

Neither are we.

This is the approach Trump must take with the whole defense industry. We're spending almost a trillion dollars per year when you add up all our military spending, including medical costs and all the spending hidden in other departments like energy. Yet our soldiers are still in combat using equipment that's outdated or never worked in the first place.[20]

The swamp doesn't get any deeper than the defense contracting industry. I don't have anything against defense contractors per se, but they've been given such free rein for so long they've run amok. Between the contractors just looking to maximize profits, like any business, and the sellouts in Congress, the interests of the soldiers in combat have been completely forgotten.

The contractors aren't stupid. They've located themselves strategically in enough congressional districts that just about every congressman has some interest in constantly increasing defense spending. Say no to a contractor and you're killing jobs in your district and jeopardizing reelection. And let's not kid ourselves, all our so-called representatives care about is getting reelected, regardless of whether they actually do any good for their districts, their states, or their nation.

That's why Congress continues to buy equipment the Pentagon itself says it doesn't need. Army Chief of Staff General Raymond Odierno has been telling Congress for years to stop buying tanks. He said the same thing last year that he had already said in 2012. Odierno told Congress it was spending "hundreds of millions of dollars on tanks that we simply don't have the structure for anymore."[21]

That's a perfect example of our government in action. They want to campaign on how they're supporting our troops, so they keep buying tanks the Army doesn't even want every year, as if we're still fighting Rommel in the African desert. We're not. We're fighting a new kind of enemy that hides among civilian populations and strikes at civilians in our own country. We don't need tanks for that. Sometimes I want to walk onto the floor of Congress and start shaking people. Wake up!

But let's not forget what's really behind us. Yes, there is plenty of stupidity in Congress, but there is more to this story than that. Use my most important three-word advice: Follow the money. You'll find components for those tanks manufactured in many congressional districts and lobbyists for the manufacturer telling every one of those congressmen that if they want to keep their cushy jobs in Washington, they have to keep those people employed.

At least the tanks the Army doesn't need actually work, which is more than I can say for the F-35 fighter jet. Former RAND author John Stillion says the F-35 "can't turn, can't climb, can't run."[22] Other than that, it's working just fine. I suppose I shouldn't nitpick poor Lockheed Martin about a few glitches. They've only been working on this for twenty years, and spent $1.3 trillion of our money on a plane that can't fly and is consistently outperformed by the ancient F-16. That's right, I said $1.3 *trillion*.

While trillions are being spent on disasters like the F-35, our special forces are in combat trying to win a war with faulty rifle sights.[23] The contractor that made them settled a lawsuit for more than $26 million. That doesn't help soldiers in the field who may have been killed or maimed because they missed their intended target due to faulty rifle sights.

The soldiers can't even depend on the helmets they're wearing. Another contractor getting fat off the taxpayers to the tune of $30 million provided more than 126,000 faulty helmets to our troops.[24] Why? Because they decided they could make a little more money having the helmets built by federal prisoners, while millions of Americans remain out of work.

I could go on and on, but you get the picture. That military-industrial complex Eisenhower warned us about has completely infested the entire nation and is sucking us dry, while leaving our brave soldiers in the field with junk equipment. It's a wonder they can still win at all. But they do. The soldiers are not the problem. The swamp is the problem.

This is why Trump's Boeing tweet was so important. It doesn't matter if the plane was going to cost $3 billion or $4 billion or $2 billion. What's important was the message to the whole, corrupt defense contracting industry: The party is over. We're going to pay you well for quality products that help our troops protect the nation, but the days of $500 screwdrivers and $4 billion airplanes are over.

This rot can be extricated from the Defense Department, saving hundreds of billions of dollars and making our military stronger and better equipped at the same time. All it takes is a president who isn't wholly owned by the corporations that perpetrate it.

The last step in rebuilding the military is to stop using it like a Whac-A-Mole hammer in every godforsaken backwater some do-gooder liberal or neocon wants to invade. No matter how well equipped, well trained, and devoted the troops are, no military can hold up under the constant deployments ours has been asked to support for going on two decades now. We need to destroy ISIS and then we need to take a fresh look at every military deployment around the world. It's time to stop being the world's policemen, paid for by the blood of our troops and the treasure of our taxpayers. That's a part of Trump's War I'll talk about in the next chapter.

SAVAGE SOLUTIONS

★ Stand firm on peace with Russia

★ Combat the war propaganda
with the bully pulpit

★ Destroy ISIS and then leave
the Middle East

★ Bring our troops home from
unnecessary deployments

CHAPTER SEVEN

TRUMP'S WAR AGAINST THE WAR MACHINE

A MAN OF PEACE

Just after the election, I saw Mel Gibson's movie *Hacksaw Ridge*. It's about U.S. Army medic Desmond T. Doss, who served at the vicious Battle of Okinawa in World War II but refused to kill anyone. He became the first man in American history to win the Medal of Honor without firing a shot.

This was the perfect movie to see in the context of Donald Trump as an anti-war president. While I was watching this moving film, Trump was speaking to Russian president Vladimir Putin, even though Trump hadn't even been sworn in yet. The two men vowed to work together.

It was a sigh of relief for me. The left should have been celebrating Trump instead of rioting in the streets. You know why? Because we almost had a war with Russia, thanks to the psychopath who previously occupied the White House, the man who thought he was the greatest thing since the cure for polio.

He was ginning up a war with Russia and the neolibs and the neocons were salivating.

Candidate Trump was on my show a month before the election and said he'd meet with Vladimir Putin, if he could, even before he was inaugurated. That's how badly Trump wanted to tamp down war talk. The crazy feminist sorority that surrounded Obama was dying for a war with Russia.

I led Trump to that commitment with a series of questions I asked him during that show. I've been writing about the demonization of Putin and Russia for years in my books. Putin is no angel and Russia's interests don't always coincide with ours. But that doesn't mean we must be enemies or give the forces of darkness in Washington another war to get rich on while the rest of us suffer and our soldiers die for nothing. That's why I wanted a commitment from Trump to talk to Putin at the earliest possible opportunity. I got it.

What happened was predictable. The media went berserk the next day. All the little girls and the little boys in the media were running around saying, "Oh, Trump's going to step on Obama's foreign policy!" Let's hope he does, early and often.

Do you realize that if Trump does nothing else, he's already done more than any other president would have given us, especially the hysteric Hillary Clinton, who wanted a war in order to satisfy the bloodlust of her followers?

I'm an anti-war conservative. I know you don't understand what those words mean because you think liberals are anti-war. But they're not. As you can see in the streets of America, they are the violent fascists of our time, using the drug-addicted children as their shock troops, the same way ISIS uses civilians as human shields. All these left-wing organizations represent the true danger, not Trump.

One of the reasons I worked so hard to get Trump elected is I believe he will be a man of peace. Put everything else aside. The most important thing in this world is not the economy. It's peace. Domestic peace, international peace, peace between individuals, and peace between nations is far more important than gross domestic product or low interest rates.

Hundreds of years ago, Thomas Hobbes said the very first law of nature is to seek peace.[1] That is the essence of true conservatism. And I'm not just talking about the absence of military war on the battlefield. I'm talking about peace between individuals and groups within society. It's truly the opposite of progressivism, which seeks nothing but conflict. They promote conflict between people of different racial groups, different sexual orientations, and different income levels. They even promote conflict between men and women.

The spoiled brats who looted and pillaged because Hatchet Hillary lost the election don't understand any of this. They don't understand the connection between armies fighting on battlefields and classes fighting within society. That's because their liberal schoolteachers and professors never taught them the true nature of government. Government is force. That's all it is. It's the pooled capacity for violence of every member of society. It's the societal equivalent of a firearm for an individual. It's only supposed to be used defensively, to protect innocent people from aggression by others.

The insane left doesn't want to limit government, this violent institution, to defending the innocent. They politicize everything. They want to transform peaceful, voluntary exchanges of property into violent, coerced redistributions. They wage war against voluntary associations and force people to associate against their will. They won't even allow peace in the expression of one's own thoughts. If a confused boy or girl can't choose one of the two sexes to "identify as," they want to force you to refer to them with a whole new set of pronouns.[2] Under Obama, we were all Thomas Mores being forced to say the words the king orders us to say.

That's why true conservatives oppose everything the left stands for, domestically and internationally. We oppose liberalism in the name of peace. We oppose it because the government can achieve income equality only by seizing wealth at the point of a gun from those who legitimately earned it. The government can force people who don't wish to associate with each other to do so only at the point of a gun. It can make people say words they don't believe are true only at the point of a gun. To organize society this way is to perpetuate a constant state of war. Look at our streets. They're succeeding.

THE LIBERAL WARMONGERS

Just as they cannot achieve their warped version of equality within society peacefully, neither can they achieve worldwide equality peacefully. That's why the left has taken this nation to war constantly for the past one hundred years. It is beyond their comprehension that some alien cultures may not be ready for their brand of pure democracy. Some may not want it. But they can't just leave these societies alone to work things out on their own. Just like they couldn't leave a devoutly Christian baker in peace and let a gay couple take their business elsewhere, they can't leave foreign societies in peace when they don't live up to the liberal ideal of absolute equality.

In this insane pursuit, liberals constantly violate that first law of nature. They constantly seek war, instead of peace. Before George H. W. Bush, it was liberals who started all the wars in the twentieth century. I'll bet you didn't realize that, either. Look it up. It's true. Not only do liberals seek absolute equality between the sexes and absolute income equality, but they seek worldwide political equality, regardless of whether alien cultures want to be equal to Americans or not.

This is what was behind Hillary Clinton's unhinged reign as secretary of state. She went around the Middle East with a flamethrower, apparently believing she could burn down dictatorships and the flower of democracy would sprout from the ashes. She's been in bed with the savages in Saudi Arabia for so long she couldn't see how crazy it was to expect anything but what we got after Ghaddafi was gone in Libya: jihadist anarchy.

She wanted to do the same thing in Syria, regardless of the consequences. Not only would toppling Assad have put ISIS in charge of Syria; it would have resulted in a war with Russia. Even Joint Chiefs Chairman General Joseph Dunford said that and he's an Obama appointee.[3] She didn't care. The plight of 250,000 Syrians in Aleppo was more important than the lives of millions of Americans that would be lost in a war with Russia.

Of course, that war wouldn't merely be an unintended consequence of "liberating" the Syrians. It also fits right into their justification for every other war. They believe it's our job to liberate the Russians, too, from the oppressive Putin regime. According to the liberal warmongers, Putin is the new Hitler because he prosecuted sexual anarchists when they desecrated a Christian church. Russia is Nazi Germany because they're no longer communists; they're a market economy. This despite the Nazis being national *socialists,* not capitalists. They despise Putin because he's trying to defend Russia's borders, language, and culture from the same violent, uncivilized assault ours are under.

The hypocrisy of these people is astounding. Throughout the twentieth century, they looked the other way while communist dictators murdered hundreds of millions of people. When Stalin purged twenty million political opponents, there was no outcry from the left. That's because Stalin was a benevolent communist fighting "income inequality." It was the same for Mao Tse-tung. He may have killed eighty million, forty million of whom simply starved to death under his "Great Leap Forward." Liberals still praise him as a great leader to this day.

Stalin, Mao, and Castro are all inspiring, benevolent leaders to the lunatic left, but Putin is an aggressive dictator who must be resisted, on the battlefield, if necessary. Why? I'll give you the real reason. Putin is a conservative who has resurrected Russia's culture from the dustbin of history. He's restored its ancient, Judeo-Christian institutions and its market economy. He isn't afraid to call the Islamofascists what they are. And he won't sit idly by while the United States brings NATO to Russia's borders and threatens to take away her ports and wreck her economy.

Putin committed the deadliest sin against the godless liberal religion when he reinstituted religious study in Russian public schools.[4] Liberals think our First Amendment guarantees freedom from religion, but it doesn't. It guarantees there will be no national religion, and guarantees the freedom to practice one's own religion.

The Russians are actually more consistent with our First Amendment than we are. They don't require students to study any particular religion. They can choose to study Orthodox Christianity, Islam, Judaism, or Buddhism. Those who don't wish to study religion can take courses on the "foundations of religious culture" or "fundamentals of public ethics."[5]

It's the same policy John Adams wrote into the original Massachusetts state constitution. The state was allowed to require religious instruction in schools, but what the students actually studied was left up to the local districts. They were allowed to elect the instructors and decide on their own what was taught.

The point is children need a moral compass to direct their lives. Religion provided that to American schoolchildren for hundreds of years, until the progressives destroyed it. It was what guided them as adults to live in peace with each other. Progressives eliminated it from our schools and with it societal peace. Look at the violence and disorder all over society today. It comes from generations educated without any moral guidance.

Just as liberals have been at war with religion within our own society, they are at war with it internationally. They ignored the atrocities of the Soviet Union because it prohibited religion. They demonize the restored Russia because it recognizes that society cannot live without religion or some equivalent set of moral principles. As John Adams said of our own Constitution, "[I]t was made only for a moral and religious people. It is wholly inadequate to the government of any other."[6]

Being pro-religion isn't Putin's only sin against the liberal religion. He's also mocked the climate change hoax in the past, although he's recently sold out to the envirofascists,[7] and he opposes abortion.[8] Worst of all, he isn't a communist. He even lectured Obama about the evils of socialism at a Davos conference, although his wise advice went unheeded.[9]

These are the real reasons the left hates Putin. Yes, he's a former KGB agent who may have "disappeared" a few political opponents. I don't know if those accusations are true or not. As I said, he's no angel. But he's been a voice of reason on the world stage while Emperor Obama and his Hatchet Woman Hillary Clinton destroyed the international order and set barbaric jihadists loose all over the Middle East. And just like Trump, Putin refuses to bow to the globalist elites who want to run the world out of Washington, D.C.

We've avoided the feminist sorority's war with Russia for the moment, but Trump is going to be under pressure to start it from them and their echo chamber media for his entire presidency. The liberal warmongers won't rest until the entire world is an egalitarian, socialist wasteland.

THE NEOCONS

Don't expect support from the sellout Republicans against the liberal warmongers. There are some who supported Trump, but the party and Congress are still infested with neoconservatives who are just as bloodthirsty as the liberals, albeit for different reasons. Where the liberals believe they can make the whole world equal through "humanitarian war," the neocons have a much more traditional goal: They want to rule the entire world. Global hegemony not only fulfills their lust for power; it helps their crony capitalist friends on Wall Street and in corporate America.

The first thing you must understand about the neoconservatives is they're not really conservatives. The movement was founded by liberals[10] who left the party because it became too anti-war over Vietnam. These people don't care about limited government or conservative values. They're all for big welfare programs like Medicare Part D as long as they are free to wage constant war all over the planet.

The terrorist attack of September 11, 2001, was the greatest thing ever to happen to these faux conservatives because it gave them an excuse to push for wars they'd wanted for an entire decade.[11] They had been writing letters to Bill Clinton demanding he invade Iraq for practically Clinton's entire presidency. Luckily, Bill was too busy chasing interns around the Oval Office desk to get around to it. Besides, he had his own, liberal, "humanitarian war" to wage in Yugoslavia. Liberals call setting Islamofascists free to decimate relatively free countries humanitarian.

But the neoconservatives were all for Obama and Clinton wrecking the Middle East. They just didn't think they were doing it right. If you don't believe me, look up the Project for a New American Century (PNAC). That was the neocons' think tank in the 1990s and it laid out their entire plan.[12] You won't find their original website, because they've taken it down, but there are researchers who've preserved their awful ideas in mirror sites.

PNAC talked about overthrowing Saddam Hussein long before 9/11 and how the United States had about twenty years after the fall of the Soviet Union to do whatever it wanted on the international stage, before any new superpower was likely to emerge to challenge them. They said the United States should greatly increase military spending and use the war machine to "challenge regimes hostile to our interests and values." That's just neocon-speak for war and regime change.

It's also a very succinct statement of their philosophy.

Regimes hostile to their values refers to the liberal dream of remaking the whole world into a progressive social democracy. As I said, these are liberals at heart, although I don't think the neoconservatives really care about liberating oppressed people. They do care about hegemony and corporatism, and "hostile to our interests" refers to regimes that don't go along with their globalist economic plans. The neocons added the interests of their friends at multinational corporations to liberal humanitarian war insanity. That allows them to sell wars for profit as humanitarian at the same time. Do you remember George W. Bush flip-flopping all over the place about why we invaded Iraq?

First, it was weapons of mass destruction that didn't exist. Then it was to bring democracy to the poor, oppressed Iraqis, who now wish they could have Saddam Hussein back to continue oppressing the ninth-century throwbacks who are chopping their heads off. Meanwhile, everyone suspected the war was all about oil. That's neoconservatism in a nutshell. They talk about security; they talk about liberating oppressed people; but in the end, they're in the back pockets of the multinationals who don't care about the interests of average Americans.

Just like the liberals, the neoconservatives have been spoiling for a war with Russia, but for different reasons. One reason is that Russia has partially rebounded from the economic devastation that resulted from seventy-four years of communism. They not only have a growing economy based on fossil fuels; they have a new sense of national pride now that they're not slaves to the Marxist commissars. For the neocons, any independent nation exhibiting economic strength is a potential threat to their global rule.

When Russia was a down-and-out wasteland after the Soviet Union fell, the neocons didn't consider it a threat. But now it's a rejuvenated country under a strong, conservative leader who isn't falling-down drunk in the Kremlin like his predecessor. And though Russia still only has an economy the size of Italy's, they do have tens of thousands of nuclear weapons, something Putin hasn't been afraid to point out.[13]

The neocons have been working for twenty years to keep Russia from reemerging as the world power it always was, even before the Communists took over. They talk about Putin being aggressive and seeking to expand Russia's borders. You should treat that as an insult to your intelligence. If you want to see what's expanded, take a look at maps of NATO in 1991 and today.[14] NATO has moved right up to Russia's borders, including virtually all the former Soviet satellites that provided a "buffer zone" to it during the Soviet era. Let's not forget NATO's primary reason to exist: to fight a war against Russia. Russia looks at expanding NATO this way as aggression against them, not the other way around.

Many Americans don't know this, because their knowledge of history doesn't extend back past Beyoncé's first CD, but the West made promises[15] to Russia back in 1990 when Gorbachev agreed to the reunification of Germany. Then-secretary of state James Baker said NATO would not move "one inch eastward." The Russians kept their part of the bargain; U.S.-led NATO did not. Yet all we hear from the liberals is how Trump is the devil for threatening not to honor America's commitments. How about honoring one that could still prevent a nuclear war?

The neocons didn't care about honoring commitments to Russia when Russia was too weak to object. They'd been kicking them while they were down for twenty years, hoping to extend that unchallenged period they talked about in their think tank papers. Now that Russia has recovered some of her strength, the stakes are getting higher. Trump is not only being fair and honorable in proposing more equitable treatment of Russia; he's being pragmatic. The United States cannot continue to treat this nuclear power like a doormat forever.

That brings us to one of the real reasons for the revolutions in Ukraine and Syria. Both the neocons and the liberals want you to believe the United States is merely supporting the oppressed people in those two countries. I'll bet you haven't noticed what both countries have in common: They're each home to one of Russia's very few warm-water ports. If you think that's a coincidence, you're kidding yourself.

Russia is a largely landlocked nation and much of its history has centered on its quest to secure ports that don't freeze over during wintertime. They've had one at Tartus, Syria, for more than fifty years and another at Sevastopol, Ukraine, for even longer. The neocons would love to take them away from

Russia and cripple her sea trade and defenses. Why do you think the United States and NATO have supported regime change in both countries?

Now you understand why Hillary Clinton was so adamant about deposing Bashar al-Assad in Syria. Syria is Russia's ally. Russia has a port there. It was Russia's only presence in the Middle East until the neocons and liberals sided with the jihadists to try to overthrow Assad. That's when Russia stepped in. They aren't going to give up their port in Syria without a fight.

But it's not just about a Russian port. The neocons always have some corporate interest in mind and this is no exception. They don't hate Assad merely because he's friendly with Putin. He's also stood in the way of the multinational corporations' plans for a natural gas pipeline through Syria to Europe.[16] The pipeline would run from Qatar through Saudi Arabia and eventually to Europe through Turkey. Along the way, it would have to pass through Syria.

The big loser in this scenario would be Russia. Right now, Russia has a virtual monopoly in the European natural gas market, which the Europeans claim Russia takes advantage of or will in the future. They may be right. It's a matter of opinion.

What's not a matter of opinion is that it is up to Syria whether to decide to allow a pipeline to run through its country or not, just as the United States reserves the right to decide whether the Keystone pipeline runs through its own country. The neocons don't care. Their misinterpretation of the United

States being an "exceptional nation" is that the rules every other nation follows don't apply to it. If Syria won't go along with their corporatist plans for a pipeline, neocons are happy to start a war there to overthrow the government and put one in that will cooperate.

The neocons would love to destabilize Syria, allowing the jihadists to take over.

Of course, the warmongers and sellouts will deny all of this. "Putin is the aggressor, he's the one invading Crimea!" they'll say. I hope you will consider everything I've said, take five minutes to look at a map, and ask yourself who you believe. Is it just a coincidence the United States is deeply entangled in regime change conflicts in those two places for humanitarian reasons? If that's true, why are we still supporting Saudi Arabia, whose government chops off more heads every month than ISIS does all year?

THE WAR PROFITEERS

I know it may be difficult to keep track of all the varieties of parasite infesting the swamp in Washington, D.C. Most people in Obama's America are too busy working twice as hard to take home half as much to their families, thanks to a wrecked economy that's replaced breadwinner factory jobs with minimum wage "service sector" employment, for those who can find work at all. It's my job to stay on top of these things for you, and give you one man's informed opinion on who the enemies within are and what they'll be up to next.

Longtime listeners of my show, *The Savage Nation,* and those who have read my previous books know I've always given three little words of advice to anyone trying to make sense of anything Washington is doing: Follow the money. Forget liberal, conservative, neoconservative, and the rest of the various -isms. Whenever the government is up to no good, you will usually find someone making money—a lot of money—from whatever the latest scheme turns out to be.

The war machine is no different. Do you remember when Trump got booed at a presidential debate last year in South Carolina? He had the temerity to say the Iraq War was a mistake and the United States should work with Russia to fight ISIS in Syria and Iraq. The live audience booed and Trump told the millions watching on television the truth. "That's Jeb's special interests and lobbyists talking."[17] He was right. That's just who they were.

They were likely members of the multibillion-dollar defense contractor lobby, which has spent well over $100 million per year for the past decade.[18] They were powerful enough to pack the live audience for the debate, leaving only a few tickets for Trump and his family. And when Trump criticized the Iraq War and suggested the United States soften its insane stance toward Russia, they booed. Peace is good for America, but bad for business for the Lockheed Martins and Raytheons of the world.

They didn't just heckle Trump at primary debates, either. They invested their ill-gotten gains backing the candidates who would keep the gravy train rolling. I probably don't have to tell you Hillary Clinton was their overwhelming favorite, receiving 50 percent more in contributions as of April 2016 than even "bomb them until the sand glows in the dark" Ted Cruz.[19] They knew Hatchet Hillary would be reliable in keeping demand for their products high.

By the way, Ted Cruz only came in third in the defense contractor campaign contributions lottery. Bernie Sanders received slightly more than Cruz did, which should tell you something about the authenticity of his anti-war rhetoric.

Donald Trump received the least amount from the defense lobby, less than 3 percent of what Clinton hauled in as of last April. So, in response to all the hysterical liberals screeching about Trump getting us into a nuclear war, I'll repeat those three little words: Follow the money. The money said Trump was a bad bet for the merchants of death, meaning he was a good bet for America.

THE BATTLE PLAN

Just like Trump's War in general, the War Against the War Machine didn't end with the defeat of Hillary Clinton. The liberals, neocons, and the war profiteers who align with both will never stop pushing for more war. And they'll have the lying media on their side, from the *War Street Journal* to the *New York Crimes,* calling Trump everything from a racist to a traitor whenever he tries to alter the Establishment warmonger foreign policy.

Trump will have four things to fight back with. The first three are the truth, the bully pulpit, and the support of the tens of millions of true patriots who sent him to Washington in the first place. He'll need the Savage Nation to stand by his side, especially now that we've confirmed that even the opinion polls can't be trusted.

The accord with Russia is an important first step. Trump is already under attack for it. He must continue to talk to Putin and reach an understanding, first about the Middle East and then Eastern Europe. While Trump and I are both men of peace, we see eye to eye on ISIS. It must be destroyed in the name of peace and civilization. It would be relatively easy with the United States and Russia working together, instead of fighting a proxy war against each other and pretending they're fighting the terrorists.

But once ISIS is gone, it's time to leave the Middle East for good. I'm well aware of the danger that another group may come along to fill the void left by ISIS, but we can't stay there forever. If we're ever going to start an America-first foreign policy, we're going to have to stop defending every living soul on the planet.

There are many rich countries in the Middle East who have plenty to lose if another ISIS threatens the stability of the Middle East and the United States isn't there to protect them. Let them fight their own battles for a change. They may be a little less likely to burn our flag and bomb our cities once the Islamofascists are their problem.

You can expect the entire War Machine to erupt at the suggestion. I can already hear Bill Kristol, in his whiny voice, saying we can't afford to allow the Middle East to become "destabilized." What a laugh. After fifteen years of war, the Middle East is the most unstable it has ever been. Libya is on the verge of jihadist anarchy. Syria is in flames. ISIS still controls parts of Iraq.

Nevertheless, Trump still has a fourth weapon in his arsenal when it comes to military decisions: He's the commander in chief of the armed forces. He's not the commander in chief of the whole country. That's what Emperor Barry thinks the presidency is. But Trump is legitimately empowered by the Constitution to issue orders to the armed forces.

Strict constructionists will argue he is not supposed to order the military into offensive combat without a declaration of war from Congress, but that's not what we're talking about here. We're talking about ordering the troops out of combat in a war that wasn't declared. So, the constitutionalists will have nothing to say here. Trump can not only leave the Middle East once ISIS is destroyed; he can make good on his promises to reevaluate all the commitments around the world that are bleeding us dry and keeping us in a constant state of war.

No matter how much the liberals and the neocons want to paint Trump as a dictator, on this they have no case. But they will use all propaganda means at their disposal to discredit him. Doing the right thing is never easy. It's hard.

Trump is going to have to muster the same iron will he displayed at that debate in South Carolina while being booed by everyone he could hear and harassed by a hostile debate moderator. He's going to have to call the war lobby out as he did then, even if seems like the whole world is against him. He has to call the war profiteers out and name names.

How refreshing would it be for a president to be honest with the American people about the real reasons for the war propaganda they're subjected to daily and who stands to make billions on the war they're told they must fight? Imagine if Trump gave an address during an all-out push for war, supported by the media, and said, "Folks, those are Lockheed Martin's lobbyists you're hearing from on television and reading in the newspaper. They're planting these stories so they can cash in on another unnecessary war."

Moments like that, when he told the truth every honest person in this country knew but no one in the media would dare say, won him the election. The truth is a powerful weapon. He's going to have to have the strength to tell it for four long years, during which he'll be excoriated by everyone who stands to gain from distorting it. He must have the strength to call out congressmen who are bought off by profiteers who've placed their operations strategically throughout congressional districts to ensure the spending never stops and the wars never end.

We, the Savage Nation, must be strong ourselves. We're going to have to have the strength to stand by Trump when the warmongers tell every lie they can make up about him to try to undermine our support. We already know what they'll do. They'll call him and us racists, bigots, isolationists, and anything else they can think of. We overcame it for a year during the campaign. Can we do it for four or eight more years?

We must. The soldiers who fought at Hacksaw Ridge and places like it endured four years of war. We can, too. Like them, we'll be fighting a war to restore peace. That's what it will take to put America first again in Washington, D.C.

SAVAGE SOLUTIONS

★ Ignore the think tanks on
trade and the wall

★ Punish RINOs at the ballot
box in primaries

★ Make sure GOP doesn't mean
Grand Old Party but Government
of the People.

★ Et tu, Brutus? Trump must beware
of some who are close to him.

CHAPTER EIGHT

TRUMP'S WAR AGAINST
THE RINOS*

In a speech in December, Obama blamed talk radio for spreading "Russian propaganda."[1] He said "domestic propagandists" and talk radio was the reason his party lost the election.

He was right about one thing. Talk radio was a significant contributor to their defeat. That's why the emperor went out in shame with his tail between his legs. We exposed him and his comrades for what they were.

My last book, *Scorched Earth,* helped elect Donald Trump. That book exposed the Democrat-socialist machine for what it is. This was the book that even the intelligentsia on the left, notably *Salon* magazine, said was the architectural

---

* "RINO" originally stood for "Republicans in Name Only," meaning a Republican who campaigned on conservative principles but then acted like a progressive once in power. I use the term in that sense, although the Republican Party has become so replete with liberal internationalists the acronym is somewhat a misnomer.

plan for Donald Trump. They called me the "godfather of Trumpamania."

It's true I predicted the chaos that became Obama's legacy. Does that make me a propagandist, pointing out the division that eight years under Emperor Barry gave us? I asked several questions before the election:

As cops are being killed on a regular basis thanks to the evil former president and the hatred he expressed toward the police, has our great country become, in some respects, a Third World nation of terror? Answer: yes.

How many terrorist events did we have during his presidency? Answer: many. I trust you haven't forgotten the riots, the mobs, Black Lives Matter, and Baltimore almost burning to the ground. I haven't. Neither have I forgotten Ferguson, Missouri, and the rest of the chaos Obama encouraged.

I said in *Scorched Earth* that our Constitution had been trampled by a divisive president, that open borders were poisoning America, that we were one bad election from losing America forever. We were.

Hundreds of thousands of people read that book, maybe more. That means you, the Savage Nation, were the difference between Trump winning or losing the election. My evidence for this bold statement can be verified by the fact that Trump came on my radio show the day of the election. He asked me to motivate all of the millions who listened to me. I happen to know he chose *The Savage Nation* for his only radio appearance on Election Day, because he needed every Eddie and Edith to go out and vote for him.

Now, if you want to call it propaganda, go ahead. But if you want to prove it, you have to disprove the allegations I made. I opened that book with a quote from a French scholar, André Piganiol, who wrote, "Roman civilization did not pass peacefully away. It was assassinated."

Obama, Hillary, and the radical left were assassinating the United States of America. Then Trump came along and told us everything we wanted to hear. Do you remember the first thing he said that got your attention? I do. He said he would build that wall on the southern border that I've been saying we need for decades. And every time he said, "I'll build that wall," the crowds got bigger.

He also said he was going to ban the entry of Muslims into the United States. He later clarified he meant immigrants and refugees from countries with a high concentration of radical Islamists, but we all know what he was really saying. He was saying he wasn't going to allow our enemies to pour into the country, as Comrade Merkel has done in Germany.

We all cheered that promise, too, not because we're racists, but because we want to live. We don't want twelve-year-old Muslims planting bombs in our city centers, as an Iraqi boy did in Germany last Christmas.[2] That was an Iraqi who was born in Germany but became "strongly radicalized" while living there. What can you expect from people brought directly in from countries at ground zero for Islamofascism?

Merkel, the psychotic fascist who might as well be Hillary Clinton's twin sister, brought more than a million of them into Germany in 2015 alone.[3] Now Germany is a "no-go zone."

Sweden is a no-go zone. Every nation that has been similarly invaded by Muslims, thanks to these liberal psychotics, has become a no-go zone. That means if you're a civilized human being, it's no longer safe for you to go there.

Those of us with an iota of common sense look at Europe and say, "No thanks." This past election, we saw the corruption and suicidal policies of liberalism in Germany, Sweden, and France and said, "No, not here."

Then, along came a presidential candidate who said it with us and declared he would not allow what's happened to Europe to happen to America. He was called every name under the sun for saying it, but he didn't buckle. We elected him.

Now it's time to see if we're going to get that wall he promised and if he makes good on not facilitating an invasion of America by jihadists. Those were the two major reasons we voted for him, in addition to bringing back jobs for the millions of unemployed and underemployed workers.

In each of my last several books, I said we needed a businessman to run the country more like a business. Many of you agreed. Of course, we can't run the nation purely like a business, because businesses are ruthless. Businesses are heartless. Businesses have no feelings. If America were run purely like a business, the poor would starve to death and the crippled would die in the snow. Corporations couldn't care less about the next man's welfare.

I always warn against academic theories being taken too far and ignoring reality. We need the nation run in a more *businesslike* fashion. That would mean fiscal responsibility and common sense. But let's not throw out the liberal pedantic academics and replace them with conservative pedantic academics who think the real world is an Ayn Rand novel.

Scorched Earth is a reasonable book, written by a reasonable man. It was also somewhat prophetic. In it I said that after eight years of Obama, there was an irrefutable case that our nation had been undermined by terrorists from within, terrorists from without, anarchists, a president and Congress with contempt for the Constitution and the law, and a complicit, liberal media.

Every one of those ideas resonated with you and was magnified by candidate Trump. He had very bright people working with him who would listen to talk radio, especially *The Savage Nation,* right on WABC in New York, where the Trump campaign was headquartered. They took notes and wrote the speeches that carried Trump to the White House. I thank God I finally found a candidate who expressed what I believe in. I'm glad he won. I will always be thankful for that success.

However we must be cautious, because we know politics corrupts absolutely. We saw the evil Republican National Committee try to hijack the Trump administration from the get-go. They have not been wholly unsuccessful.

They got Reince Priebus into the inner circle. I strongly suspect this was the result of a deal Trump had to make last April to have any chance to win. If you remember, the party was fighting Trump's nomination with everything it had. Trump probably had to agree to let Rinso come into the administration, being the operative that he is, and pick some of the appointments.

We've already seen some of the fallout from that deal, if it was made as I suspect. As one of the primary movers in getting Trump elected, I feel obligated to tell you that if we don't stand up now, we risk losing everything we fought for within six months. The Republican Party elites will take back everything we voted for unless we vociferously stand up to them starting now.

I've been standing up since the day Rinso got appointed chief of staff. On November 14, 2016, I wrote the article[4] that probably got me banned from the Trump administration for the duration of his presidency. I said it was starting to look like Jeb Bush won the election, instead of being laughed out of the primary race. I subtitled it, "From RINOs to Rinso in One Election."

I know I paid a price for that, but I don't care. I'm not looking for anything personally from the Trump administration. I'm still happy he won and will continue to support him.

But what I will not do is support the evildoers in the Republican Party like Mitch McConnell, the most backstabbing SOB the party has ever seen. He and John Boehner already betrayed us in 2012. They rode into power on our support and a day later stabbed us in the back.

That's exactly what they're trying to do now, since Donald Trump won. The subtitle of *Scorched Earth* is very important: *Restoring the Country After Obama.* Have we restored America? No, not yet. Trump just took office. The wall hasn't been built. ISIS hasn't been defeated. The economic reforms haven't been completed yet. No federal departments have been eliminated.

Our job for 2017 and beyond is enormous. It's bigger than it was before the election. Our battle has just begun. We can't become complacent, settle back, and say, "Trump won; now I can relax." Every minute of every day, even while you're sleeping, the creeping nightmare that is the Republican Party takes over more territory within the Trump administration. We have to stand vigilant and support Trump against them. If we allow the party elites to succeed, we may as well have never elected Trump in the first place.

THE PARTY VS. THE PEOPLE

Don't get me wrong. This is not a criticism of Trump himself or his intentions. Don't forget that while he hired the insider Rinso to be chief of staff, he also brought in real conservatives, some of whom have more important roles than chief of staff, if they can survive.

The chief of staff exerts the biggest influence on who is going to execute the president's agenda, but the true conservatives Trump has nominated, like the generals, must exert a stronger influence on what that agenda is. They should be the ones most trusted by the president. Hopefully, they will be the ones Trump will turn to when he isn't sure Rinso is doing what he wants him to do, rather than taking direction from the sellouts in the Republican Party.

I hope you noticed there was no liberal backlash to Rinso's appointment. That's because Rinso is one of the sellouts the liberals know won't really oppose the progressive agenda where it really counts. For example, he'll go along with amnesty for illegals as long as he can give it a phony name like "immigration reform" and throw in a few talking points that make it sound like there is some difference from what Nancy Pelosi or Chuck Schumer might propose.

Those are the moments it will be so important to have real conservatives in the administration, with the president's ear. They will be the ones who tell the president, behind closed doors, that the enemies within are at work.

But unlike their indifference to Rinso's appointment, the chief strategist, Stephen Bannon, was immediately met with the kind of outrageous lies usually reserved for conservative elected officials. The first was that he was a white supremacist.[5] This smear wasn't just vomited out by far-left publications like *Occupy Democrats* or *Salon*,[6] the latter adding anti-Semite and misogynist to the list of Bannon's supposed evils. CNN,[7] the *Washington Post*,[8] and the *New York Times*[9] all blared some version of the same smear within a day of his appointment.

They say when you're taking flak, you must be over the target. They even called him a Nazi, something I anticipated in my book *Government Zero*, which I wrote before Trump even announced he was running in 2015. I knew then that any conservative calling for a nationalist movement would be smeared as a Nazi. But the left always forgets one, crucial distinction: The Nazis were national socialists, not capitalists. Hitler denounced capitalism and implemented precisely the kind of centrally planned, top-down socialist economy the left in this country has been trying to force on us for one hundred years.

It's not surprising the chief strategist's answer to the charge could have come right out of my book. "I'm not a white nationalist, I'm a nationalist. I'm an economic nationalist," Bannon said.[10] I wish he would have added, "because I'm not a social- ist." That's the key difference between the nationalism I have been speaking and writing about for more than two decades and Hitler's version. Socialism is a philosophy of brute force as the answer to all questions, economic or social. It's the socialists on the left who want to run society like a dictator, not Trump.

We can deal with the left yelling "racist!" and "dictator!" for four years. We're used to it. Let's be honest, we've all some- what enjoyed them melting down like spoiled children since election night last November. The real danger to the Trump administration comes from within the Republican Party. And right from the beginning, there has been conflict between the true representatives of the people and the party insiders within the Trump administration.[11]

Even *Politico* recognized what all of you who comprise the Savage Nation already knew. The battle lines are not drawn between Republicans and Democrats anymore. They are drawn between the Washington insiders and their connected special interests and everybody else. Within Trump's administration, the insiders are led by Rinso Priebus and those representing the people by the generals and other conservative appointees. With the conservative insiders go our hopes for a Trump administra- tion that remains true to the ideas that got him elected.

REPUBLICAN TRADE TRAITORS

During the presidential campaign, Trump made frequent mention of Bill Clinton signing NAFTA. Obviously, he wanted to remind Middle America it was the Democratic nominee's husband who had put them out of work. And don't forget she was for TPP until Trump began rising in the polls opposing it. She called it "the gold standard" of trade deals.[12] Do you remember that? Then she flip-flopped and said she doesn't support it.[13]

But let's also not forget who gave birth to this disaster. The first version of the treaty was signed by Republican president George H. W. Bush in December 1992. It then passed Congress with overwhelming Republican support and Clinton signed the final, modified version.[14] Republicans voted in favor of this sellout deal, 132–43. Democrats voted in favor, 156–102.[15]

It was Republicans who stood with Obama to sell us out again in 2015, when chief sellout Mitch McConnell helped ram fast-track trade promotion authority (TPA) for Obama through the Senate over the objections of Democrats led by Harry Reid and Nancy Pelosi. That's how bad McConnell is. Reid and Pelosi were actually fighting on our side, albeit for the wrong reasons.[16]

The Republicans in Congress are so in the pocket of special interests that they were willing to give Obama enormous power in negotiating trade. TPA allowed him to send trade deals to Congress for an up or down vote and prohibited filibusters in the Senate, among other expanded powers. It was supposed to be the precursor to Obama ramming the Trans-Pacific Partnership (TPP) through Congress, even though it was dominated by Republicans.

If you think TPP has gone away for good just because Trump signed the executive order, think again. Most of the same Republican trade traitors who gave Obama fast-track authority are still in Congress. Lame duck George H. W. Bush didn't get to sign the final version of NAFTA, but a president of the opposing party did so the year after he left office. That's just a little too coincidental for comfort.

I'm not saying Trump will go back on his promise to renegotiate NAFTA or rescind his executive order on TPP. But he will be under tremendous pressure from his own party, which supported Obama against the Democrats on TPP. Republicans in Congress may try to make superficial changes to TPP and get it signed under a different name. Rinso will be in the White House, whispering lies into Trump's ear about how it's different than it was before. If conservatives aren't there to counter Rinso, they just might be successful.

Trying to trick Trump into signing a repackaged TPP may not work, but the RINOs have other tools at their disposal. Before Trump even took office, they vowed to oppose any tariffs he proposes as incentives for businesses to keep jobs in the United States.[17] That's tantamount to opposing renegotiating the deals at all. How can Trump negotiate if his threats have no teeth?

It's just like what Trump said of the Iran deal. The Iranians knew Obama wasn't going to walk away from the negotiating table, so they made no real concessions. Why should they have? They knew they could get their money back along with anything else they wanted and, unlike Obama, they negotiated purely in their own country's interests. Then they started violating the treaty before the ink was dry because they knew Obama's history at enforcing "red lines."

If Canada, Mexico, and the Asian signatories to TPP know Trump can't impose tariffs on them, he will be in an impossible negotiating position. In a perfect world, I'd love no tariffs on anything. But if we're ever going to level the playing field on international trade, our trade partners have to believe the threat of tariffs is real. We may even have to levy one or two to send the message that we're serious. Otherwise, we'll accomplish nothing on trade.

Not every Republican who supports these disastrous trade deals is a sellout per se. Some of them believe such deals are good for America. Contrary to what they might think, I understand their point of view. In the cozy confines of the classroom or the think tank, NAFTA and TPP work just fine.

Unfortunately, the real world is not a classroom or a think tank. A lot of these Republicans have never walked to their second job through the slush. They've never ridden a city bus to work. They don't know what it's like to try to put food on the table under "free trade."

Trump's economic adviser Stephen Moore used to be one of them. He's a brilliant economist who went right from the university to the think tank. He's supported deals like NAFTA and TPP all his life, until he went out campaigning for Trump. Meeting real Americans trying to make a living in corporate-owned America changed his mind.[18] It's a credit to him that his mind was open to change.

But when he told the Republicans in Congress they were no longer Reagan's party, but Trump's populist party, they didn't want to hear it.[19] They're still cashing too many corporate donation checks or too attached to their textbooks. They may need the same tough medicine as our trade partners. Let a few of them get thrown out in primaries during the next election and you'll soon see the rest get on board, if they want to stay in Washington.

Ronald Reagan did the nation a great service thirty-five years ago. After five decades of almost exclusively Democratic governance, the country had become far too socialist. We needed a man like Reagan to come in and set industry and business loose from the shackles that academic socialists had put on them. We still need Trump to undo some of what Obama has put back in place.

But this is 2017, not 1981. Reagan is dead and we now need to undo some of the damage academic conservatives have done to our country. By treating the economy like it exists in a classroom instead of the real world, they've put millions out of work and rendered millions more underemployed. By being too purist in their free-market ideology, they actually helped socialists like Obama, who promised the unemployed government help while they were down.

It's no accident a lot of the people who voted for Obama four years ago voted for Trump in 2012. They don't care about ideology. They care about what works. And for them, NAFTA hasn't worked. Neither would TPP have worked. They're smart enough to know it and motivated enough to punish elected officials who won't face reality.

A WALL OR A FENCE OR
A VIRTUAL WALL?

If I had to pick one campaign promise Donald Trump made that he absolutely, positively must keep, it's building the wall on our southern border. That is the promise that started the whole Trump movement. As important as trade is, his enormous crowds didn't chant, "Fix our trade!" at his rallies. They chanted, "Build that wall!" That was the rallying point for Trump supporters in every state. The people of Iowa may be different from the people of Texas in many ways, but they have one thing in common: They're all Americans.

Without a border, there is no America.

We've had Republicans campaign on securing the border for thirty years, but when they get into office, suddenly there are more important things to do. That's because when they're campaigning, they're trying to please us, but once they're in, they're trying to please lobbyists.

I'm not as concerned about lobbyists with Trump as I am about who he has running his departments. On the campaign trail, he stuck to his guns on building the wall, even when people within his campaign wavered. He was emphatic. He said he would build the wall and he would get Mexico to pay for it. End of story.

Or was it?

Now he has Rick Perry running the Department of Commerce[20] and Perry doesn't seem so sure his boss is really going to build a wall. Even last summer, while saying he supported Trump for president, he said the wall wasn't really going to happen. "It's a wall, but it's a technological wall; it's a digital wall," he said.[21]

I thought the glasses were supposed to make him look smarter. I have news for Perry: Saying you support Trump but the wall isn't going to happen cancels out any effect the glasses might have. Will he fall into line now that he's running one of the federal departments he said four years ago he'd eliminate as president? We'll see.

If you think you can at least count on Perry's fellow Texans in Congress, think again. The *Texas Tribune* polled[22] the thirty-eight members of Congress from Texas in December, more than 70 percent of whom are Republican. Almost none of them supported the wall Trump promised to build. Republican representative Pete Sessions said Trump's promise was just "an analogy."[23]

Senator John Cornyn said he'd support about seven hundred miles of fence in urban areas, per the 2006 Secure Fence Act, but then started talking about "eyes in the sky" and "boots on the ground."[24]

I have news for you, Senator. The people have heard this before. We have boots on the ground and eyes in the sky already. They're not working. We were promised a *wall*. Not eyes, not boots, not a fence, not a virtual wall. We were promised a wall and you'd better support Trump on building it or there will be even more surprises at the next midterm election than there were last November.

Ten of the twenty-five Republican House representatives from Texas didn't even respond to the survey. That says it all for them. When they're asked to comment on the single, most important issue of the presidential campaign and they don't even respond, you know what they're going to do when the time comes to vote.

Most of the rest were wishy-washy at best. They said they'd support a wall in some places, a fence in others, and electronic security in other places. In other words, they gave themselves room to bail out when the time comes to vote and the heat is on.

The closest we got to a full endorsement of Trump's wall by a Texas Republican came from Representative Mike McCaul. In a December 2, 2016, op-ed[25] for Fox News, he said, "We are going to build the wall. Period." But when asked by the *Texas Tribune* if that meant he supported a contiguous wall along the entire border, his spokeswoman declined to comment.[26] It doesn't say he didn't respond because he was too busy. He *declined* to comment. Why?

So, out of thirty-six House representatives and two senators from Texas, we have one "maybe" on supporting Trump's wall. And this is the most conservative border state in the union. What do you think you'd find if you surveyed Republicans in liberal New Mexico? Would it be any different in Arizona?

Don't think the academics won't weigh in against Trump on this. A wall on the border is going to require some private landowners to sell their land to the government. The government may even have to force their hands with eminent domain.[27] That will give Republicans another excuse to weasel out of keeping their promises to the people. "We must defend the sanctity of private property," they'll say.

That's another pedantic trope that sounds great in the think tank. But you tell me how much sanctity that private property will retain when Mexican drug gangs or Islamic terrorists decide to walk over the unprotected border and set up camp on it. What are the think tankers going to do for those ranchers when the next El Chapo decides their ranches might make a good entry point for his drug exports?

This is why I was so concerned the minute Rinso Priebus was made chief of staff. Do you see the connection? You have a Congress riddled with RINO Republicans and a chief of staff fresh off running the RINO RNC. You have Mr. Wall's-Never-Gonna-Happen Rick Perry running Commerce. All around him, Trump has people in his own party ready to stab him and us in the back when the Democrats put the heat on over building the wall.

Against all of that, you have loyalists in the administration and Trump himself. It reminds me of the three hundred Spartans, defending the pass against thousands of Persians during the Battle of Thermopylae 2,500 years ago. Can they hold on against the onslaught? Or will the enemy overwhelm them?

The Greeks prevailed, against all odds, in their ancient battle. But they didn't have to worry about traitors in their own ranks. Trump does. That's why we must stand by Trump. I will be there, day in and day out, speaking out on my show, *The Savage Nation,* against the RINOs. I'll need you to stand with me. Without a border, we don't have a nation. It may be up to us to make sure we do.

SAVAGE SOLUTIONS

★ Fund research by global
warming skeptics.

★ Promote conservative
conservationism over progressive
environmentalism.

★ Exercise caution and care in repealing
environmental regulations.

★ Restore real science at the
NIH, CDC, and FDA.

CHAPTER NINE

TRUMP'S WAR TO RESTORE REAL SCIENCE

President Trump appointed the CEO of ExxonMobil to be secretary of state. He has enormous power.

Rex Tillerson is an Eagle Scout. It's very important you understand why that's important. It means he's been in touch with the earth. He knows something more about the earth than the average doctrinaire knee-jerk conservative who rarely steps outside his own comfort zone, whether the radio studio or a bulletproof house, without bodyguards.

So Tillerson has done his share of investigating the earth. He is probably a warmist to some extent. And you're going to hear more about this from the Trump administration. I can guarantee you. The meetings between Al Gore and Ivanka Trump and the appointment of Tillerson almost guarantee what's coming. It may shock many of you, but Trump is going to come out and say, "Yeah, there is warming, but . . ."

I believe they may play it both ways. They'll whipsaw you. They'll say, just as ExxonMobil did, "Yes, there is some evidence of man-made global warming, but we don't believe in carbon credits."

Now, having told you what I believe may be coming from the administration, I'm going to give you scientific evidence on some of these issues and prove to you beyond a reasonable doubt that there's almost nothing we can do to stop the warming trend the liberals are always talking about, because there is no warming trend.

In fact, there may be a cooling trend. But I don't want to scare people with that.

I want to talk about all the evidence against the conclusions presented by the great Ph.D. scientist Leo DiCaprio in Trump Tower in December 2016. I have to assume that between portraying playboys, drug dealers, murderers, and all-around bad boys, Leo DiCaprio somehow earned a doctorate along the way, given the pronouncements we hear him making. While flying on his private planes and sailing on his yacht,[1] he became an expert on global warming.

Leo should spend an afternoon on dry land, reading some of the actual science. He can start with my book *Government Zero,* in which I wrote extensively about independent research, notably the Vostok ice core samples. Those samples are evidence that must be included in any and all discussions about so-called man-made global warming.

The samples were obtained by drilling down into the ice above Lake Vostok in Antarctica to a depth of ten thousand feet. French and Russian scientists obtained deep core samples allowing them to look at, among other things, the history of temperature and carbon dioxide over the past 420,000 years.

I won't rehash all the information I provided in the other book, but let me give you the highlights. These samples prove, for one, that CO_2 is not causing global warming. They suggest precisely the opposite, because they show that increases in CO_2 in the past always occurred *after* average global temperatures rose.

They also show that hundreds of thousands of years ago, both global temperatures and CO_2 levels were much higher than they are today.

I don't think I have to try too hard to prove to most readers of this book that global warming is a hoax fabricated for political and monetary ends. But I do want you to know the science backs up that claim 100 percent. You may have doubts because all you've heard for the past eight years is "the science is settled" and that virtually every climate scientist agrees.

Being a scientist myself, just writing the words "the science is settled" galls me. One thing every real scientist knows is nothing is ever settled. If that were true, we'd never have heard of Albert Einstein. Newtonian physics would have simply been "settled science."

Let me let you in on a little secret. Most of these "climate scientists" are frauds. Climate science is a discipline fabricated completely for political reasons. I know this because back when I was doing real science in rain forests all over the world, almost nobody referred to themselves as "climate scientists." The people who cared about the environment were conservationists, like me, not environmentalists.

As Richard Lindzen, the Alfred P. Sloan Professor of Meteorology at MIT and a member of the National Academy of Sciences, has said, "Even in 1990 no one at MIT called themselves a 'climate scientist,' and then all of a sudden everyone was. They only entered it because of the bucks; they realized it was a gravy train. You have to get it back to the people who only care about the science."[2]

Trump's election may be changing the way the wind blows in this area. Regardless of his pick for secretary of state, Trump himself has expressed skepticism about the global warming hoax in the past and that's all we really need. Unlike the pseudoscientists in the Intergovernmental Panel on Climate Change (IPCC), I don't suggest the other side of the debate be silenced or imprisoned. I have a more reasonable suggestion for the Trump administration: Fund all climate science research to include the skeptics.

By all means continue to study global temperatures and other weather phenomena with reasonable funding from the federal government. But the funding has to include those who have valid concerns or criticisms of what has become "conventional wisdom" on climate.

I believe this would mark the beginning of the end of the global warming hoax. The reason so many scientists are willing to go along with this preposterous theory is that they are dependent upon government money. Balance the funding and we'll see a sudden uptick in skepticism about the real effects of man's activities on climate. Once the two theories compete on a level playing field based on real evidence and honest science, I'm confident the truth will prevail.

Once it does, conservatives should reclaim their leading role in truly preserving the environment.

CONSERVATISM AND CONSERVATION

Global warming may be a lie, but ecosystems are not. That's the real science of the environment. I've been a lifelong conservationist; but I'm not an environmentalist. There's a huge difference between the two.

Environmentalists use the animals, land, air, and water as political tools to advance a global socialist agenda. A conservationist is something quite different. In case you haven't noticed, *conservationist* and *conservative* come from the same root word. The conservationist movement in this country was originally led by conservatives like Teddy Roosevelt, who understood that conserving the earth was every bit as important as conserving the social, cultural, and political traditions that form the basis of our liberty.

We on the conservative side of the band should own the environment. We shouldn't have let the Marxists take control of this issue, with the scare tactics that have, frankly, come back to bite them. Other than the academics, and the businessmen who make a fortune off the global green mafia, very few people believe any of the statements that are being made. Eddie isn't as dumb as the liberal elites think he is.

We all know that the evidence has been skewed, lied about. Made up. The "hockey stick" data, for example, is shown to be completely fraudulent.[3]

Does that mean that we as conservatives should just walk away from the whole issue and laugh about it? And go about eating our cheeseburgers and say anyone who wants to save the trees or save the air or save the waters or save the elephants or save the whales is a commie wacko?

Well, do so at your own risk of being a moron. If you want to think like a Neanderthal from another era, go ahead. Sit in your chair, smoke a cigar, drink your scotch, and laugh at anyone who wants to save the whales. Call them environmental wackos. You can laugh, but nature will have the last laugh.

Slaughtering wildlife is one thing. Hunting for food is another. And conserving what is not yours to kill is yet another. Protecting ecosystems and species is protecting yourself. By safeguarding the biodiversity of our balanced, ocean ecosystems, including the whale, you are protecting yourself and your descendants. That's hard for the average Neanderthal to understand. But just remember, the original Neanderthals are extinct.

Within the microcosm of conservative politics, I own the environmental issue. There is certainly no one else in talk radio who has my credentials to talk about it.

Seven collections of my plants are in museums around the world. That's important, because if you're a plant collector and you observe botanical species over a long period of time, and compare them with past samples of these botanical species, you get to see certain things. I've done so and made certain observations.

I've worked in the environmental field since the 1970s. In fact, one of my earliest and most popular books was *Plant a Tree: A Plan for the Regreening of America*. I worked on that for three years, going city to city, state to state, to devise plans for regreening America. I was like a Johnny Appleseed in those days.

So, I've been deeply involved in this. I've saved portions of rain forests here and there. I'm not a Johnny-come-lately to the conservation movement.

WHY CONSERVATIVES SHOULD SAVE THE WHALES

I want to save the whales. I'll bet you never thought you'd hear that from the most conservative talk show host on the radio. You've been told only whacked-out liberals care about anything to do with nature, but that's a lie.

Many of you may never have heard about the early days of the ecology movement, which would be considered quaint by today's standards. If you studied ecology in my day, you came to understand that we're part of a large ecosystem. Even if you live in an insulated world of your own making, you're part of a large harmonium of living creatures. The earth itself is a living organism.

When you come to understand what deep ecology really means, you realize that if you poison the earth, whatever your reasons may be, you're poisoning yourself. When you destroy the eggshell of an eagle and the eagle can no longer reproduce, you've destroyed yourself. You are the eagle. And someday, the same poison that killed the eagle will kill you.

Why in 2017 do we permit these throwbacks from Japan, Russia, Norway, and Finland to kill whales? There is no reason for it. It's pure, unadulterated throwback behavior. Effectively enforcing international laws to protect these magnificent creatures would do far more good than wasting resources on the nonexistent global warming "crisis."

This ties in to the Trump presidency in many different ways. Trump's secretary of state nominee Rex Tillerson has gone on record saying he does believe there is evidence of global warming, but . . . The "but" is whatever he wants it to be. It's a clever way of triangulating the opposition. You throw them a bone by saying their positions have validity, but then you don't do anything about it.

Instead of employing that tactic, I want the Trump administration to redirect the environmental movement away from the Marxists and back to its conservative, conservationist roots. Just because I know the global warming hoax is false doesn't mean I like pollution. Nobody hates it more than I do. I've run all over the globe to get away from pollution.

I remember living in Queens when I was young. I left because the air was polluted and I couldn't stand it. It was that polluted because there were no environmental laws to prevent people from burning garbage in their apartment building incinerators. I'd wake up in Queens to this tremendous soot that was falling all over the street, which I was inhaling. I knew that if I stayed there, I'd get sick and die a premature death. I left for more pristine lands.

Where are we today with environmental regulations? Have we gone too far or not far enough? We certainly have the wrong regulations in a lot of areas. That's because the liberals have been in charge and they pass environmental regulations to attack free enterprise, not protect the environment. But where will Trump go?

Despite his statements in the past, I believe Trump is going to move radically in directions that will surprise you. He's going to embrace the Al Gore view of global warming. That's why he had Gore and Leo DiCaprio in the tower. He's going to push the big lie and then back off and not do anything about it. He'll have the liberals completely neutralized. They won't be able to say Trump is a global warming denier and they won't be able to get the Republican Congress to pass anything meaningful. It's ingenious when you think about it, but it doesn't help conservatives reclaim the conservation movement they rightfully own.

Protecting the environment is patriotic. It is a duty, to your country, to the human race, and to God. By protecting the environment, you're honoring creation and demonstrating the respect that underlies a conservative's religious and political background.

Whales are the largest animals on the planet. Killing them isn't easy; it's very hard. Whale hunting is unimaginably cruel. Whales are social animals. They know when they're being killed. Their friends in the pod know when a mother is being killed and pulled apart by these vermin from Japan, Norway, and Finland.

Whalers are the last remnant of a Neanderthal past. In a way, they are worse than ISIS, because the whales have no guns. They have no way to protect themselves. And they are some of the gentlest creatures on the planet.

Just ask anyone who travels to California or Mexico to go whale watching, where they know the whales are safe. The whales swim up to the tour boats and open their big eyes, which are the size of saucers. They look back at the people looking at them because they're social animals.

Whales love human beings and we reward them for their

love and their trust by butchering them in the most brutal way you can ever imagine. It has to stop.

Back in December, I had a guest on my show who is actually doing something about this problem. Paul Watson founded the Sea Shepherd Conservation Society to take direct action on protecting marine wildlife and ecosystems from poachers. His group operates on a tiny fraction of the budget Greenpeace operates on, but accomplishes far more.

Watson's group is controversial. They have been called vigilantes and worse by detractors for taking the law into their own hands. Admittedly, their practices walk a fine line. But they exist for only one reason: Governments, including our own, have failed in their duty to enforce international laws protecting whales and other endangered species. The poachers must be stopped.

NOT ALL ENVIRONMENTAL REGULATIONS ARE COMMUNIST

I read a heartbreaking story[4] a few months back. It was about thousands of snow geese dying when they landed on a toxic, open pit mine while trying to escape a snowstorm in Montana. Twenty-seven years of copper mining had laced the pit with arsenic, iron, zinc, and sulfuric acid. This was a mine that had been closed for more than thirty years, becoming a Superfund cleanup site soon after it closed.

Ten thousand geese landed in this poisoned pond of toxic waste and many of them died. They died because we have criminals in the business world who have created hazardous waste and neglected to clean up after themselves. This is why we need very strong environmental laws.

I realize Trump has appointed a leading critic of the Environmental Protection Agency, Oklahoma attorney Scott Pruitt, to lead the agency. That's a very good thing because the EPA has to be brought under control. However, I will stand vigil at my microphone every day on *The Savage Nation* warning America against going back seventy years and erasing all the environmental laws. We'd be committing a crime against the earth and against our animal friends.

We cannot go backward in order to go forward. I agree the EPA shouldn't even exist, but we cannot let for-profit businesses have free rein over the air, water, and land, with no controls on how they use or abuse them. For those dogmatic conservatives who disagree, I'll remind them there was a time when pollution was so bad rivers actually caught on fire.[5] There are still places in the world where it happens.[6] The smog in Los Angeles was so bad in the 1960s that you couldn't see the mountains.[7]

When it was found that the eggs of eagles were being destroyed by DDT, because the shells were too thin to support the gestation and birth of the bird, DDT was banned.

If you don't understand that you are the eagle, you understand nothing. Within the ecological chain of life, we are the eagle. It was only by understanding the eagle was going to die that we were going to die next. Where do you think the cancer epidemic is coming from? It's coming from the air we breathe, the food we eat, and the water we drink, which are all filled with toxins.

Creating an unconstitutional agency may not have been the answer, but something had to be done. And let's not forget the EPA was created by a Republican.

We must take care of our animal friends and not poison them. We must not go back to turning our bays into sludge and our rivers and streams into flammable hazardous waste dumps. We must not go back to turning our air into soot-filled landscapes. We must not rape our forests. I am very much like Teddy Roosevelt in that regard.

We must be very careful because we have a polar opposite of Obama in the executive branch in many ways. We have people coming into very high positions who are the opposite of the so-called progressives Obama appointed. For the most part, that's a good thing.

I see Trump as very much a fiscal conservative and a security conservative. His appointments for national security and the departments of State, Health and Human Services, and Defense are all very good people. But we have to be very careful we don't eliminate laws and regulations that protect our little friends with wings, fins, and fur from the rapacious vermin who would kill them all off for a dollar's profit.

When it comes to most of the policies we've suffered under for the past eight years, including social policies, we need to do a complete 180. But in terms of environmental policy, we must be careful we do not go back a hundred years and make the mistakes that were made before.

CLEAN UP THE NIH AND CDC

In 2015, during one of Donald Trump's many appearances on my radio show, *The Savage Nation,* I rhetorically offered to head up the National Institutes of Health if Trump won. I said,

"When you become president, I want you to consider appointing me to head of the NIH. I will make sure that America has real science and real medicine again in this country because I know the corruption. I know how to clean it up and I know how to make real research work again."[8]

Trump replied very positively, saying, "You know, you'd get common sense if that were the case because I hear so much about the NIH and it's terrible."

It was just two like-minded people talking about the abysmal lack of real science being done at the agency, which has been completely politicized, just like the CDC. Neither of us considered it a serious proposition. But the liberal media went berserk, excoriating Trump for even considering such a "deplorable" right-winger as Michael Savage to head up the sacred agency.

In truth, I *would* bring a lot of common sense to the agency, along with a lot of pink slips, if it were under my direction. But as I've said many times, I am not cut out to be a bureaucrat. I am a writer, a thinker, and a radio talk show host. That is where I belong and that is where I intend to stay.

Nevertheless, Trump needs someone in that job who would approach the agency the same way I would, as a scientist interested in public health, first and foremost. He needs to clean house there and at the CDC, which has falsified scientific data for Obama's entire term to hide how destructive his immigration policies have been.

The good news is Thomas Frieden resigned as head of the CDC.[9] This was the man, appointed by Obama in 2009, who oversaw the complete eradication of any scientific methodology at that agency, in my opinion. Under his leadership, we saw outbreaks of measles, tuberculosis, EV-D68, and other new or previously eradicated diseases. And what did Frieden's CDC do in virtually each case? Blame the victims. Blame anti-vaccination groups and not even consider that the source of the diseases might be immigrants.

Let me be clear on one thing: I am not anti-vaccine. Somehow the liberal media has created that story out of my saying precisely the opposite to a caller on my radio show in 2015. The caller asked if it was true that pharmaceutical companies put aluminum and mercury in vaccines and if they were dangerous. I'll give you my exact words, direct from a transcript of the show.

All right. This is a very serious question. There are vaccines which still contain a form of mercury, although there are reports that some manufacturers have removed the mercury from the vaccinations. Now, you're asking about a very big topic. *Do I believe in vaccinations? Yes.* Do I believe in all the vaccinations? Not necessarily. So, which vaccination are we talking about? (Emphasis added)[10]

The man eventually told me his daughter had not had any vaccinations. Here is what I told him:

Well, you've got to be very cautious. If you don't permit your beautiful child to have a vaccine, you're putting her at risk of a disease, so, you know, be careful. And it's going to require a lot more research on your part, but don't put your daughter at risk for these diseases. They were brought in by illegal aliens, these new diseases, or the old diseases which are now resurgent, and now we have to protect our children.[11]

If you can somehow conclude my advice to the caller to have his child vaccinated proves I am an anti-vaxxer, then I must diagnosis you as suffering from that mental disorder called liberalism. Like everything else related to medicine, health, and nutrition, I approach vaccinations like the *scientist* I am. I look at the known data and draw the best conclusions I can, always ready to consider new, even contradictory data.

I don't pick a camp based on my political beliefs and believe whatever the talking heads in that camp tell me to. And when it comes to public health questions, my priority is always what is best for public health, not my political beliefs. That's what was missing at the NIH and CDC under Obama.

So, you can understand my frustration at Trump's decision to appoint Robert F. Kennedy Jr. to chair a vaccine safety commission.[12] I know a lot more about science than RFK Jr. This is a man who has likened vaccines to the Holocaust. Why would Trump bring a man like this into his inner circle? That's not advancing the cause of restoring real science at the federal government level, in my opinion.

While I believe most vaccinations are beneficial to public health, I don't believe the small group of people who refuse to get their children vaccinated is the sole cause of the recent outbreaks of these new and previously eradicated diseases. Like any trained scientist, I wouldn't draw a conclusion like that unless I could control for all other reasonably likely causes.

So, when a president suddenly floods his country with

immigrants and refugees from countries with high infection rates for tuberculosis and other previously eradicated diseases and there are subsequent outbreaks of those same diseases, I would find it impossible to ignore the possibility the immigrants brought the diseases in. But that is exactly what the CDC did. They were completely disinterested in investigating the origin of the diseases, except in the one case where they were confident the source was tourists.[13] For the Disneyland measles outbreak, they were able to trace the source of the disease within weeks, proving it can be done. I should know; I'm a trained epidemiologist.

But for many of the other outbreaks, the source of the disease was a mystery, if the outbreak was acknowledged at all. As of this writing, the CDC still claims it is "concerned about AFM, a serious illness that we do not know the cause of or how to prevent it."[14] *AFM* stands for acute flaccid myelitis, a condition that causes polio-like symptoms in children and which "in 2014 coincided with a national outbreak of severe respiratory illness among people caused by enterovirus D68 (EV-D68),"[15] according to the CDC's website.

Maybe it's just a coincidence that disease outbreaks that don't reflect poorly on Obama's immigration policies are easy to trace, but those that one would naturally suspect were brought in by Obama's illegal immigrants and refugees are a complete mystery. But I doubt it.

Trump has always recognized the danger of allowing deadly diseases to enter our country. But he's going to be under constant pressure to buckle on this issue from anyone with a political or financial interest in destroying our borders. Obama's "Ebola Czar" Ron Klain has already weighed in,[16] criticizing Trump for suggesting we should employ the first rule of infectious disease control: Don't let the disease into the country in the first place.

We avoided an Ebola outbreak in this country despite Obama's disregard for that rule, not because of it. But you can be sure this dubious success will be cited over and over to attempt to discredit any attempt by the Trump administration to enact stricter measures on illegal immigration and the more intensive screening or quarantining of persons arriving in the United States from countries with high infection rates of communicable diseases.

In addition to following the first rule of infectious disease control, Trump's immigration policies should also follow the second: If infected or high-risk individuals do enter the country, contain the infection geographically. In plain English, don't ship refugees from countries rampant with infectious diseases to every corner of our own. No rational person would believe a president would do such a thing to his own country, if he weren't here to see it. But Obama did.

Trump's pick for secretary of Health and Human Services, Tom Price, is a solid pick. He is a physician and will oversee the CDC and NIH. But he's mainly known for his opposition to Obamacare. Repealing and replacing that monstrosity will clearly be his focus. We'll have to see how much emphasis he puts on reorienting the NIH and CDC back toward doing real science.

SAVAGE SOLUTIONS

★ Root out the socialist propaganda
Obama concealed in the National
Defense Authorization Act.

★ Jail anarchists who cross
state lines to incite unrest.

★ Shield religion from persecution
by passing the First Amendment
Defense Act.

CHAPTER TEN

TRUMP'S WAR FOR THE FIRST AMENDMENT

Trump's victory over Clinton has resulted in liberals throwing childlike tantrums all over the world. Since last November 8, we've heard a dozen stories about why Trump's victory wasn't legitimate. First, it was the Electoral College, an institution liberals have no problem with when a Democrat wins.[1] Then it was Russian propaganda, which deceptive left-wing conspiracy theorists alleged co-opted hundreds of conservative and libertarian news outlets to influence voting results.[2]

And, of course, when all else fails, the left just chalks up rejection of it's suicidal policies like open borders to racism and bigotry. Anyone who voted for Trump must be a racist or a bigot, even those Trump voters who voted for Obama in 2012.[3]

What the left-wingers propose to do about this catastrophe for their socialist agenda ranges from the humorous to the ominous. On the humorous side, there is a proposed ballot measure for California to secede from the union.[4] "Yes California," the group that sponsored the measure, has been around for more than two years. But a spokesman for the group said it accelerated its plans to get secession on the ballot because of Trump's victory.

I put this liberal tantrum in the humorous category because it's never going to happen. But it's interesting from a historical perspective because it's not the first or even the second time a secession movement resulted from a presidential election. In fact, there is a relevance here to my subject in this chapter that you may not be aware of.

The first thing everyone thinks of when they hear the word *secession* is the Civil War. Everyone knows the first seven states of the Confederacy seceded as a direct result of Lincoln's election. That was the first time a secession movement succeeded at the state level, but it wasn't the first time several states considered leaving over the election of a president.

The first time it happened was 1800, when Thomas Jefferson was elected. That election and subsequent secession movement is much more relevant to 2016 than the Civil War. In 1800, it was the big-government party, the Federalists, who lost. And the control freaks in New England, the original "progressives," threw the same kind of tantrum liberals are throwing now. They eventually had a convention to vote on secession during Madison's administration, but they were already talking about it immediately after Jefferson's election, just as Yes California is talking about it now.

Jefferson addressed the controversy during his first inaugural with some of the greatest words in any speech ever given by a U.S. president. He said, "We are all Republicans, we are all Federalists. If there be any among us who would wish to dissolve this Union or to change its republican form, let them stand undisturbed as monuments of the safety with which error of opinion may be tolerated where reason is left free to combat it."[5]

Take a moment to consider those immortal words. Here was a president who had just taken office after what remains one of the most controversial elections in history. His party had won a resounding victory, but Jefferson himself had finished in a tie with a rival from his own party, Aaron Burr. It took dozens of ballots in the House of Representatives and some political intrigue by Jefferson's fiercest rival, Alexander Hamilton, just to get him elected.

So, the 1800 election was at least as contentious as 2016, probably more so. But Jefferson still sought to unite the country, just as Trump did on election night when he said, "For those who have chosen not to support me in the past, of which there were a few people, I'm reaching out to you for your guidance and your help so that we can work together and unify our great country."[6]

Contrast that with Obama's speech[7] after the 2012 election, which he won. Did you hear him asking Republicans for their guidance and help? Of course not. He did the obligatory sit-down with the losing opponent and then, even after losing the Senate in 2014, arrogantly legislated around the wishes of Congress with his "pen and phone."

But the main reason I brought up Jefferson's speech was his principled defense of free speech. Here was a president facing the possibility of states seceding from the Union, just as Lincoln did later, but still did not seek to use government power to silence them, so long as "reason is left free to combat it."

That last part is important. Everyone is a staunch supporter of their own free speech, but not of those who disagree with them. Free speech doesn't mean you have a right to immunity from disagreement. You have a right to say whatever you wish, but so do those who may vilify you for what you've said.

Let me spell it out for the liberals. When you say something idiotic and someone replies, "That's idiotic," that's not suppressing your freedom of speech. It's him exercising his own.

I've been on the radio for more than twenty years and believe me, I've been called a lot worse than idiotic. I've never shied away from responding to my detractors, sometimes in devastating fashion, but I've never tried to silence them, even though my opponents have not granted me the same respect.

Trump has also endured false accusations, insults, and slanders of all sorts since announcing his run for the presidency in 2015. They've called him a dictator. They've made up fake news about him. They've boycotted his inauguration. But despite all of it, when push came to shove, Trump stood up for free speech and freedom of the press, just as I have so many times in the past.

Trump called his first news conference in several months on January 11. The briefing and Q&A session covered many topics, but one of them was the "fake news" published by *BuzzFeed*[8] and CNN[9] regarding sexually depraved acts Russian intelligence supposedly filmed Trump engaging in while in a hotel in Russia. By the time of the news conference, the story had been completely discredited by all but the most delusional of Trump's opponents.

In that context, a reporter asked Trump what he wanted to do about it. The first part of the question is inaudible, but it reads, "(inaudible) published fake news and all the problems that we've seen throughout the media over the course of the election, what reforms do you recommend for this industry here?"[10]

Liberals love the word *reform.* So do RINOs. It's invariably their euphemism for some new form of government theft or regulation. Whenever you hear a progressive or a RINO use the word *reform,* you can bet your wealth or your freedom will soon be under attack.

This was no exception. I'm not sure whether the reporter was trying to bait Trump or just didn't know any other way to respond, as most liberals don't, to behavior he didn't approve of, other than bringing government power to bear against it. Trump's answer probably surprised some of those in attendance, but it didn't surprise me.

"Well, I don't recommend reforms. I recommend people that are—that have some moral compass . . . They're very, very dishonest people, but I think it's just something we're going to have to live with."[11]

Of course, we heard nothing about this moment in the media. The man with more incentive to attack freedom of the press than virtually anyone on the planet made a principled stand in its defense, just as I have so many times in the past.

I've actually been banned from an entire nation—Britain—just for telling truths its government didn't want to hear. But that only affected me personally. What Obama and Congress did to us last December is much more ominous.

THE NEW MINISTRY OF TRUTH

By late December in the last year of any other president's second term, respect for the electorate usually outweighs activism, but not for Emperor Barry or the sellouts who remain in Congress. Christmas fell on a Sunday last year and late on the Friday preceding it, when no one was paying attention, Obama signed the National Defense Authorization Act (NDAA) for fiscal year 2017 into law.[12]

That might not sound controversial, as Congress passes an NDAA every fiscal year. It's the congressional authorization to fund the military. But funding the military isn't why Obama waited until just before a holiday to sign it. Hidden within the bill was a provision that for all intents and purposes creates a U.S. government Ministry of Truth, right out of Orwell's *1984*.

Fanatical liberal Rahm Emanuel famously said, "You never want a serious crisis to go to waste. Things that we had postponed for too long, that were long-term, are now immediate and must be dealt with. This crisis provides the opportunity for us to do things that you could not do before."[13] The crisis Emanuel was talking about at the time was the 2008 financial meltdown. The opportunity for Obama was to impose his socialist economic policies on a nation in shock from the mostly government-caused Great Recession.

Well, if you haven't noticed, Trump's election itself is a crisis for the liberal power structure. But since they can't come out and admit that they don't really care about democracy when the other side wins, they have manufactured a crisis called "Russia hacked the election." We're supposed to believe Trump is president only because Russian intelligence hacked the Democratic National Committee email server and basically confirmed what we already knew about Hillary Clinton: that she is an unprincipled, opportunistic liar who cares little for the people who vote for her or what they want her to do in office.

Just as the neoconservatives dusted off the already-written provisions of what became the Patriot Act after 9/11, the neoconservative ventriloquists and their liberal fellow travelers have dusted off a bill creating a de facto Ministry of Truth introduced last summer,[14] well before the "fake news" narrative was even scripted, and used this latest, completely phony "crisis" to get it through Congress and signed by the president.

The new law[15] begins by basically codifying the anti-Russia propaganda the Obama administration and his liberal and neoconservative supporters spouted for the past eight years. It then authorizes Congress to create a "Center for Information Analysis and Response," the purpose of which is "whole-of-government initiatives to expose and counter foreign information operations."

There is more lawyerly doubletalk about what this center will do, but I'll translate it for you. It's supposed to counter anything it deems as foreign propaganda with propaganda of its own, using the vast resources of the federal government put at its disposal by the bill.

That might not sound so bad until you remember the Establishment has decided that any support for Trump in the media is de facto Russian propaganda. For them, this means my radio show, *The Savage Nation,* may need to be "exposed and countered."

Where does countering end? I don't know. I don't particularly want to find out. U.S. government-funded propaganda campaigns against my show or other conservative media sounds bad enough. Had Hillary Clinton been elected, I'm sure it wouldn't have stopped there. But just because Trump is in the White House, don't think there won't be pressure to enforce this chillingly Orwellian law. As Trump tries to keep the promises that got him elected, particularly repairing our relationship with Russia, expect accusations of foreign influence aimed at any conservative media supporting him.

The Establishment will try to make everyone believe that to support Trump's 2016 campaign platform is to support foreign adversaries trying to influence U.S. policy. In other words, "War is Peace. Freedom is slavery. Ignorance is strength." We are going to have to push back hard at any sign Congress is trying to pressure the Trump administration to enforce this unconstitutional provision of the NDAA.

SOROS' BROWNSHIRTS

Just as the First Amendment does not allow the government to suppress dissent, it does not sanction using violence to promote one's message. It specifically protects "the right of the people *peaceably* to assemble, and to petition the Government for a redress of grievances." Yet Obama and his cohorts in the media have repeatedly characterized the domestic terrorism perpetrated by groups like Black Lives Matter as peaceful protest, even when innocent bystanders have been assaulted, shops looted, and whole neighborhoods burned to the ground.[16]

When liberals of all races and creeds began rioting after Trump's election, O did the same thing. He actually stood on foreign soil and called the riots "one of the great things about our democracy."[17] I'm not fabricating this. This divisive serpent had become so arrogant, so unafraid of any consequences for the damage he'd done to this nation, that he would look into the camera and say outrageous things like that, knowing an adoring media would back him up.

He had the media and half the electorate so hypnotized for eight years that I don't doubt many people have trouble distinguishing his progressive fantasies from reality. Many well-meaning people no doubt believe that what we've seen over the past few years in Ferguson, Baltimore, New York, and elsewhere has something to do with free speech or the First Amendment.

It doesn't. When you write an article or a blog, appear on a television show, or even assemble peacefully in a public forum meant for that purpose, you are exercising rights the First Amendment protects. But the moment you pick up a brick and throw it through a window, or join a mob blocking an expressway, which violates someone else's right to liberty, or especially when you commit a violent act against an innocent bystander, you are no longer exercising your First Amendment rights. You are now violating the rights of others, something the First Amendment does not allow you to do.

Let's not forget who is starting the riots. These are not spontaneous demonstrations by people who live in the neighborhoods where the riots occur. They are paid agents provocateurs, sometimes brought in from outside to riot, loot, and assault innocent victims. They represent the same threat to freedom of speech as the original Brownshirts and Blackshirts in 1920s Germany and Italy, respectively. Like those fascist paramilitary groups, the new brownshirts don't seek to exercise free speech but to repress it.

If you doubt what I'm saying, I invite you to attend a Black Lives Matter rally and express a dissenting opinion. Try to point out to those "peaceful protesters" that most of the police shootings reported in the media as racially motivated turned out to be justified, not to mention the millions of unreported police interactions that occur every day without inappropriate force or bias.

Of course, I am speaking hypothetically. Please do not test the theory based on what I said. I don't want to see anyone get hurt. I think everyone reading this book knows they wouldn't be met with an invitation to sit down and talk under the circumstances I described above.

But that is what free speech really means, the freedom to express an unpopular opinion without fear of violent retribution, either from the government, from civilian gangs, or from individuals.

Let's not forget the opinion I described isn't even unpopular. It might be at a Black Lives Matter rally, but Trump's election was very much an affirmation that most people in America know the overwhelming majority of cops aren't racists. That's just another left-wing fiction the media shamelessly promotes, even in the face of overwhelming evidence to the contrary.

Just before the new year, we heard directly from the chief financial architect of Black Lives Matter and a host of other anti-American organizations I named in my last book, *Scorched Earth*. I am talking, of course, about George Soros, whom I consider one of the most evil men on the planet.

Soros penned an essay[18] in which he briefly summarized what we can expect to be the left's talking points and agenda for the foreseeable future during Trump's administration. In it he trots out the usual progressive tropes about inequality and the greed of the wealthy undermining the liberal utopias America and Europe supposedly were before Brexit and Trump's election.

It's always hard to tell if you're dealing with evil or stupidity when listening to the lunatic ravings of liberals. But not with Soros. We know he's not stupid. That only leaves one explanation for the lies he told in his essay, which of course had all of the liberal media tripping over each other to acknowledge its supposed brilliance and insight.

Like the Devil himself in the movie *The Exorcist,* Soros mixes lies with the truth to deceive the envious, the lazy, and the incompetent into believing the only problem with Western civilization is a "lack of redistributive policies." He correctly observes the crash of 2008 resulted in Europe being "transformed into a relationship between creditors and debtors, where the debtors had difficulties in meeting their obligations and the creditors set the conditions the debtors had to obey." But like every socialist who ever lived, he places the blame on the creditors and portrays the debtors who borrowed money to live beyond their means as the victims!

Ironically, Soros says his family didn't flee Hungary until 1947, when the country was under communist control. His Jewish family had survived the Nazi occupation thanks to his father's wits, but they didn't leave until the communists took over. Why didn't they stay? Certainly, there wasn't a "lack of redistributive policies" under the communists. They redistribute at 100 percent. When you read the ravings of liberals carefully, their logic inevitably falls apart.

This is the man who gave $33 million to Black Lives Matter[19] and who funds MoveOn.org and the rest of his so-called Open Society Foundations. They should be called the anti-American Foundations, because every one of them seeks to break up the foundation of American culture. More than fifty groups directly funded by Soros organized the "spontaneous" Women's March the day after Trump's inauguration.[20] Another hundred are hard at work every day, agitating for left-wing causes.

Sir Arthur Conan Doyle called his fictional character Dr. Moriarty, of the Sherlock Holmes stories, "the Napoleon of

Crime." Well, George Soros is the Napoleon of American socialism. The sheer number of subversive organizations that have received funding from this man is staggering. I am listing them here so you understand just what we're up against. They include:[21]

Advancement Project
Air America Radio
All of Us or None
Alliance for Justice
America Coming Together
America Votes
America's Voice
American Bar Association Commission on Immigration
    Policy
American Bridge 21st Century
American Civil Liberties Union
American Constitution Society for Law and Policy
American Family Voices
American Federation of Teachers
American Friends Service Committee
American Immigration Council
American Immigration Law Foundation
American Independent News Network
American Institute for Social Justice
American Library Association
The American Prospect Inc.
Amnesty International

Applied Research Center
Arab American Institute Foundation
Aspen Institute
Association of Community Organizations for Reform Now
Ballot Initiative Strategy Center
Bill of Rights Defense Committee
Black Alliance for Just Immigration
Blueprint North Carolina
Brennan Center for Justice
Brookings Institution
Campaign for America's Future
Campaign for Better Health Care
Campaign for Youth Justice
Campus Progress
Casa de Maryland
Catalist
Catholics for Choice
Catholics in Alliance for the Common Good
Center for American Progress
Center for Community Change
Center for Constitutional Rights
Center for Economic and Policy Research
Center for Reproductive Rights
Center for Responsible Lending
Center on Budget and Policy Priorities
Center on Wisconsin Strategy (COWS)
Change America Now
Citizens for Responsibility and Ethics in Washington

Coalition for an International Criminal Court
Common Cause
Constitution Project
Defenders of Wildlife Action Fund
Democracy Alliance
Democracy 21
Democracy Now!
Democratic Justice Fund
Democratic Party
Demos
Drum Major Institute
Earthjustice
Economic Policy Institute
Electronic Privacy Information Center
Ella Baker Center for Human Rights
EMILY's List
Energy Action Coalition
Equal Justice USA
Fair Immigration Reform Movement
Faithful America
Feminist Majority
Four Freedoms Fund
Free Exchange on Campus
Free Press
Funding Exchange
Gamaliel Foundation
Gisha: Center for the Legal Protection of Freedom of
    Movement

Global Centre for the Responsibility to Protect
Global Exchange
Grantmakers Without Borders
Green For All
Health Care for America Now
Human Rights Campaign
Human Rights First
Human Rights Watch
I'lam
Immigrant Defense Project
Immigrant Legal Resource Center
Immigrant Workers Citizenship Project
Immigration Advocates Network
Immigration Policy Center
Independent Media Center
Independent Media Institute
Institute for America's Future
Institute for New Economic Thinking
Institute for Policy Studies
Institute for Public Accuracy
Institute for Women's Policy Research
International Crisis Group
J Street
Jewish Funds for Justice
Joint Victory Campaign 2004
Justice at Stake
LatinoJustice PRLDF
Lawyers Committee for Civil Rights Under Law

League of United Latin American Citizens
League of Women Voters Education Fund
League of Young Voters
Lynne Stewart Defense Committee
Machsom Watch
MADRE
Malcolm X Grassroots Movement
Massachusetts Immigrant and Refugee Advocacy
    Coalition
Media Fund
Media Matters for America
Mercy Corps
Mexican American Legal Defense and Education Fund
Meyer, Suozzi, English & Klein, PC
Midwest Academy
Migration Policy Institute
Military Families Speak Out
Missourians Organizing for Reform and Empowerment
MoveOn.org
Ms. Foundation for Women
NARAL Pro-Choice America
NAACP Legal Defense and Education Fund
The Nation Institute
National Abortion Federation
National Coalition to Abolish the Death Penalty
National Committee for Responsive Philanthropy
National Committee for Voting Integrity
National Council for Research on Women

National Council of La Raza
National Council of Women's Organizations
National Immigration Forum
National Immigration Law Center
National Lawyers Guild
National Organization for Women
National Partnership for Women and Families
National Priorities Project
National Public Radio
National Security Archive Fund
National Women's Law Center
Natural Resources Defense Council
New America Foundation
New Israel Fund
NewsCorpWatch
Pacifica Foundation
Peace and Security Funders Group
Peace Development Fund
People for the American Way
People Improving Communities Through Organizing
Physicians for Human Rights
Physicians for Social Responsibility
Planned Parenthood
Ploughshares Fund
Prepare New York
Presidential Climate Action Project
Prison Moratorium Project
Progressive Change Campaign Committee

Progressive States Network
Project Vote
Pro Publica
Proteus Fund
Public Citizen Foundation
Public Justice Center
Rebuild and Renew America Now (a.k.a. Unity '09)
Res Publica
Secretary of State Project
Sentencing Project
Social Justice Leadership
Shadow Democratic Party
Sojourners
Southern Poverty Law Center
State Voices
Talking Transition
Think Progress
Thunder Road Group
Tides Foundation and Tides Center
U.S. Public Interest Research Group
Universal Healthcare Action Network
Urban Institute
USAction Education Fund
Voto Latino
We Are America Alliance
Working Families Party
World Organization Against Torture
YWCA World Office

As I said, I've never called for government action against anyone spending their own money as they wish, even to promote socialist nonsense, as long as reason is left free to combat it.

But when violent revolutionaries seek to tear down the pillars of civil society and assault anyone who dissents from their nihilistic view, then there is a role for the government to step in and defend life, liberty, and property against those who wish to destroy them.

Law and order are the first foundations of civilization. Without them, it doesn't matter how technologically advanced or wealthy a society is. Trump promised on the campaign trail and during his acceptance speech at the RNC that he would restore law and order in America society. That doesn't just mean supporting the police instead of tacitly condoning violence against them, as the Community Organizer in Chief did for eight years in Washington. It also means making our streets and highways safe from the domestic terrorism masquerading as "peaceful protest" we've endured during most of those years. Which means Trump must investigate and prosecute groups and individuals who violate federal law by crossing state lines to incite unrest.

THE BATTLE FOR RELIGIOUS FREEDOM

There were many who were surprised that Donald Trump enjoyed such overwhelming support from white evangelicals.[22] After all, Trump isn't exactly the poster child for a devout Christian lifestyle. But I wasn't surprised. Trump pledged[23] to protect religious freedom, which had been under unprecedented assault during the previous eight years. Evangelicals may not have believed Trump was a model Christian, but they believed he'd keep that promise.

The very first freedom protected in the First Amendment is not free speech. It is religious freedom. For the founding fathers, this was the most important freedom. They believed the fate of one's soul was so important that only the individual could decide matters of conscience.

Have you ever noticed that the Constitution requires all representatives, executive and judicial officers, and even representatives in state legislatures to be bound by oath *or affirmation* to support the Constitution? The reason there is an alternative to taking an oath is that some religions forbid taking oaths and the founders would not require anyone—not even the president—to violate the dictates of his conscience on religious matters.

The founders believed in the right of conscience so strongly that they excused those whose religious beliefs forbade it even from fighting in defensive wars. But for the past century, this first of all rights has been under constant attack by the progressive movement, never more so than under the man we had in the White House for the past eight years.

Before Obama, most of the attacks on religious freedom were based on completely misreading the first ten words of the First Amendment and completely ignoring the next six. The first ten words, "Congress shall make no law respecting an establishment of religion," simply meant Congress couldn't create a national religion, like the Church of England. It had nothing to do with a "separation of church and state."

We know this for two reasons. First, the words "separation of church and state" appear nowhere in any of our founding documents. Second, some states had their own state religions at the time the Constitution was ratified. That was the whole reason they wanted Congress prohibited from creating a state religion—because it would invalidate their own!

So, the entire progressive movement to ban any reference to religion in public places is based on a misunderstanding at best, a bald-faced lie at worst. The words "or prohibit the free exercise thereof" means people are not supposed to be prohibited from freely expressing their religion. It doesn't say, "except in public places." People prayed in public schools for hundreds of years in America until the progressives laid siege to the First Amendment.

They all but erased God from any publicly owned property during the twentieth century. But the freedom to follow one's conscience according to one's religious beliefs remained sacrosanct on private property. That all changed when O took the oath of office.

Over the past several years, we've seen the right of conscience under constant assault by progressives, using the gay rights agenda as their bludgeon. The first nationally recognized case was the Christian bakers who politely refused to bake a wedding cake for a gay wedding, based on their deeply held religious beliefs that marriage can only be between a man and a woman. The gay couple reported the bakery to the State of Oregon Labor Board, whose commissioner awarded the gay couple $135,000 and slapped a gag order on the defendants, in addition to the monetary judgment.[24]

You have to hand it to the liberals. When they violate the Constitution, they really go all the way. Not only were the bakers' First Amendment rights to freedom of religion and speech violated, but they were judged by a member of the executive branch, which violates Oregon's constitution,[25] in which all judicial power is vested in a court system, consisting of a Supreme Court, circuit courts, county courts, justices of the peace, and municipal courts.

In concert with his left-wing street brigades, Emperor Barry Hussein launched an assault on Christian employers via that monstrosity known as Obamacare. After promising the American people that Obamacare would not be used for funding abortions, he sent his lawyers to the Supreme Court[26] to try to force the Little Sisters of the Poor to do just that in providing their employees coverage for abortion-inducing contraceptives.

The eight-person Court elected not to make a decision on the case. In what many characterized as a win for the Little Sisters, the Court "vacated" the lower court rulings[27] that had held the Little Sisters liable to provide the coverage, and asked them to reconsider. I didn't consider it a true win for religious liberty because the lower courts could use some other voodoo reasoning to make the same decision all over again, sending it back to the Supreme Court, this time possibly for a liberal justice to apply the coup de grâce.

It was just one more aspect of our culture, one more foundation of Western civilization, that Hillary Clinton was poised to destroy if she were allowed to ascend to the White House last November. When you think about it, what she might have done to religious liberty through executive orders or the next Supreme Court nomination is as bad as the war with Russia she may have dragged us into.

All of that changed with the election of Donald Trump. Not only will Trump and the Republicans repeal Obamacare, but Senator Mike Lee (R-Utah) will reintroduce the First Amendment Defense Act (FADA), which prohibits the federal government from "discriminating against people or organizations due to their opposition to same-sex marriage."[28] That's going to derail the progressive plan to blackmail churches, Christian schools, and other religious organizations into violating the tenets of their religions or lose their tax-exempt status.

The bill didn't go anywhere when it was first introduced in 2015 because even those Republicans who aren't RINOs knew Obama would veto it, as Hillary would have if she had won. But Trump will almost certainly sign the bill, which is an important step in the fight to win back the religious freedom lost during previous administrations.

By far the most important blow Trump can strike for religious freedom will be his appointments to the Supreme Court. It is here that liberal twentieth-century judges gutted the First Amendment with their bizarre "freedom from religion" doctrine.

Trump will have the opportunity to replace the late justice Antonin Scalia immediately, and three more justices who will be well into their eighties before the next election, including that destructive, uber-radical feminist Ruth Bader Ginsburg, who will be eighty-seven in 2020.[29] Trump could literally pack the Court with conservatives for the next several decades, ensuring at the very least that religious liberty suffers no more setbacks in that forum. There may even be the opportunity to reverse some of the damage.

Trump can also nullify some of Emperor Barry Hussein's worst executive orders[30] which violate religious liberty. But perhaps the most positive impact he can have on restoring religious liberty is simply to refrain from attacking it the way Obama did for eight years. Without an administration directing its attorneys to pursue cases in which religious people are persecuted, there would be far fewer opportunities for spurious rulings.

As I've said many times over the decades, a nation is defined by its borders, language, and culture. Trump must build the wall to defend our borders. And he must do everything he can to defend and restore religious liberty, the foundation upon which our culture is built.

SAVAGE SOLUTIONS

★ The problem isn't guns, it's mass shooters armed with radicalism, drugs, and mental issues.

★ Order public health agencies to conduct unbiased studies on the side effects of psychotropic drugs.

CHAPTER ELEVEN

TRUMP'S WAR FOR THE SECOND AMENDMENT

ALL QUIET ON THE GUN CONTROL FRONT—FOR NOW

Two weeks to the day before Donald Trump was inaugurated, we had another tragedy. The story has become all too familiar. A lone gunman walked into a public place, this time in an airport baggage claim area at Fort Lauderdale airport, and opened fire on random, innocent people. Five people were killed and six more injured.[1]

While the story was sadly familiar, the aftermath was not. After every other random shooting over the past several years, we've heard an immediate refrain, led by the president, from every left-wing politician, agitator, and media figure. "We must pass stricter gun control," they've told us, regardless of the reasons for the killing or whether stricter gun control would have prevented it.

This time, we heard nothing of the sort. We didn't have the usual anti-gun press conference from Obama. He told ABC mouthpiece Georgie-boy Stephanopoulos he was "heartbroken" and that tragedies like this "have happened too often during the eight years I've been president."[2] But he didn't go into his usual script about how innocent Americans who had nothing to do with the shooting should be stripped of their rights. Neither did the media. They were all strangely quiet on the subject. Of course, they did not mention the shooter was motivated by ISIS.

That quiet was the sound of a president and his fake news media who knew their attacks on this basic freedom had just been flatly rejected in the historic election the previous November. The left spent the entire transition period trying to undermine Trump's presidency before he even took the oath of office. That included hysterical protests, daily reminders that Hillary won the popular vote—at least counting all the illegal immigrants, dead people, and other noneligible voters who pulled a lever for her—and even pathetic attempts to keep Trump from taking office via the Electoral College.

But by January 6, it seemed the shellacking progressivism took from the vast majority of communities in the United States had subdued their zeal for disarming law-abiding citizens, at least for the moment. However, I caution anyone who thinks Trump being inaugurated has ended that fight. You can bet the left will regroup and again espouse the cause Hitler, Stalin, Castro, and so many other tyrants have championed. That is, seizing the people's weapons. Rendering the populations powerless to resist their tyranny.

Just as I said with Obamacare, it's not enough for us to win a momentary victory. We must recognize why the left has had success in moving their agenda forward in the first place. Just as most Americans don't want to see millions of people go without reasonable access to medical care, they also don't want to see innocent people gunned down in public places. If conservatives don't come up with a solution, the progressives will. And we know what that will be.

The socialists' success in gun control employs the same strategy as their success in health care and just about everything else. They seize on a problem, obscure the true cause, set up a straw man cause, and then propose the heavy hand of government as the only possible solution.

That's what they did with the financial meltdown of 2008, allowing them to pass Dodd-Frank and other wealth-destroying regulations. That's what they did with the global warming hoax, which gave Obama cover to mute the American oil and coal industries and further deter the general economy. That's what they did with health care, as I've already shown in a previous chapter, and that's what they want to do with the right to bear arms. When there is a tragedy that leaves well-meaning Americans vulnerable to their arguments, they seize the opportunity. "Never let a crisis go to waste."

In the absence of a recent tragedy, the left's argument for gun control is absurd on its face. They want us to believe the availability of guns and the sheer number of privately owned firearms are the reasons these tragedies happen, as if the guns themselves were the problem.

A 2016 survey[3] by the left-leaning Pew Research Center found that gun ownership by household was up 7 percent over the past two years, to 44 percent of American households.

That doesn't count the 5 percent of households who wouldn't say whether they owned a gun or not. Regardless, roughly half the population has guns. That's well over 100 million people.

That means the dozen or so people who committed the tragic crimes the left exploits to disarm us are statistically insignificant. In any kind of argument that cites the sheer number of guns as a determining factor, the number of guns used to commit these crimes is so close to zero that any statistician doing such an analysis would treat them as if they didn't even exist. What's 12 shooters divided by 100,000,000?

THE TRUE CAUSES OF MASS SHOOTINGS

The left doesn't want you to focus on at least one of the real causes of mass shootings: radical Islam. If you haven't noticed, the majority of mass shootings over the past several years hasn't been simply by lone nuts who were hearing voices. The three deadliest shootings in this country since Sandy Hook—the 2013 Washington Navy Yard shooting, the 2015 San Bernardino shooting, and the 2016 shooting at the gay nightclub in Orlando, Florida—have all been carried about by perpetrators connected to radical Islam.

The latter two incidents were publicized as such because the motivation was undeniable. The shooters themselves confirmed they were murdering innocent people in the name of their so-called religion. But I'll bet you didn't know Aaron Alexis, the Washington Navy Yard shooter, created a website called "Mohammad Salem."[4] He did. Look it up for yourself.

It was buried in the reporting on the incident at the time, but you can still find it if you look for it.

That means that all of the deadliest shootings in America since Sandy Hook were committed by shooters who were either overtly or secretly radical Islamists.

The Obama administration and its left-wing media propaganda machine never missed an opportunity to bury radical Islam when they could. It was no different in January with the Fort Lauderdale shooter, Esteban Santiago Ruiz. The FBI reported it had found no jihadi content on his social media accounts, despite widespread rumors he had expressed jihadi views online.[5]

I don't know who was assigned to that case. Maybe it was someone Obama the party animal put in there. But they seemed to have missed that obscure social media platform called Myspace, where Ruiz registered under the name "Aashiq Hammad."[6] His account included pictures of himself in Islamic clothing, recording Islamic music and downloading terrorist propaganda. The alternative media site *Got News* had all of this one day after the shooting, while the FBI was still trying to determine Ruiz's motivation weeks later.

Of course, the media had to find some motivation other than radical Islam. We did get a halfhearted attempt to blame guns. Gabby Gifford's Americans for Responsible Solutions called the tragedy a "painful reminder of our nation's gun violence crisis."[7] The Brady Campaign lashed out at Senator Marco Rubio (R-Fla.), saying "Tell hypocritical politicians to take action and pass life-saving gun laws! We need solutions not more prayers."[8]

But the story the media consolidated around was that Ruiz was suffering from PTSD after his experiences in the Iraq War. That's not an entirely unhelpful conclusion for the gun-grabbing left. If mental illness is part of the reason, they can pass laws saying anyone who is mentally ill is prohibited from owning a gun. And, of course, it will be far-left liberal psychiatrists and psychologists who will determine who is mentally ill, which will be everyone who wants a gun. It's a little like Catch-22.

There's only one problem with the official story. Ruiz created his Aashiq Hammad Myspace account in 2007, a full three years before he went to Iraq. So, maybe his mental illness was radical Islam itself. What else can you call the desire to live by the barbaric rules of AD 800, where apostates are beheaded and homosexuals thrown off rooftops?

Self-described former Palestinian terrorist Walid Shoebat says there is clear photo evidence Ruiz was a jihadi sleeper agent.[9] Shoebat had pictures of the shooter wearing a kaffiyeh while serving in the army and raising his index finger in a recognizable jihadi gesture. "And if the Nazi has a Seig Heil and cutting their sides of their hair, the Islamist uses the sabbabah (index finger) and lets the beard go while trimming the mustache,"[10] wrote Shoebat on the day of the shooting.

Certainly, Ruiz was mentally ill. But the suppression by the media of Ruiz's obvious jihadi sentiments is just another example of them distracting you from the true causes of tragedies, especially when it's radical Islam. We suffered under a president who wouldn't even say those two words together for eight years. But he was always willing to exploit tragedy to push more gun control.

Donald Trump made it absolutely clear in his inauguration speech that the days of covering up for radical Islam were over, at least in the White House. "We will reinforce old alliances and form new ones—and unite the civilized world against radical Islamic terrorism, which we will eradicate completely from the face of the Earth," Trump thundered from the Capitol balcony.[11] "Radical Islamic terrorism" reverberated like a cannon shot over the entire nation.

Trump stood firm on protecting the Second Amendment throughout his campaign and these words from his speech confirm he is determined to recognize the true cause of incidents like the one in Fort Lauderdale. To do so you must be willing to say the words. If there is a mass shooting during his tenure, and unfortunately its likely there will be, he must stand firm in saying "radical Islam" instead of "guns" if the perpetrator is another sleeper cell.

WHAT ABOUT THE DRUGS?

Certainly, I don't mean to imply that every mass shooter is a radical Islamic terrorist. There is no such evidence for the Sandy Hook shooter or many other perpetrators of similar crimes. But do you know what virtually all of them who were not jihadists had in common? They were all taking or had recently been taking psychotropic drugs.[12]

This goes all the way back to the shootings at Columbine High School in Littleton, Colorado, in 1999, perpetrated by Eric Harris, who was prescribed Zoloft and afterward Luvox, and Dylan Klebold, whose medical records have never been released.[13] The list includes Mitchell Scott Johnson and Andrew Douglas Golden, the two schoolboys who perpetrated the deadliest mass shooting at an American middle school; Steven Kazmierczak, who shot twenty-two people at Northern Illinois University, killing five; Asa Coon, who shot five people at a Cleveland high school; and many more.[14]

The shooters in virtually every high-profile mass shooting were taking or had previously taken drugs whose side effects include suicidal thoughts and/or other violent behavior.[15] Yet, after every mass shooting, the media invariably focuses on guns as the chief cause, despite the more than 100 million gun owners who weren't taking this class of drugs and didn't kill anyone. Rarely will you see the medications the shooter was taken mentioned other than in passing and sometimes not at all. Never does the media suggest a direct cause-effect relationship between the medications the shooter was taking and his crime.

One of the few exceptions to this was the reporting on Adam Lanza, the Sandy Hook Elementary School shooter. In his case, the media narrative was that Lanza should have been taking psychotropic drugs but his mother had neglected to comply with his psychiatrist.[16] And where did the liberal media go with that? That guns must be banned for anyone with mental health issues, that the government must fund more mental health care, and that these dangerous drugs may have prevented the shooting.

As I wrote in an earlier chapter, I'm trained as a scientist. I certainly don't deny the beneficial effects these drugs can have on people with serious mental illnesses. Perhaps Adam Lanza was someone who should have been taking these medications but wasn't, although there is some evidence that refutes that narrative.[17] It's certainly an uncontroversial statement that suddenly discontinuing these drugs can lead to erratic or violent behavior, among other side effects.

My main point is that on the days these tragedies occurred, tens of millions of Americans were carrying guns on the streets, into stores, restaurants, and other public places that do not prohibit them, and only one in those tens of millions committed a mass shooting. You don't have to be a trained scientist to conclude that access to firearms was not the causative factor in the tragedy.

Neither is the mere presence of "mental illness." That's a rather expansive term that we should be careful about permitting to work its way into any kind of legislation. There are many, many more people who could be described as suffering from minor mental illnesses who will not commit violence against others because of it. And you can bet your paycheck that if the government is allowed to get an expansive definition of mental illness into gun legislation, the liberal mental health industry will try to diagnose every single gun owner with some sort of mental illness. Perhaps they will invent the term *gunophilia*!

No, it was not even merely the presence of mental illness that these mass shooters all had in common. It was being treated for mental illness, appropriately or not, with controversial psychotropic drugs.

I'm not suggesting any of the mass shooters were inappropriately prescribed these drugs. There is no way to know one way or another without an intensive study of each of their case histories. But we do know there is widespread concern these drugs are being overprescribed.[18] Aside from their relationship to mass shootings, use of this class of drugs also leads to more overdose deaths than heroin.[19]

What public health agencies like the FDA and NIH should be looking at is whether the inappropriate prescription of these drugs, especially to grammar school–aged boys who are just acting like normal boys, are systematically building more Adam Lanzas and Steven Kazmierczaks. At the very least, logic dictates that the more people who are prescribed with drugs with side effects that include suicidal thoughts and violent behavior, the more violence and suicides we should expect to see.

This is just another reason Trump must restore real science to the public health agencies. This is an area where there is obviously a problem, but not one with an easy solution. Many people need these drugs to live normal, reasonably healthy lives. Yet the drugs' side effects can be dangerous and there is an undeniable correlation to mass shootings.

The next time someone who has been prescribed these drugs commits a high-profile act of violence, Trump needs to use the bully pulpit to call attention to the real cause. After eight years of solidarity between the president and media against the Second Amendment, Trump must be the first president to say the words "psychotropic drugs," just as he boldly said "radical Islam" in his inauguration speech.

By telling the truth about these shootings, Trump can kill two birds with one stone: protect the Second Amendment, and drain that part of the swamp occupied by drug companies getting government cover and subsidies to push dangerous drugs on children who don't need them.

SAVAGE SOLUTIONS

★ Study the global agenda of the
intelligence community.

★ Back Trump's plan to end the
new Cold War with Russia.

★ Learn how to recognize fake news.

CHAPTER TWELVE

TRUMP'S WAR AGAINST THE DEEP STATE

On January 11, President-elect Donald Trump conceded "as far as hacking, I think it was Russia, but I think we also get hacked by other countries and other people."[1] It was a significant victory for the Deep State in its all-out war against Trump and everything he represents.

During the same week, the intelligence community, together with its friends in the media, had trumpeted both the Director of National Intelligence (DNI) report on Russia hacking the election and the fake news story about Trump's alleged sexual misbehavior in a Russian hotel in 2013. This is the kind of pressure Trump is going to have to face day in, day out, for the duration of his presidency.

Those of you who regularly listen to my radio show, *The Savage Nation,* are probably familiar with the term *Deep State,* but some of you may not be. I know there are millions of people who previously had ignored politics for decades, convinced they would remain forgotten men and women, not caring who won elections. Trump's victory has brought millions of new enlistees to our fight to save the greatest nation on earth. So, for those newcomers reading this book, I'm going to tell you something about how daunting our task is. As I've said throughout, winning an election was only the beginning.

Every four to eight years, Americans elect a new president, who then appoints a cabinet and a host of other officers to high-level jobs running the federal government. If the new president is from a different political party than the one who preceded him, the average voter believes everything will change. In reality, very little ever does.

That's because the president doesn't replace the vast majority of the 1.4 million[2] civilian government employees. Most of them are career people who serve under multiple presidents from both major parties. They get a new boss three or four management levels above them on the chain of command, but go on doing their jobs the same way, for the most part, regardless of who wins.

I'm not suggesting anything sinister about this, per se. The majority of these employees are doing routine jobs, like delivering the mail, processing Social Security checks, doing food inspections, or maintaining national parks. Our elections are not primarily about what they do or how they do it. Yes, the government is always behind the private sector in terms of innovation and efficiency, but how many different ways can you empty the garbage cans at Yellowstone Park?

But between the janitor at Yellowstone and the secretary of defense there is a significant layer of people who do make a difference and don't for the most part get replaced with a new president. They work in the intelligence agencies, the Defense Department, and in other key agencies. They are also career government workers, immersed in Washington culture and ideology. It is this entrenched class that is partially responsible for the uniformity with which the federal government operates, particularly in terms of foreign policy, no matter who gets elected.

Yes, it may veer to the right or the left somewhat, depending upon the president. Under Obama, it veered so far left that it caused significant damage to America interests around the world. But the ideological framework remains. Washington is still dominated by globalists who seek to turn America into a European social democracy domestically and an empire internationally.

I'm not talking about a traditional empire, where a conquering country subjugates vast territory politically. Rather, it is an empire run by globalist elites, multinational corporations, and international bodies of bureaucrats, like the European Union. Within such an empire, national borders are an impediment to "progress," as are the cultures of the various nations within them, including our own. The American culture, with its historical emphasis on individual liberty, free enterprise, and Judeo-Christian morality, stands in the way of the progressive globalist vision.

Many people define the Deep State as merely the layer of federal employees I've just described, especially in the intelligence and Defense departments. But I define it more broadly, to include the connected business interests, including defense contractors and financial speculators, their lobbyists, consultants, the social engineers, and the media. The media are an especially important component of the Deep State, because they manufacture tacit consent to the globalists' plans.

A lot of people might describe this as a "conspiracy theory," which has become a meaningless slur of any and all dissent. I don't look at it that way. Anyone who has listened to my show knows I'm not terribly interested in theories. I'm interested in reality. The reality is globalist Washington is the center of a *culture,* not a conspiracy. It's a culture with values, just like American culture, but its values are different.

Where American values include individual liberty, free enterprise, and Judeo-Christian values, the globalist culture includes collectivism, multiculturalism, managed corporate trade, and hedonistic sexual freedom. We can have a philosophical argument about whether one set of values is better than the other in the abstract, but this much is clear: They cannot coexist. They are mutually exclusive.

Moreover, history has shown that one of them works and one of them doesn't. The dustbin of history is full of multiculturalist empires that succumbed to economic elitism and rampant hedonism before collapsing. The Roman Empire is only the most obvious example.

This is the true nature of Trump's War. As I've always said, it all comes down to borders, language, and culture. The nationalists who elected Donald Trump are fighting to save ours. The globalists in the Deep State are committed to destroying them to further their agenda. They couldn't stop Trump's election, so they are determined to neuter his presidency.

That's what the campaign to convince the American people that Russia hacked the election is about. They seek to create a narrative in which Trump not only lost the popular vote, but he only won the electoral vote because a foreign enemy wanted him in the White House. It's a new wrinkle on an old narrative in which Vladimir Putin is the new Stalin, who both oppresses his own people and seeks to rebuild the former Soviet Union via military conquest of Eastern Europe. They've now fit Trump into this narrative as Putin's unwitting dupe, naively appeasing him after Putin all but placed him in the White House himself.

The official story has a lot of holes. It is imperative we punch through them to get to the truth.

DID RUSSIA REALLY HACK THE ELECTION?

Five days before the January 11 press conference, and just two weeks before his inauguration, Donald Trump was presented with an intelligence report[3] claiming Vladimir Putin had directed a cyberattack with the intention of influencing the U.S. election. The report said the cyberattack did not target or compromise any systems involved in vote tallying, but did hack the DNC's email server and provide the infamous Podesta emails to WikiLeaks. So, even if Russia did what the Democrats and the media say they did, not a single vote for Hillary or Trump was added or subtracted.

The report, presented with all the usual official government trappings, seemed to partially confirm the media narrative trumpeted since the election that Trump's victory represented Moscow's will over the American people's.

But buried in the reporting on the release of this report was an important detail. The version of the report released to the public "lacked the evidence that intelligence officials said was included in a classified version, which they described as information on the sources and methods used to collect the information about Mr. Putin and his associates."[4] In other words, the public was provided with the conclusions the intelligence agencies drew but not the evidence they drew them from.

Of course, the public is led to believe the evidence must be concealed for national security reasons. That's very convenient. The voters who elected Trump are told there is proof his election wasn't completely legitimate, but they are not allowed to see the evidence. They are just supposed to take the word of people like James Clapper, who have already lied to them in the past about what the Deep State is up to.

Like the rest of the public, I have not been able to examine the evidence the intelligence agencies say they have. So I cannot dismiss out of hand the possibility Russia was behind the hacking of the DNC. But there is a lot of circumstantial evidence suggesting serious problems with that conclusion. The first clue came from Trump himself.

Immediately before reviewing the report, Trump tweeted, "The Democratic National Committee would not allow the FBI to study or see its computer info after it was supposedly hacked by Russia . . ."[5]

Trump was referring to a revelation that would be made public by FBI director James Comey *after the DNI report was released* that the FBI was not given direct access to the DNC server in order to investigate the claims of Russian hacking. Comey testified that the FBI had made repeated requests for that access, but the DNC refused.[6] He said his agency had to rely on the findings of a "highly respected private company" in conducting its investigation.

If that already has you a little suspicious, just wait. It gets better. Do you know who the highly respected private company was that had sole access to the DNC server? It was a company called CrowdStrike, which was given $100 million by Google capital to investigate Russian hacking of the DNC.[7] And we all know where Google's political sympathies lie. The chairman of its parent company, Alphabet Inc., is a longtime Hillary Clinton supporter and Democratic Party donor.[8]

It gets better. CrowdStrike was founded by cybersecurity experts George Kurtz and Dmitri Alperovitch. Alperovitch is noteworthy because cybersecurity is not his only interest. He's also a fellow at the Atlantic Council, a think tank that lists "Ukraine in Europe"[9] among its initiatives.

Can you believe this? The entire U.S. intelligence community may be relying on information provided by a private cybersecurity firm, founded by an anti-Russian activist and funded by Google. And we're supposed to take this firm's findings at their word. Why wasn't the FBI allowed to examine the DNC server directly and verify CrowdStrike's findings?

Well, it turns out they didn't even need to examine the server anyway. According to William Binney, former technical director, World Geopolitical & Military Analysis, National Security Agency, "the NSA would know where and how any 'hacked' emails from the DNC, HRC or any other servers were routed through the network."[10]

Based on that knowledge and all the weasel words various U.S. intelligence officers are using, like "our best guess" or "our opinion," or "our estimate," which indicate the allegedly hacked emails cannot be traced, Binney doesn't believe the DNC email server was hacked at all. He believes the evidence points to a leak inside the DNC!

The more we learn about this fake intelligence report, the wiser Donald Trump looks in utterly mistrusting the intelligence community. Again, we don't know if Trump saw evidence we are not privy to. Perhaps they have direct evidence independent of CrowdStrike's. But my gut tells me they don't. It all fits just a little too conveniently into the anti-Russia narrative the Deep State was already pushing for years before the election.

Despite the serious question marks surrounding the DNI report, the globalist media has written the official story as if it were established truth. Unfortunately, Trump's concession helped them do so. It's as dishonest as the "settled science" narrative on global warming, but the media know most people will only remember the sound bites.

That, my friends, is the Deep State in action.

Despite conceding the possibility the Russians did, in fact, hack the DNC, Trump remained defiant, attacking the intelligence community and the media for the completely discredited "honey trap" story the intelligence community leaked and the media printed. Trump compared the tactics to Nazi Germany, referring to Joseph Goebbels' infamous propaganda machine. He's right. It's the same tactics used by all oppressive governments, from Hitler's to Stalin's to the totalitarian state that once ruled East Germany.

The American Deep State is no different and it doesn't brook resistance. That couldn't have been made clearer than by the ominous warning from globalist operative Senator Chuck Schumer. "You take on the intelligence community, they have six ways from Sunday at getting back at you. So, even for a practical, supposedly hard-nosed businessman, he's being really dumb to do this," said Schumer.[11]

Democrat apparatchiks like Schumer are using all the technology we have today and the methodology of the Stasi in Eastern Europe. We thought the Stasi were gone, but little did we know that Charles Schumer, of all people, would be using the tactics of the Stasi, along with the neocon ventriloquists here in America.

Let's never forget what the 2016 intelligence agencies were. They were primarily men and women appointed by Barack Obama. So it was really Obama attacking Trump with fake stories in an effort to undermine his presidency before he even took the oath of office.

Of course, they had fellow travelers on the Republican side, like McCain and his fellow neocon ventriloquists in the media,who are all still anti-Russia a quarter century after the Cold War ended. They are still trying to start a war with Russia by any and all means. And they have the support of most of the globalist media, who have mindlessly parroted the anti-Putin propaganda from Obama's inauguration to Trump's.

The media has done far more damage invading the minds of Americans and others around the world than Putin did in invading Crimea, which asked for his help.[12] It's been an all-out assault on the mind-space of millions by CNN, ABC, CBS, NBC, etc.

This story is by no means over. The globalists will keep it alive as a sword of Damocles over Trump's head for his entire administration. Whenever Trump tries to improve relations with Russia, they will accuse him of appeasing the dictator who planted him in the White House.

We're going to have to be vigilant in supporting him and reminding people of the truth. Even if the Russians did hack the DNC, all they leaked was the truth. No one is accusing the Russians of hacking the voting machines. The report expressly says they didn't. The most they are guilty of is what Edward Snowden is guilty of: providing America proof of the lies, corruption, and evil of the globalist elites.

THE PHONY HONEY TRAP STORY

We can't let our friends and neighbors forget all the verifiably phony stories the Deep State put out about Trump, either. Do you remember the one about Trump encouraging violence against dissenters at his rallies? That turned out to be false. In fact, a conservative spy inside the DNC let us in on the truth behind that story: The DNC paid operatives, some of them mentally ill, to initiate violence at Trump rallies.[13]

Then there was the fiction about Trump being filmed in a Russian hotel room with prostitutes, engaging in some especially lurid sexual behavior. This one sounded like a fabrication from the beginning, but someone within the intelligence community leaked it and some of the media chose to publish it.

What struck me about this story is how many of the key "fake news" elements it shared with the Russian hacking story. That they both contained the same key elements lead me to doubt them both.

First, both stories were sensational, which was particularly difficult with the sex scandal. Trump had already survived evidence that he's no choirboy in this area. Most politicians can be taken down with merely an accusation of adultery or some other indiscretion. That wasn't going to work with Trump, so it had to be something even more outrageous. That's why the story had to involve "golden showers" or something sufficiently more salacious than any accusations made during the campaign, substantiated or not, that Trump had already survived politically.

Second, the story fit neatly into the Deep State's preexisting narrative about Russia. He wasn't allegedly caught on camera in Brazil or India or even China, which are all countries Trump does business in.[14] No, it had to be Russia, providing another piece of "evidence" that Russia is now or will in the future exercise control over Trump.

Third, the claims are completely unverifiable by the public. We were told they have evidence but they can't show it to us because of national security. With this one, we now know there just never was any evidence whatsoever.

Even the official story regarding the source of this "fake news" discredits it. According to the mainstream media, the dossier was compiled by ex-MI6 agent Christopher Steele and "was prepared under contract to both Republican and Democratic adversaries of Mr. Trump."[15] That in and of itself doesn't mean the story is false. Political operatives hire people to dig up dirt on opponents all the time. A lot of it turns out to be true.

But Steele's information was so dubious that even the globalist *New York Times* called it "unsubstantiated information from anonymous sources, a practice that fueled some of the so-called fake news—false rumors passed off as legitimate journalism—that proliferated during the presidential election."[16]

This story became so discredited that James Clapper, the director of national intelligence who once told Congress the NSA didn't collect any type of data at all on millions or hundreds of millions of Americans, put out a statement saying "this document is not a U.S. Intelligence Community product and that I do not believe the leaks came from within the IC."[17] He very well may have been lying again. It doesn't really matter, because even if it came from Congress, they're all on the same team.

INVESTIGATING THE FBI

As late as January, Obama and his allies were also still fighting the election itself. They released news of a new investigation of the FBI[18] for having told us what Hillary Clinton was actually doing. The fanatics in the media supported him. Right up to January 20, they seemed to honestly believe they could undo the election and put Hillary in the White House instead of Donald Trump.

Speaking of the poor gal, she was seen stumbling out of a restaurant about a week before Trump's inauguration. Apparently, after destroying her party and being unable to run again, her difficulty in traversing flat surfaces persisted, even months after her grueling campaign was over.

She had been seen dining with some old, loser actors at a midtown Manhattan restaurant. A reporter snapped a picture of an aide holding an umbrella for her as she attempted to enter her van. She seemed to be unsteady on her feet, which was nothing new. She was also unsteady during the campaign, which was another reason we didn't vote for her.

I don't want to go back into the whole email controversy and, apparently, neither does anyone in the Trump administration. I only bring up this investigation as another example of the Deep State's war on Trump's presidency. It has the same overarching theme: Donald Trump would not have won the election if not for the intervention of sinister interests that swayed the otherwise sensible, reliably progressive American public to vote for this unforgivably nationalist conservative candidate.

In the Russian hacking story, it's a foreign government that influenced the election. In this one, it's a rogue element within our own. In both cases, the globalists are pushing the same narrative. Donald Trump is an illegitimate president in every way. They're hoping if you hear it enough, in enough different contexts, you'll begin to accept it, something like subliminal advertising. There's a more familiar word for it in political contexts: *propaganda*.

I don't know what Comey's motivations were. He may have been pro-Trump or anti-Clinton. Or he may have just felt compelled to tell the truth, which would have the same results as being pro-Trump or anti-Clinton. At some point, he'll either be quietly cleared or very publicly thrown under the bus. It doesn't really matter, because either way, the seed of doubt regarding Trump's legitimacy has been planted. That's the only reason for announcing the investigation or continuing to publicize it.

CAN LIBERALS READ A MAP?

While Americans were distracted with the phony, salacious sex scandal story about Trump, the snake Barry O sent an armored brigade into Poland. This was the biggest military buildup since the Cold War ended[19] and Mr. Nobel Peace Prize had the audacity to do it one week before his presidency mercifully ended.

Obama tried to provoke a war with Russia right up until the day he walked out the door of the White House for the last time. I really wasn't sure at times how far he was willing to go. Would he fire missiles at Russia before he left, like a juvenile delinquent throwing stink bombs into the school he's been thrown out of?

Does anyone want more aggression against Russia, other than the Reaganites who still think we're living in the Cold War era, before the Berlin Wall fell? Anyone who does is on the same side as Obama. Obama, McCain, and the rest of the neocons all play for the same team.

Of course CNN, mouthpiece of the Deep State, blared the headline "Poland Welcomes US Troops as Part of NATO Buildup."[20] Obama's fellow globalist, Polish prime minister

Beata Szydlo, said it was a great day and would help ensure Poland's security. Do you see what they're up to? It's all the-ater to plant the seed in the minds of the American public that Russia was an imminent threat to Poland, even though noth-ing could be more ludicrous. Did Russia threaten to invade Poland? No! This was a complete fabrication of Obama's Deep State of lies and fearmongering.

I never said the snake didn't have cunning. By making this move just days before Trump takes office, he has created the conditions for an all-out propaganda war on Trump's presi-dency during its first few weeks. Do you remember the hys-terics during the campaign when Trump suggested NATO nations had to start paying their fair share of the security bill or take responsibility for their own defense?[21]

Well, now they have manufactured a phony crisis by send-ing armored troop divisions into Poland. If Trump orders the troops out, every dishonest media outlet in this country will bellow "Donald Trump abandons NATO allies!" They will say Trump is bending to Putin's will, citing all the phony stories they planted before his inauguration to set him up for those accusations later.

If, on the other hand, Trump does not pull the troops out, it will be a sore spot that will undermine the friendlier relations he is trying to establish. Putin was very patient during the transition, even amid statements from Trump's own cabinet appointees backing the aggressive move.[22] But one can't expect him to just sit and take it forever. Sooner or later, he's going to insist the troops be removed. At the very least it will put a strain on what Trump is trying to accomplish with Russian relations.

That doesn't mean Putin is trying to "break NATO," as Trump's defense secretary, James Mattis, indicated.[23] It means Putin, unlike our last president, recognizes his duty to act in the best interests of his home country. If there were Russian troops just across the Rio Grande in Mexico, you can be sure the U.S. president would show much less restraint than Putin showed in January.

Lost in all the noise and melodrama will be this one, salient fact: Putin was never going to invade Poland or the Baltic states. Not before Obama's act of naked aggression and not now. Putin himself called the idea "madness" in an interview with Bloomberg.[24] That doesn't mean I take everything Putin says as the gospel truth. He's simply making a lot more sense on this subject than anyone in Washington. The combined population of the NATO countries is 600 million. The population of Russia is 146 million. He knows invading a NATO country would be suicide, with only nuclear war as a last resort. He may not be an angel, but he's not insane.

The neocon ventriloquists and their liberal fellow travelers aren't insane, either. They may be evil, but not stupid. I don't know that I can say the same for the millions of liberal *voters* who suddenly think Bill Kristol and John McCain are men of genius. Because that's who they're lining up with when they start parroting the "Putin is an aggressor" narrative.

I have a recommendation for all those perhaps well-meaning but extremely misinformed liberals who are jumping on the anti-Russia bandwagon just because they don't like Trump. Look at a map. I don't mean a map of California wine country or outlet malls on Long Island. I mean a map of the world. They used to cover the walls in history class when I went to school. I know many liberals have never seen a map of the world because their classrooms had nothing but posters about "white privilege" and global warming. But sometimes a picture can indeed say more than a thousand words.

A quick look is very telling when you find places like Ukraine, Poland, Georgia, and Estonia. They all have two things in common. They're all on the Russian border. That's number one. Number two is they're all places where the U.S. government has been involved in stirring up trouble over the past eight years.

Everybody has probably forgotten the George W. Bush administration's attempts to bring Georgia and Ukraine into NATO.[25] I haven't. My memory doesn't have party line boundaries. The effort failed because of strong protests from Russia.[26] How could they not protest? NATO's raison d'être is to fight a war with Russia. It would be no different if Russia or China were to invite Mexico into an alliance against the United States. Do you suppose the U.S. government might view that as an aggressive act? Would you?

The *New York Times* had a completely different opinion of Vladimir Putin the last time a Republican was president. After a Cheney speech criticizing Russia for "lack of democracy" and "energy blackmail," the *Times* noted Putin's response and opined, "Putin is a statesman, and Cheney is not."[27]

The globalists did manage to get Estonia into NATO. Find that country on the map. Not only does the tiny state bordering Russia now belong to an anti-Russian alliance, but it hosted a massive NATO military exercise last summer within striking distance of St. Petersburg. In order to join the force of more than 14,000 multinational NATO troops, 1,200 U.S. troops in more than 400 vehicles marched into Estonia using the same road Hitler used to invade Russia during World War II.[28]

So, NATO has massed troops in Estonia and now Poland. It has actively sought to overthrow the governments of Russian allies Syria and Ukraine, and succeeded with the latter. It has attempted to deprive Russia of both its year-round warm-water ports. Yet millions of Americans believe Russia is the aggressor on the world stage. That is the power of the Deep State's propaganda machine.

Now you understand what Donald Trump meant when he said, in relation to Russia, "Common sense says this cycle, this horrible cycle of hostility must end and ideally will end soon."[29] He was talking about the hostility toward Russia. In the same speech, he said he wanted to "discuss how we can upgrade NATO's outdated mission and structure, grown out of the Cold War to confront our shared challenges, including migration and Islamic terrorism."[30]

No rational person would find either of those statements objectionable. In terms of the interests of the American people and the citizens in all the respective countries, they're not. But to the interests of the globalists of the Deep State, they're a declaration of war. They represented notice from Donald

Trump that the neoconservative dream of ruling the entire planet would come to an end under his administration. He was threatening to take their primary vehicle for world domination, NATO, and redirect it toward defeating the true threat to Western civilization, radical Islam.

Russia is our natural ally in that fight. They face an even graver threat from radical Islam than we do, considering the closer proximity of Islamic nations to their borders. Who could doubt that ISIS would be no more than an unpleasant memory by now if the United States and Russia were truly fighting it together, instead of proxy-fighting each other over the Assad regime in Syria?

It all comes back to Donald Trump and whether he'll be able to govern at all. The forces against him have been trying to see that he can't since November 9, 2016. That's why he has a war on his hands, not with foreign nations, but with the evil forces trying to destroy him from within. The Deep State will use all means at its disposal to undermine him and protect the globalist empire they've built under Democrat and RINO administrations going back decades. We're going to have to stand by Trump against them if we're going to reclaim this nation and its government.

CHAPTER THIRTEEN

THE BATTLE PLAN

While many others were writing about how Trump managed to get elected, I saw what Trump would face in trying to do what we elected him to do. There is no other word for it but a war. But it is not just Trump's War. It is our war. The final battle for the heart and soul of our nation. The worldwide left-wing movement had almost won. From the Vatican, to the media, to the imposters who seized power in every Western nation, they almost had it all. And then an earthquake called Brexit shook England. The second shock to the plotters of a new world Soviet era was the upset victory of a brash businessman aborting their final takeover of America.

The new nationalism that is sweeping the West came through loud and clear in Trump's inaugural address, which dispensed with rhetorical niceties and told even the former presidents in attendance they had been part of a system that had sold out America to enrich itself and its connected special interests. Never has a president made such a statement on the day of his inauguration.

While his courage was admirable, I couldn't help thinking about Gary Cooper's character in the 1952 film *High Noon*. I don't mean Cooper at the end, when he defiantly throws his sheriff's badge in the dirt after defeating Frank Miller and his gang. I am referring to the scene when he leaves his office to face them down, after every man in town has deserted him. The camera pans back as Cooper walks the empty streets of the town and one can't help feeling that no one has ever been more alone against a seemingly undefeatable enemy than him.

In a way, Trump looked like a man in very much the same position as he thundered away on the Capitol balcony, with the former presidents and other members of the Establishment smirking patronizingly behind him. Outside, George Soros' paid brownshirts were already rioting in the streets. The media and intelligence community had been waging war against his presidency since before it even began. A large portion of his own party were opposed to basic planks of his platform, and even some of his good, conservative cabinet appointees had backpedaled a bit under the pressure put on by the Establishment Senate.

Despite these forces against the new nationalism of Donald Trump I am hopeful for his presidency. Let's not forget that, although real life is not a movie, Gary Cooper won in the end. And Trump isn't as alone as the sheriff was. There are true conservative representatives in Congress, previously betrayed by the RINO leadership, whom Trump has already reached out to and begun to work with.

Most important, Trump has us, the Savage Nation, who have stood by him through the first stage of the war to get him elected. Let's not forget we all have pens and phones, too, and we must not fear using them. Keep the pressure on your representatives to back Trump on the most important mandates we gave him: build the wall, restore the borders, fix trade and the economy, lower taxes, rebuild the military, empower the police, restore law and order to the streets, and invigorate our American culture.

There is only one thing politicians fear: public opinion. When it starts mounting against them, they will cut and run in an instant to save their jobs. That's why I've said displaying this book prominently on your coffee table and even on your desk at work, if you can, sends a strong message that you stand with Trump and all patriotic Americans seeking to take the government back from the entrenched bureaucrats and the streets back from the highly organized, well-funded agitators.

As Trump said himself during his speech, "This is your day. This is your celebration. And this, the United States of America, is your country."[1] That means this is our fight and requires our leadership as much as his. Blind worship will not help him or us.

BEWARE THE TRUE BELIEVERS

We know about the intolerant left, but now something is emerging in the wake of Trump's victory. There's intolerance on the right. You can't say anything against decisions Trump is making without facing some type of vitriol from the True Believers.

There was a book written about this type of psychological behavior with that exact title, *The True Believer: Thoughts* on the Nature of Mass Movements, by Eric Hoffer. It describes the fanaticism of people who are consumed by one idea without taking a step back to see what's really going on, and how those dynamics feed a mass movement. That's what we're seeing with Trump. I was the only one in the conservative, libertarian sphere who objected to the dangerous act of Trump publicly taking a call from the president of Taiwan during the transition phase.

Look who was behind it. The lobbyist Bob Dole said he was instrumental in making that call happen. Edwin Feulner, former president of the Heritage Foundation, was said to have been a crucial figure in setting up the communication channels between Trump and Taipei. These are people who served Reagan, and who supported George W. Bush's Middle East policy. Where did that get us other than to publicly humiliate and antagonize China? And they were aided by True Believers who claimed that any criticism of Trump is a sign of disloyalty.

I can't go along with this groupthink that says everything Trump is doing is the right thing. I have to analyze these situations as an openly independent commentator. I believe Trump endangered our relationship with China. It's not the same as reaching out to a dictator in Cuba. Castro had no power to do damage to us the way China can. It's not the same as reaching out to Russia to say we can talk about peace in a region. It's deliberately poking a big bear that we need to have a working relationship with. They own trillions of our debt. They're manipulating currency so we can't compete with them. But we must negotiate with them privately, as we have been and will do with Russia since Trump was elected. It was a grave error to publicly humiliate and challenge China.

The smart thing to do is to let them save face. You'll hear that from anyone who knows the Chinese mindset, who know how to get things done with China at the bargaining table. Trump should have listened to skilled people before making or taking that call with Taiwan's leader.

China is on a war footing. They are rapidly building up their military. They have been at cyberwar with us for many years. They have hacked many of our military secrets. To purposely try to show them up is the exact wrong way to deal with them. But the whole Republican Establishment is pointing him in this direction. And anyone who speaks up is ridiculed, excommunicated. The force of social media is used against them. It's the lobbyists like Dole who have to reanalyze and step back before criticizing independent critics. The RNC Beltway bandits, the war machine, the military-industrial complex must not be allowed to dictate foreign policy.

The True Believers must not get swept up in a mass movement where they can see no wrong being done. We must avoid becoming as equally intolerant as those on the left. Constructive criticism is our duty to our principles of borders, language, culture, and peace.

This worship of any politician is akin to a fundamentalist religious mindset. To the True Believer, either you believe or you don't believe. Either you believe in God or you don't believe in God. Either you believe in a politician or you don't believe in a politician. Here is where the danger resides. Just as there are no absolutes in science, there is no absolutely pure, correct political system. We've seen what happens when a dictator insists on imposing his political views on the masses.

North Korea, Cuba. To a lesser degree, we saw this under Obama, where there was no opposition. We must remain vigilant with the man we elected to ensure that our hope for him and America does not become blind worship.

I'll continue to do my job as a member of the Fourth Estate. I'll be a thorn in the government's side when I have to be, along with my audience of millions of radio listeners who worked hard to elect Trump. It is the average voter, the Eddies and Ediths out there who actually pushed those dots for Trump in those election booths, who must make the difference. They have to resist the temptation to become True Believers and help keep Trump on course to do what we sent him to Washington to do.

SAVAGE SOLUTIONS

Throughout this book, I've provided bullet points at the beginning of each chapter summarizing the specific solutions we're looking for in each area of governance. Unlike the radical, hate-filled feminists, communists, and illegal aliens who threw tantrums the day after the inauguration, we know what we need Trump to accomplish if we are to win Trump's War. This book will not have accomplished its goal if it does not lead to action.

I'm collating all the Savage Solutions here, by category, to provide you with a quick reference to return to during the heat of battle in the years to come. I hope you will keep it handy as a guide. The propaganda Trump and his administration will be subjected to will be very much like the "fog of war" on a real battlefield. This list of solutions will provide clarity when the empire of lies has even honest conservatives doubting themselves. We can return to this list and ask ourselves, Are we accomplishing what we set out to accomplish or aren't we?

In 1776, Thomas Paine wrote, "We have it in our power to begin the world over again."[2] That's just as true for us today. Much like those first American revolutionaries, we seek to both reclaim a sociopolitical structure wrecked by the government in a distant capital and build a new, better America for the century ahead. We have chosen our general. Here is our battle plan.

The Economy
- Cut taxes, unshackle American corporations and citizens
- Quit NAFTA at once, just as he did with TPP
- Employment mandate for America: foreigners need not apply
- Immediately rebuild infrastructure through private investment

Repealing Obamacare
- Recognize the health care system was broken before Obamacare and why
- Fix the crony capitalist FDA
- Mandate insurance availability for individuals across state lines
- Raise the eligibility age of Medicare
- Mandate co-pays for Medicare and Medicaid

Restoring Our Borders
- World War III is being waged by undocumented, unvetted immigrants. Start fighting back!
- Purge our shores of enemy combatants and limit World War III to Europe
- Build the border wall now
- Fire the bleeding hearts at CDC and restore sensible public health protocols
- Abolish sanctuary cities and deport the illegal vermin who are killing our citizens

Restoring Our Culture
- Kill Common Core at the state level
- Restore civics classes at the local level
- Abolish the Department of Education
- Use the bully pulpit to preach Americanism

Restoring the Military
- To beef up the military, man up the military
- Help wounded warriors, not sexually confused enlistees
- It's biology, not misogyny: gender equality has no place in the armed services
- Make the VA more transparent and accountable via the Accountability First and Appeals Modernization Act and the Caring for our Heroes in the 21st Century Act

Defeating the War Machine
- Stand firm on peace with Russia
- Combat the war propaganda with the bully pulpit

- Destroy ISIS and then leave the Middle East
- Bring our troops home from unnecessary deployments

Defeating the RINOs
- Ignore the think tanks on trade and the wall
- Punish RINOs at the ballot box in primaries
- Make sure GOP doesn't mean Grand Old Party but Government of the People
- Et tu, Brutus? Trump must beware

Restoring Real Science
- Fund research by global warming skeptics
- Promote conservative conservationism over progressive environmentalism
- Exercise caution and care in repealing environmental regulations
- Restore real science at the NIH, CDC, and FDA

Defending the First Amendment
- Root out the socialist propaganda Obama concealed in the National Defense Authorization Act
- Jail anarchists who cross state lines to incite unrest
- Shield religion from persecution by passing the First Amendment Defense Act

Defending the Second Amendment
- The problem isn't guns, it's mass shooters armed with radicalism, drugs, and mental issues

• Order public health agencies to conduct unbiased
studies on the side effects of psychotropic drugs

Defeating the Deep State
• Study the global agenda of the intelligence community
• Back Trump's plan to end the new Cold War with Russia
• Learn how to recognize fake news

In addition to his day-one executive orders to pull out of
TPP, defund international organizations that perform abortions, and put a hiring freeze on nonmilitary federal workers, Trump wrote subsequent orders to build the wall, defund
sanctuary cities, hire five thousand more border guards, and
end the "catch and release" policy for illegal immigrants.[3]

That and more was accomplished in the first days of
Trump's presidency. It was a victory for you, the Savage
Nation, who have supported my message of Borders, Language, and Culture for more than twenty-two years. Make no
mistake, Trump was reading from our playbook.

I am proud to have done so much to get Donald Trump
elected. But the war is just beginning. There will be more riots,
more propaganda, more backroom betrayals, and more international intrigue from the globalists.

Remember, it was God's will that this underdog, Donald
Trump, defeated the vast armies of the New World Order. We
must pray for him and for our nation while standing strong
against the global forces of collectivism.

ENDNOTES

CHAPTER ONE: TRUMP'S WAR AGAINST THE ENEMY WITHIN

1 Terry Ward, "Update: Anti-Trump Protests Block Traffic in Major U.S. Cities," *WHSV*, November 9, 2016, http://www.whsv.com/content/news/Anti-Trump-protests-block-New-York-street-at-Trump-Tower-400624121.html.

2 Kimberly Veklerov, "Photojournalist Attacked While Covering Trump Protest in Oakland," *San Francisco Chronicle*, November 10, 2016, http://www.sfchronicle.com/crime/article/Photojournalist-attacked-while-covering-Trump-10606690.php.

3 Amber Randall, "Black Guys Assault White Man While Shouting Anti-Trump Slogans [VIDEO]," *Daily Caller*, November 10, 2016, http://dailycaller.com/2016/11/10/hillary-supporters-assault-white-trump-supporter-video/.

4 Rachel Stoltzfoos, "Media That Warned of Trump Riots Now Covers Hillary 'Protests,'" *Daily Caller*, November 10, 2016, http://dailycaller.com/2016/11/10/media-that-warned-of-trump-riots-now-covers-hillary-protests/.

5 Valerie Richardson, "Republicans Call on Clinton, Obama to Reel in Soros-Linked 'Professional' Anti-Trump Protesters," *Washington Times,* November 14, 2016, http://www.washingtontimes.com/news/2016/nov/14/republicans-call-clinton-obama-reel-professional-a/.

6 Tyler Durden, "Anti-Trump Protests: Proof of Professional Activist Involvement," Zero Hedge, November 13, 2016, http://www.zerohedge.com/news/2016-11-13/anti-trump-protests-proof-professional-activist-involvement.

7 Elisabeth Bumiller, "CORPORATE CONDUCT: THE PRESIDENT; Bush Signs Bill Aimed at Fraud In Corporations," *New York Times*, July 31, 2002, http://www.nytimes.com/2002/07/31/business/corporate-conduct-the-president-bush-signs-bill-aimed-at-fraud-in-corporations.html.

8 Sheryl Gay Stolberg, "A Private, Blunter Bush Declares, 'Wall Street Got Drunk,'" *New York Times*, July 23, 2008, http://www.nytimes.com/2008/07/23/washington/23bush.html.

9 Bridget Johnson, "McConnell: Trump's 'Drain the Swamp' Term-Limits Vow Going Nowhere in the Senate," PJ Media, November 9, 2016, https://pjmedia.com/news-and-politics/2016/11/09/mcconnell-trumps-drain-the-swamp-term-limits-vow-going-nowhere-in-the-senate/2/.

10 Don Hawkins, "No, D.C. Isn't Really Built on a Swamp," *Washington Post,* August 29, 2014, https://www.washingtonpost.com/posteverything/wp/2014/08/29/no-dc-isnt-really-built-on-a-swamp/?utm_term=.8de6c6d2b92b.

11 David Johnson and Jeff Zeleny, "Congressman Sought Bribes, Indictment Says," *New York Times,* June 5, 2007, http: www.nytimes.com /2007/06/05/ washington/05jefferson.html?ex=1338782400&en=f8ac6372594c21f5&ei=5124&partner=permalink &exprod =permalink.

12 Michael Democker, "William Jefferson Verdict: Guilty on 11 of 16 Counts," *Times-Picayune,* August 5, 2009, http://www.nola.com/news/index.ssf/2009/08/william_jefferson_verdict_guil.html.

13 Paul Kane, "Trump Takes Aim at House Republicans, and They Run for Cover," *Washington Post*, January 3, 2016, https://www.washingtonpost.com/powerpost/trump-takes-aim-at-house-republicans-and-they-run-for-cover/2017/01/03/fb530ad2-d1fb-11e6-9cb0-54ab630851e8_story.html?utm_term=.ec62b424593c.

14 Becca Stanek, "Newt Gingrich Admits Trump Probably Can't Get Mexico to Pay for His Wall. 'But It Was a Great Campaign Device,'" *The Week*, November 10, 2016, http://theweek.com/speedreads/661335/newt-gingrich-admits-trump-probably-cant-mexico-pay-wall-but-great-campaign-device.

15 Chelsea Bailey, "Donald Trump Says Border Wall May Be Part Fence, Hints at Mass Incarcerations," NBC News, November 13, 2016.

16 Jessica Taylor, "Trump's Cabinet Picks Break with Him on At Least 10 Major Issues." NPR, January 13, 2017, http://www.npr.org/2017/01/13/509588590/trumps-cabinet-picks-break-with-him-on-at-least-10-major-issues.

17 Ibid.

18 Ibid.

19 Donald Trump, Twitter, January 13, 2017, https://twitter.com/realDonaldTrump/status/819858926455967744.

20 Jeremy Diamond. "Trump's Latest Executive Order: Banning People from 7 Countries and More," CNN, January 29, 2017, http://www.cnn.com/2017/01/27/politics/donald-trump-refugees-executive-order/index.html.

21 Georgett Roberts, Jennifer Bain, and Kathianne Boniello, "Federal Judge Grants Stay for Those Detained under Trump's Travel Ban," New York Post, January 28, 2017, http://nypost.com/2017/01/28/federal-judge-grants-emergency-stay-for-those-detained-under-trumps-travel-ban/.

22 Andrew C. McCarthy. "Trump's Exclusion of Aliens from Specific Countries Is Legal." National Review, January 30, 2017. http://www.nationalreview.com/article/ 444371/donald-trump-executive-order-ban-entry-seven-muslim-majority-countries-legal

CHAPTER TWO: TRUMP'S ECONOMIC WAR

1 M. Angeles Villarreal and Ian Ferguson, "The North American Free Trade Agreement (NAFTA)," Congressional Research Service, April 16, 2015, https://www.fas.org/sgp/crs/row/R42965.pdf.

2 Aaron Klein, "Hagel Pushes Wealth Redistribution to Third World," *WorldNetDaily,* January 19, 2013, http://www.wnd.com/2013/01/hagel-pushes-wealth-redistribution-to-third-world/.

3 Jorge Villarreal, "To Stop Climate Change, Don't Just Cut Carbon. Redistribute Wealth," Moyers and Company, August 12, 2016, http://billmoyers.com/story/stop-climate-change-dont-just-cut-carbon-redistribute-wealth/.

4 Mike Siegel, "Trade Agreements Are Not Free Trade," *Daily Caller*, September 13, 2016, http://dailycaller.com/2016/09/13/trade-agreements-are-not-free-trade/.

5 Matthew Davis and Martyn Brown, "From Ferrets to Fish...New EU Laws That Are Ruining Britain," *Daily Express,* June 24, 2014, http://www.express.co.uk/news/politics/484419/New-EU-laws-ruining-Britain.

6 Ibid.

7 Lucy Pasha-Robinson, "Marine Le Pen Takes Huge Lead over Nicolas Sarkozy in French First Round Presidential Election Poll," *Independent,* November 20, 2016, http://www.independent.co.uk/news/world/europe/marine-le-pen-poll-election-odds-latest-french-presidential-lead-sarkozy-a7428126.html.

8 Paul Wells, "Nationalist Movements Could Smother Justin Trudeau: Paul Wells," *The Star,* November 25, 2016, https://www.thestar.com/news/canada/2016/11/25/nationalist-movements-could-smother-justin-trudeau-paul-wells.html.

9 William Maudlin, "Obama Administration Gives Up on Pacific Trade Deal,"

Wall Street Journal, November 11, 2016, http://www.wsj.com/articles/obama-administration-gives-up-on-pacific-trade-deal-1478895824.

10 Candace Smith, "Trump Says He Will Withdraw from TPP on Day 1, Mum on Building the Wall," ABC News, November 21, 2016, http://abcnews.go.com/Politics/trump-withdraw-tpp-day-mum-building-wall/story?id=43703187.

11 Barnini Chakraborty, "Trump Signs Executive Order Withdrawing US from TPP Trade Deal," Fox News, January 23, 2016, http://www.foxnews.com/politics/2017/01/23/trump-signs-executive-order-withdrawing-us-from-tpp-trade-deal.html.

12 Ibid.

13 Martin Sullivan, "The Truth About Corporate Tax Rates," *Forbes,* March 25, 2015, http://www.forbes.com/sites/taxanalysts/2015/03/25/the-truth-about-corporate-tax-rates/#9e29ed720a54.

14 Pascal-Emmanuel Gobry, "Attention Bernie Sanders: Europe Gave Up on Its Socialist Paradise Years Ago," *The Week,* January 22, 2016, http://theweek.com/articles/600512/attention-bernie-sanders-europe-gave-socialist-paradise-years-ago.

15 Jason Russell, "Look at How Many Pages Are in the Federal Tax Code," *Washington Examiner,* April 15, 2016, http://www.washingtonexaminer.com/look-at-how-many-pages-are-in-the-federal-tax-code/article/2563032.

16 "Federal Individual Income Tax Rates History. Nominal Dollars, Income Years 1913–2013," Tax Foundation, http://taxfoundation.org/sites/default/files/docs/fed_individual_rate_history_nominal.pdf.

17 Trump-Pence 2016 official website, https://www.donaldjtrump.com/press-releases/fact-sheet-donald-j.-trumps-pro-growth-economic-policy-will-create-25-milli.

18 Robert Wood, "Trump as Tax Code King and Hedge Fund Slayer," *Forbes,* August 31, 2015, http://www.forbes.com/sites/robertwood/2015/08/31/trump-as-tax-code-king-and-hedge-fund-slayer/#660608f10264.

19 Portia Crowe, "Hedge Fund Manager David Tepper Comes Out in Support of Hillary Clinton," *Business Insider,* November 7, 2016, http://www.businessinsider.com/1-david-tepper-on-hillary-clinton-us-election-2016-11.

20 Curtis Dubay, "The Sneaky Way Obama Is Hiking Death Taxes," *Daily Signal,* August 17, 2016, http://dailysignal.com/2016/08/17/the-sneaky-way-obama-is-hiking-death-taxes/.

21 "The Ten Planks of the Communist Manifesto," Laissez-Faire Republic, http://laissez-fairerepublic.com/tenplanks.html.

22 Wilbur Ross, "Trump Versus Clinton on Infrastructure," white paper, October 27, 2016, http://peternavarro.com/sitebuildercontent/sitebuilderfiles/infrastructurereport.pdf.

23 William Graham Sumner, "The Forgotten Man," http://www.swarthmore.edu/SocSci/rbannis1/AIH19th/Sumner.Forgotten.html.

24 Bernie Sanders, "Let's Rebuild our Infrastructure, Not Provide Tax Breaks to Big Corporations and Wall Street," November 21, 2016, https://medium.com/senator-bernie-sanders/lets-rebuild-our-infrastructure-not-provide-tax-breaks-to-big-corporations-and-wall-street-f7d3ab463717#.l5r3f6je5.

25 Paul Krugman, "Build He Won't," *New York Times,* November. 21, 2016, http://www.nytimes.com/2016/11/21/opinion/build-he-wont.html?_r=0.

26 Jim Powell, "No President Obama, It Was Private Business That Made Our Roads and Bridges Possible," *Forbes,* July 29, 2012, http://www.forbes.com/sites/

jimpowell/2012/07/29/no-president-obama-it-was-private-business-that-made-our-roads-and-bridges-possible/2/#4fb5ff0a659d.

27 Seymour Dunbar, *A History of Travel in America,* vol. 1 (Indianapolis: Bobbs-Merrill, 1915), pp. 321–22.

28 Leonard Gilroy and Adam Summers, "Detailing Foreign Management of US Infrastructure," Reason Foundation, March 1, 2006, http://reason.org/news/show/detailing-foreign-management-o.

29 Bridget Johnson, "McConnell: Trump's 'Drain the Swamp' Term-Limits Vow Going Nowhere in the Senate," PJ Media, November 9, 2016, https://pjmedia.com/news-and-politics/2016/11/09/mcconnell-trumps-drain-the-swamp-term-limits-vow-going-nowhere-in-the-senate/2/.

30 Russel Berman, "Trump Tries to Bend Republicans on Infrastructure," *Atlantic,* November 15, 2016, http://www.theatlantic.com/politics/archive/2016/11/trumps-infrastructure-challenge-to-republicans/507656/.

31 Larry Getlen, "How the Privatization of Our Oceans Is Sinking Fishermen," *New York Post,* November 27, 2016, http://nypost.com/2016/11/27/how-the-privatization-of-our-oceans-is-sinking-fishermen/.

CHAPTER THREE: TRUMP'S WAR TO REPEAL OBAMACARE

1 Byron York, "No, House Republicans Haven't Voted 50 times to Repeal Obamacare," *Washington Examiner,* March 15, 2014, http://www.washingtonexaminer.com/no-house-republicans-havent-voted-50-times-to-repeal-obamacare/article/2545733.

2 Kelsey Snell and David Weigel, "Conservatives Ready to Support $1 Trillion Hole in the Budget," January 5, 2017, https://www.washingtonpost.com/powerpost/conservatives-ready-to-support-1-trillion-hole-in-the-budget/2017/01/05/76d4bf34-d391-11e6-a783-cd3fa950f2fd_story.html?utm_term=.faac46c081aa.

3 "Rand Paul Only Republican to Vote 'No' as Senate Takes First Step to Repeal Obamacare," *Lexington Herald Leader,* January 12, 2017, http://www.kentucky.com/news/politics-government/article126091309.html#storylink=cpy.

4 Cristiano Lima, "Rand Paul: Trump 'Fully Supports My Plan to Replace Obamacare,'" *Politico,* January 6, 2017, http://www.politico.com/story/2017/01/rand-paul-trump-fully-supports-my-plan-to-replace-obamacare-233307.

5 Senator Rand Paul, "Rand Paul: Repeal All of Obamacare and Replace Immediately," Rare, January 2, 2017, http://rare.us/story/rand-paul-repeal-all-of-obamacare-and-replace-immediately/.

6 Robert Costa and Amy Goldstein, "Trump Vows 'Insurance for Everybody' in Obamacare Replacement Plan," *Washington Post*, January 15, 2017, https://www.washingtonpost.com/politics/trump-vows-insurance-for-everybody-in-obamacare-replacement-plan/2017/01/15/5f2b1e18-db5d-11e6-ad42-f3375f271c9c.

7 "Transcript: Donald Trump Announces Plans to Form Presidential Exploratory Committee," CNN, October 8, 1999, http://www.cnn.com/ALLPOLITICS/stories/1999/10/08/trump.transcript/.

8 "National Health Expenditures 2015 Highlights," Centers for Medicare and Medicaid Services, https://www.cms.gov/Research-Statistics-Data-and-Systems/Statistics-Trends-and-Reports/NationalHealthExpendData/Downloads/highlights.pdf.

9 Andy Kiersz and Lydia Ramsey, "People Are Furious About the Price of the EpiPen—Here's How Much It's increased in the Last Decade," *Business Insider,* August 25, 2016. http://www.businessinsider.com/how-much-price-of-mylans-epipen-has-increased-2016-8.

10 Sydney Lupkin, "FDA Fees on Industry Haven't Fixed Delays in Generic Drug Approvals," NPR, September 1, 2016, http://www.npr.org/sections/health-shots/2016/09/01/492235796/fda-fees-on-industry-havent-fixed-delays-in-generic-drug-approvals.

11 Ibid.

12 "Funding," European Medicines Agency official website, http://www.ema.europa.eu/ema/index.jsp?curl=pages/about_us/general/general_content_000130.jsp&mid=WC0b01ac0580029336.

13 "Fiscal Year 2016 President's Budget," U.S. Food and Drug Administration, http://www.fda.gov/downloads/AboutFDA/ReportsManualsForms/Reports/BudgetReports/UCM432650.pdf.

14 Daniel Takash, "FDA Cracks Down on Dietary Supplements," *The Hill,* September 1, 2015, http://thehill.com/blogs/congress-blog/healthcare/252327-fda-cracks-down-on-dietary-supplements.

15 "Industry Profile: Summary, 2016," OpenSecrets.Org, https://www.opensecrets.org/lobby/indusclient.php?id=h04.

16 "Trump Gets Down to Business on *60 Minutes,*" CBS News, September 27, 2015, http://www.cbsnews.com/news/donald-trump-60-minutes-scott-pelley/.

17 "Fiscal Year 2016 Budget of the U.S. Government," The White House, https://www.whitehouse.gov/sites/default/files/omb/budget/fy2016/assets/budget.pdf.

18 "Federal Receipt and Outlay Summary," Tax Policy Center, http://www.taxpolicycenter.org/statistics/federal-receipt-and-outlay-summary.

19 Paul Bedard, "Boom: Trump Eyes 10% Spending Cuts, 20% Slash of Federal Workers," *Washington Examiner,* January 17, 2017, http://www.washingtonexaminer.com/boom-trump-eyes-10-spending-cuts-20-slash-of-federal-workers/article/2612037.

20 "Fiscal Year 2016 Budget of the U.S. Government," The White House, https://www.whitehouse.gov/sites/default/files/omb/budget/fy2016/assets/budget.pdf.

21 Kristina Wong, "National Security Experts Sound Alarm on Long-Term Debt," *The Hill,* May 10, 2016, http://thehill.com/policy/defense/279320-prominent-group-says-long-term-debt-the-single-greatest-threat-to-us-national.

22 Larry Light, "Federal Watchdog: U.S. Government Spending 'Unsustainable,'" CBS News, January 17, 2017, http://www.cbsnews.com/news/gao-federal-spending-revenue-unsustainable/.

23 "Life Expectancy in the USA, 1900–98," University of California, Berkeley, http://u.demog.berkeley.edu/~andrew/1918/figure2.html.

24 "Life Expectancy," U.S. Centers for Disease Control and Prevention, https://www.cdc.gov/nchs/fastats/life-expectancy.htm.

25 "The Number of Workers per Medicare Beneficiary Is Falling," Heritage Foundation, http://www.heritage.org/multimedia/infographic/2012/05/medicare-at-risk/the-number-of-workers-per-medicare-beneficiary-is-falling.

26 "Cost Sharing Out of Pocket Costs," Medicaid.gov, https://www.medicaid.gov/medicaid/cost-sharing/out-of-pocket-costs/index.html.

CHAPTER FOUR: THE WAR FOR OUR BORDERS

1 Laura Jarrett and Gloria Borger, "Obama Commutes Sentence of Chelsea Manning," CNN, January 18, 2017, http://www.cnn.com/2017/01/17/politics/chelsea-manning-sentence-commuted/.

2 Andy Eckardt, Alastair Jamieson, and Carlo Angerer, "Berlin Truck Attack: Christmas Market Suspect Released Due to Insufficient Evidence," NBC News,

December 20, 2016, http://www.nbcnews.com/storyline/berlin-truck-attack/berlin-truck-attack-pakistan-migrant-christmas-market-suspect-n698131.

3 Claudio Lavanga, F. Brinley Bruton, and Eoghan MacGuire, "Berlin Truck Attack Suspect Anis Amri Shot Dead in Milan: Officials," NBC News, December 23, 2016, http://www.nbcnews.com/storyline/berlin-truck-attack/berlin-truck-attack-suspect-anis-amri-shot-dead-milan-officials-n699431.

4 "Berlin Truck Killer Amri 'Had 14 Identities' in Germany," BBC News, January 5, 2017, http://www.bbc.com/news/world-europe-38516691.

5 Claudio Lavanga, F. Brinley Bruton, and Eoghan MacGuire, "Berlin Truck Attack Suspect Anis Amri Shot Dead in Milan: Officials," NBC News, December 23, 2016, http://www.nbcnews.com/storyline/berlin-truck-attack/berlin-truck-attack-suspect-anis-amri-shot-dead-milan-officials-n699431.

6 "Assassin's Motive? Listen to His Words," *Michael Savage Newsletter*, December 20, 2016, http://www.michaelsavage.wnd.com/2016/12/michael-savage-newsletter-assassins-motive-listen-to-his-words/.

7 Daniel Sarlo, "The Economics of Mass Deportation in the Neo-Assyrian Empire under Tiglath-Pileser III," *Academia*, April 26, 2013, http://www.academia.edu/3463490/The_Economics_of_Mass_Deportation_in_the_Neo-Assyrian_Empire_under_Tiglath-Pileser_III.

8 "Trump Supporters Chant 'Build a Wall' from Crowd," video, Howard University, WHUR-FM, July 22, 2016, https://www.youtube.com/watch?v=K9Vri5ECMps.

9 "Trump Repeats Vow to Build Border Wall, but Admits 'There Could Be Some Fencing,'" *Fox News Politics*, November 14, 2016, http://www.foxnews.com/politics/2016/11/14/trump-repeats-vow-to-build-border-wall-but-admits-there-could-be-some-fencing.html.

10 "House Republicans Test Trump On his U.S.-Mexico Wall," Reuters, November 10, 2016, http://www.reuters.com/article/us-usa-election-wall-idUSKBN135175.

11 Donald Trump. "Read Donald Trump's Remarks at Carrier Plant in Indiana," *Time*, December 1, 2016, http://time.com/4588349/donald-trump-carrier-jobs-speech/.

12 Julia Edwards Ainsley. "Exclusive: Trump Team Seeks Agency Records on Border Barriers, Surveillance," Reuters, January 4, 2017, http://www.reuters.com/article/us-usa-border-trump-exclusive-idUSKBN14N0TY?il=0.

13 Manu Raju, Deirdre Walsh, and David Wright, "Trump Asking Congress, Not Mexico, to Pay for Border Wall," CNN, January 6, 2017. http://www.cnn.com/2017/01/05/politics/border-wall-house-republicans-donald-trump-taxpayers/.

14 Ibid.

15 Office of the United States Trade Representative, https://ustr.gov/countries-regions/americas/mexico.

16 Brian Bennett and Noah Bierman, "Congress Begins to Search for Funds to Help Trump Build Border Wall," *Los Angeles Times*, January 7, 2017, http://www.latimes.com/politics/la-na-pol-border-wall-20170106-story.html.

17 Debra Heine, "Trump Poised to Build Wall and Undo Obama's Executive Actions on Immigration," PJ Media, January 3, 2017, https://pjmedia.com/trending/2017/01/03/trump-poised-to-build-wall-and-undo-obamas-executive-actions-on-immigration/.

18 Paul Bedard, "ICE Releases 19,723 Criminal Illegals, 208 Convicted of Murder, 900 of Sex Crimes," *Washington Examiner*, April 28, 2016, http://www.washingtonexaminer.com/ice-releases-19723-criminal-illegals-208-convicted-of-murder-900-of-sex-crimes/article/2589785.

19 Warner Todd Huston, "Drunken Illegal Migrant Arrested for Fatal Hit-and-Run in Omaha," *Breitbart News,* April 19, 2016, http://www.breitbart.com/big-government/2016/04/19/drunken-illegal-migrant-arrested-fatal-hit-run-omaha/.

20 Katie McHugh, "Mexican Illegal Alien Deported Eight Times Charged After Fatal Hit-and-Run," *Breitbart News,* December 11, 2016, http://www.breitbart.com/big-government/2016/12/11/mexican-illegal-alien-deported-eight-times-charged-fatal-hit-run/.

21 Matt Kelley, "Illegal Immigration Under Microscope as Mother Testifies of Omaha Crash That Killed Her Daughter (AUDIO)," Nebraska Radio Network, April 19, 2016, http://nebraskaradionetwork.com/2016/04/19/mother-testifies-about-omaha-crash-that-claimed-her-only-daughter-audio/.

22 Ibid.

23 Michael Patrick Leahy, "1,565 Refugees Diagnosed with Active TB Since 2012, Three Times More Than Previously Reported," *Breitbart News,* January 2, 2017. http://www.breitbart.com/big-government/2017/01/02/1565-refugees-diagnosed-active-tb-2012-three-times-more-reported/.

24 Michael Patrick Leahy. "Six Diseases Return to US as Migration Advocates Celebrate 'World Refugee Day,'" *Breitbart News,* June 16, 2016, http://www.breitbart.com/big-government/2016/06/19/diseases-thought-eradicated-world-refugee-day/.

25 Ibid.

26 "Donald Trump Interview with Michael Savage on The Savage Nation—7/14/16," *The Savage Nation* podcast, July 14, 2016, https://www.youtube.com/watch?v=KpKBbxySg4A.

27 "Latent Tuberculosis Infection: A Guide for Primary Health Care Providers. Appendix B. Identifying Persons From High-Risk Countries," CDC website, https://www.cdc.gov/tb/publications/ltbi/appendixb.htm.

28 "High Burden Countries," Stop TB Partnership, http://www.stoptb.org/countries/tbdata.asp.

29 Ruairi Arrieta-Kenna, "Sanctuary Cities Stand Firm Against Trump," *Politico,* December 12, 2016, http://www.politico.com/story/2016/12/sanctuary-cities-trump-immigration-232449.

30 Ibid.

31 Bill Ruthhart, "How Emanuel Worked to Maximize His Meeting with Trump," *Chicago Tribune,* December 7, 2016, http://www.chicagotribune.com/news/local/politics/ct-mayor-rahm-emanuel-donald-trump-meeting-20161207-story.html.

32 J. J. Gallagher and Emily Shapiro. "Chicago's 'Out of Control' Violence Produces 762 Homicides in 2016," ABC News, January 3, 2017, http://abcnews.go.com/US/chicagos-control-violence-produces-762-homicides-2016/story?id=44402951.

CHAPTER FIVE: TRUMP'S CULTURE WARS

1 Karen Braun, "Stop CC in MI Respectfully Request President-elect Trump to 'Drain the Swamp' and Pull the Plug on Betsy DeVos," Stop Common Core in Michigan, November 28, 2016, http://stopcommoncoreinmichigan.com/2016/11/stop-cc-mi-respectfully-request-president-elect-trump-drain-swamp-pull-plug-betsy-devos/.

2 Jeremy Diamond and Jim Acosta, "Many of You Are Asking About Common Core. To Clarify, I Am Not a Supporter—Period," Fox 13 Salt Lake City, November 23, 2016, http://fox13now.com/2016/11/23/betsy-devos-clarifies-stance-on-common-core-after-being-picked-for-trumps-education-secretary/.

3 Betsy DeVos official website, http://betsydevos.com/qa/.

4 Chris Edwards, "Department of Education: Timeline of Growth," Downsizing the Federal Government, https://www.downsizinggovernment.org/education/timeline-growth#_edn17.

5 Dana Goldstein, "How Trump Could Gut Public Education," *Slate,* November 23, 2016, http://www.slate.com/articles/life/education/2016/11/how_trump_and_education_secretary_betsy_devos_could_gut_public_education.html.

6 Jeremy Diamond and Jim Acosta, "Betsy DeVos Picked for Trump's Education Secretary," CNN Politics, November 24, 2016, http://www.cnn.com/2016/11/23/politics/betsy-devos-picked-for-education-secretary/.

7 Emily Shapiro, "Injured Professor Says Won't Judge OSU Attacker: 'I'm Going Home . . . He's Dead,'" ABC News, November 29, 2016, http://abcnews.go.com/US/injured-ohio-state-professor-withholding-judgment-student-attacker/story?id=43850613.

8 Ibid.

9 Virginia Kruta, "Police Release Facebook Rant Posted by Abdul Artan Before OSU Attack—and It May Reveal His Motive," *Independent Journal Review,* November 29, 2016, http://ijr.com/2016/11/745287-make-peace-with-daesh/.

10 Debra Heine, "OSU Diversity Officer Urges Compassion for Somali Terrorist Who Attacked Students," PJ Media, November 29, 2016, https://pjmedia.com/trending/2016/11/29/osu-diversity-officer-urges-compassion-for-somali-terrorist-who-attacked-students/.

11 https://twitter.com/realDonaldTrump/status/803921522784092160.

12 Deroy Murdock, "Secret Service Agents: Hillary Is a Nightmare to Work With," *New York Post,* October 2, 2015, http://nypost.com/2015/10/02/secret-service-agents-hillary-is-a-nightmare-to-work-with/.

13 Speech, Dayton, Ohio, March 12, 2016, Donald Trump Talks About Security Scare in Dayton, Praises Secret Service, https://www.youtube.com/watch?v=yLfxrPnfR_8.

14 Travis M. Andrews, "Video Shows Group Viciously Beating Man in Chicago, Yelling, 'You Voted Trump' and 'Don't Vote Trump,'" *Washington Post,* November 11, 2016, https://www.washingtonpost.com/news/morning-mix/wp/2016/11/11/video-shows-group-beating-man-in-chicago-yelling-you-voted-trump-and-dont-vote-trump/?utm_term=.aacd74424a32.

15 Susan Jones, "Obama: 'Islam Has Been Woven Into the Fabric of Our Country Since Its Founding,'" *CNS News,* February 19, 2015, http://www.cnsnews.com/news/article/susan-jones/obama-islam-has-been-woven-fabric-our-country-its-founding.

16 Cheryl K. Chumley, "Obama Outrages by Calling 4 Jewish Victims of Paris Terror 'a Bunch of Folks' Shot Randomly," *Washington Times,* February 10, 2015, http://www.washingtontimes.com/news/2015/feb/10/obama-outrages-by-calling-4-jewish-victims-of-pari/.

17 Thomas Jefferson, "First Inaugural Address," Avalon Project, Yale Law School, http://avalon.law.yale.edu/19th_century/jefinau1.asp.

18 CNN Staff, "Here's the Full Text of Donald Trump's Victory Speech," CNN Politics, November 9, 2016, http://www.cnn.com/2016/11/09/politics/donald-trump-victory-speech/.

CHAPTER SIX: TRUMP'S WAR TO RESTORE THE MILITARY

1 John Hayward, "A Look into the Mind of Gen. James Mattis: 15 Quotes from Trump's Secretary of Defense Pick," *Breitbart News,* December 2, 2016, http://www.

breitbart.com/big-government/2016/12/02/top-15-quotes-secretary-defense-nominee-james-mattis/.

2 Ibid.

3 Ibid.

4 Secretary of Defense Ash Carter, "Department of Defense Press Briefing by Secretary Carter on Transgender Service Policies in the Pentagon Briefing Room," U.S. Department of Defense, June 30, 2016, http://www.defense.gov/News/Transcripts/Transcript-View/Article/822347/department-of-defense-press-briefing-by-secretary-carter-on-transgender-service.

5 Ibid.

6 Gaye Clark, "VA Backpedals on Gender Reassignment Surgery," *Christian Headlines*, December 2, 2016, http://www.christianheadlines.com/blog/va-backpedals-on-gender-reassignment-surgery.html.

7 Jim Garamone, "Robinson Succeeds Gortney as Northern Command, NORAD Commander," U.S. Department of Defense, May 13, 2016, http://www.defense.gov/News/Article/Article/759453/robinson-succeeds-gortney-as-northern-command-norad-commander.

8 Cheryl Pellerin, "Carter Opens All Military Occupations, Positions to Women," U.S. Department of Defense, December 3, 2015, http://www.defense.gov/News/Article/Article/632536/carter-opens-all-military-occupations-positions-to-women.

9 Tia Ghose, "Women in Combat: Physical Differences May Mean Uphill Battle," *LiveScience*, December 7, 2015, http://www.livescience.com/52998-women-combat-gender-differences.html.

10 Jonah Bennett, "Here's Exactly How the Military Could Lower Standards for Women in Combat," *Daily Caller,* March 27, 2016, http://dailycaller.com/2016/03/27/heres-exactly-how-the-military-could-lower-standards-for-women-in-combat/#ixzz4SBjIZqiM.

11 Richard Sisk, "Mattis Pick Could See Senate Clash on Women in Combat, PTSD," *Military Life,* December 1, 2016, http://www.military.com/daily-news/2016/12/01/mattis-pick-could-see-senate-clash-on-women-in-combat-ptsd.html.

12 Ibid.

13 Ash Carter, "Combat Integration: The First Year of Firsts," December 3, 2016, https://medium.com/@SecDef/combat-integration-the-first-year-of-firsts-da08f64f42a3#.nmkswigdg.

14 Oriana Pawlyk, "Air Force Confirms No Women Now in SpecOps Training," Military.com, December 7, 2016, http://www.military.com/daily-news/2016/12/07/air-force-confirms-no-women-specops-training.html.

15 Paul Ausick, "Why a Boeing 747-8 Costs $357 Million," *24/7 Wall Street,* June 3, 2014, http://247wallst.com/aerospace-defense/2014/06/03/why-a-boeing-747-8-costs-357-million/.

16 Donald Trump, Twitter account, December 6, 2016, https://twitter.com/realDonaldTrump/status/806134244384899072.

17 Luis Martinez and Becky Perlow, "Fact Checking Trump's $4B Boeing Tweet: Where That Number Came From and What the Contract Says," ABC News, December 7, 2016, http://abcnews.go.com/Politics/fact-checking-trumps-4b-boeing-tweet-number-contract/story?id=44033643.

18 Christian Davenport, "Just Before Trump Blasted Air Force One Deal, Boeing Pledged $1M for Inauguration," *Chicago Tribune,* December 9, 2016, http://www.chicagotribune.com/business/ct-boeing-trump-inauguration-20161209-story.html.

19 "FULL EVENT: Donald Trump 'THANK YOU' Rally in Fayetteville, North Carolina (12/6/2016)," Trump TV Network, December 6, 2016, https://www.youtube.com/watch?v=IUreExyfw5o.

20 Michelle Tan, "US Army Generals Criticize Outdated Deployment Model: 'We've Gotten Rusty,'" *Defense News*, March 16, 2016, http://www.defensenews.com/story/defense/show-daily/ausa-global-force/2016/03/16/us-army-generals-criticize-outdated-deployment-model-weve-gotten-rusty/81858318/.

21 Matthew Cox, "Pentagon Tells Congress to Stop Buying Equipment it Doesn't Need," Military.com, January 28, 2015, http://www.military.com/daily-news/2015/01/28/pentagon-tells-congress-to-stop-buying-equipment-it-doesnt-need.html.

22 Pascal-Emmanuel Gobry, "America's 'Everything' Fighter Jet Is a Total Disaster," *The Week,* January 27, 2016, http://theweek.com/articles/601080/americas-everything-fighter-jet-total-disaster.

23 Thomas Gibbons, "U.S. Special Operations Units Are Using Faulty Rifle Sights," *Washington Post*, April 3, 2016, https://www.washingtonpost.com/news/checkpoint/wp/2016/04/03/u-s-special-operations-units-are-using-faulty-rifle-sights/?utm_term=.2e625bd94042.

24 "Findings of Fraud and Other Irregularities Related to the Manufacture and Sale of Combat Helmets by the Federal Prison Industries and ArmorSource, LLC, to the Department of Defense," U.S. Office of the Inspector General, August 2016, https://oig.justice.gov/reports/2016/i1608.pdf.

CHAPTER SEVEN: TRUMP'S WAR AGAINST THE WAR MACHINE

1 Thomas Hobbes, *Leviathan* (Indianapolis: Hackett, 1994), p. 80.

2 Tim Ciccotta, "Transgender Activists Derail Free Speech Rally Supporting Professor Refusing to Use Gender Pronouns," *Breitbart News*, October 24, 2016, http://www.breitbart.com/tech/2016/10/24/transgender-activists-derail-free-speech-rally-supporting-professor-refusing-to-use-gender-pronouns/.

3 Russ Read, "Clinton's Syria Strategy Would 'Require' War with Russia, Congress Hears," *Daily Caller*, September 26, 2016, http://dailycaller.com/2016/09/26/clintons-syria-strategy-would-require-war-with-russia-congress-hears/#ixzz4QkSarZCm.

4 Clifford J. Levy, "Welcome or Not, Orthodoxy Is Back in Russia's Public Schools," *New York Times*, September 23, 2007, http://www.nytimes.com/2007/09/23/world/europe/23russia.html.

5 Nina Achmatova, "Religion Becomes a Compulsory Subject in All Russian Schools," *AsiaNews*, February 14, 2012, http://www.asianews.it/news-en/Religion-becomes-a-compulsory-subject-in-all-Russian-schools-23967.html.

6 John Adams, "From John Adams to Massachusetts Militia, 11 October 1798," National Archives, http://founders.archives.gov/documents/Adams/99-02-02-3102.

7 "The Road to a Paris Climate Deal," *New York Times,* December 14, 2015.

8 Ian Bateson, "Putin Signs Law Banning Advertisements for Abortion in Russia," NBC News, November 25, 2013, http://www.nbcnews.com/news/other/putin-signs-law-banning-advertisements-abortion-russia-f2D11655460.

9 Vladimir Putin, "Putin Speaks at Davos," *Wall Street Journal*, January 28, 2009, http://www.wsj.com/articles/SB123317069332125243.

10 Irving Kristol, "The Neoconservative Persuasion," *Weekly Standard*, August 25, 2003, http://www.weeklystandard.com/the-neoconservative-persuasion/article/4246#!.

11 "Were 1998 Memos a Blueprint for War?" ABC News, March 10, 2003, http://abcnews.go.com/Nightline/story?id=128491&page=1.

12 Project for a New American Century Statement of Principles, http://www. rrojasdatabank.info/pfpc/PNAC---statement%20of%20principles.pdf.

13 Colin Freeman. "Vladimir Putin: Don't Mess with Nuclear-Armed Russia," *Telegraph,* August 29, 2014, http://www.telegraph.co.uk/news/worldnews/vladimir-putin/11064209/Vladimir-Putin-Dont-mess-with-nuclear-armed-Russia.html.

14 https://upload.wikimedia.org/wikipedia/commons/thumb/4/45/History_of_NATO_ enlargement.svg/2000px-History_of_NATO_enlargement.svg.png.

15 Joshua R. Itzkowitz Shifrinson, "Russia's Got a Point: The U.S. Broke a NATO Promise," *Los Angeles Times*, May 30, 2016, http://www.latimes.com/opinion/op-ed/ la-oe-shifrinson-russia-us-nato-deal--20160530-snap-story.html.

16 Tyler Durden, "Competing Gas Pipelines Are Fueling the Syrian War & Migrant Crisis," Zero Hedge, September 10, 2015, http://www.zerohedge.com/news/2015-09-10/competing-gas-pipelines-are-fueling-syrian-war-migrant-crisis.

17 Jonathan Swan, "Trump Booed for Saying Audience Full of 'Donors and Special Interests,'" *The Hill*, February 6, 2016.

18 OpenSecrets.org, https://www.opensecrets.org/industries/indus.php?cycle=2016 &ind=D.

19 Alexander Cohen, "The Defense Industry's Surprising 2016 Favorites: Bernie & Hillary," *Politico Magazine*, April 1, 2016, http://www.politico.com/magazine/ story/2016/03/2016-election-defense-military-industry-contractors-donations-money-contributions-presidential-hillary-clinton-bernie-sanders-republican-ted-cruz-213783.

CHAPTER EIGHT: TRUMP'S WAR AGAINST THE RINOS

1 Washington Post Staff, "Transcript: Obama's End-of-Year News Conference on Syria, Russian Hacking, and More," *Washington Post*, December 16, 2016, https://www.washingtonpost.com/news/post-politics/wp/2016/12/16/transcript-obamas-end-of-year-news-conference-on-syria-russian-hacking-and-more/?utm_ term=.423e819614b1.

2 Andy Eckardt, "Christmas Market Targeted with Nail Bomb by Boy, 12: German Officials," NBC News, December 16, 2016, http://www.nbcnews.com/news/world/ christmas-market-targeted-nail-bomb-boy-12-german-officials-n696811.

3 Rick Noack, "Germany Welcomed More than 1 Million Refugees in 2015. Now, the Country Is Searching for Its Soul," *Washington Post*, May 4, 2016, https://www. washingtonpost.com/news/worldviews/wp/2016/05/04/germany-welcomed-more-than-1-million-refugees-in-2015-now-the-country-is-searching-for-its-soul/?utm_ term=.752c164b76c3.

4 Michael Savage, "Savage Warns Trump on Priebus: Looks like 'Jeb Bush Won,'" *WorldNetDaily*, November 14, 2016, http://www.wnd.com/2016/11/savage-warns-trump-on-priebus-looks-like-jeb-bush-won/#oSh03VFItdTH057j.99.

5 James DeVinne, "Trump Just Picked a White Supremacist as His Chief Policy Advisor," Occupy Democrats, November 14, 2016, http://occupydemocrats. com/2016/11/14/trump-just-picked-white-supremacist-chief-policy-advisor/.

6 Matthew Rozsa, "Steve Bannon Runs an Anti-Semitic Website, Is a Misogynist, and Will Be One of Donald Trump's Senior Advisers," *Salon*, November 14, 2016, http://www.salon.com/2016/11/14/steve-bannon-runs-an-anti-semitic-website-is-a-misogynist-and-will-be-one-of-donald-trumps-senior-advisors/.

7 Jeremy Diamond, "The Alt-Right Heads to the White House," CNN, November 14, 2016, http://www.cnn.com/2016/11/14/politics/alt-right-steve-bannon/.

8 Jerry Markon, Karen DeYoung, and Greg Miller, "Trump Faces Growing Tension with Key Republicans over National Security Issues," *Washington Post.* November

15, 2016, https://www.washingtonpost.com/politics/trump-putin-talk-of-strong-and-enduring-relationship-president-elect-prepares-to-meet-today-with-vice-president-to-discuss-cabinet/2016/11/15/081b2f40-ab2f-11e6-8b45-f8e493f06fcd_story.html?utm_term=.39c26b85c0c7.

9 Editorial Board, "Steve 'Turn On the Hate' Bannon, in the White House," *New York Times,* November 15, 2016, http://www.nytimes.com/2016/11/15/opinion/turn-on-the-hate-steve-bannon-at-the-white-house.html?_r=0.

10 Harper Neidig, "Bannon: 'I'm Not a White Nationalist, I'm a Nationalist,'" *The Hill,* November 18, 2016, http://thehill.com/homenews/administration/306785-bannon-im-not-a-white-nationalist-im-a-nationalist.

11 Alex Isenstadt and Kenneth P. Vogel, "Divisions Deepen Inside Trump Tower," *Politico,* December 14, 2016, http://www.politico.com/story/2016/12/donald-trump-divisions-tower-232607.

12 Hillary Clinton, "Remarks at Techport Australia," U.S. Department of State, November 15, 2016, https://www.state.gov/secretary/20092013clinton/rm/2012/11/200565.htm.

13 Hillary Clinton, "Hillary Clinton Says She Doesn't Support Trans-Pacific Partnership," *PBS News Hour* (video), October 7, 2015, https://www.youtube.com/watch?v=Jeh-14A8Rbc.

14 C. Eugene Emery, "NowThis News Site Says Donald Trump Wrong and Bill Clinton Didn't Sign NAFTA," PolitiFact, August 11, 2016, http://www.politifact.com/punditfact/statements/2016/aug/11/nowthis/nowthis-news-site-says-donald-trump-wrong-and-bill/.

15 "H.R. 3450 (103rd): North American Free Trade Agreement Implementation Act," govtrack, https://www.govtrack.us/congress/votes/103-1993/h575.

16 Alexander Bolton, "Senate Approves Fast-Track, Sending Trade Bill to White House," *The Hill,* June 24, 2015, http://thehill.com/homenews/senate/246035-senate-approves-fast-track-sending-trade-bill-to-white-house.

17 Jennifer Steinhauer, "House G.O.P. Signals Break with Trump over Tariff Threat," *New York Times,* December 5, 2016, http://www.nytimes.com/2016/12/05/us/politics/house-republicans-trade-trump.html.

18 Jonathan Swan, "Trump Adviser Tells House Republicans: You're No Longer Reagan's Party," *The Hill,* November 23, 2016, http://thehill.com/homenews/campaign/307462-trump-adviser-tells-house-republicans-youre-no-longer-reagans-party.

19 Ibid.

20 Amy Carter and Michael C. Bender, "Donald Trump Picks Former Texas Gov. Rick Perry as Energy Secretary," *Wall Street Journal,* December 13, 2016, http://www.wsj.com/articles/donald-trump-picks-former-texas-gov-rick-perry-as-energy-secretary-1481641430.

21 Kelly Cohen, "Rick Perry: Trump's Border Wall Is 'Not' Going to Happen," *Washington Examiner,* July 11, 2016, http://www.washingtonexaminer.com/rick-perry-trumps-border-wall-is-not-going-to-happen/article/2596124#!.

22 Abby Livingston, "Survey of Texans in Congress Finds Little Support for Full Border Wall," *Texas Tribune,* December 20, 2016, https://www.texastribune.org/2016/12/20/where-texas-congressional-delegation-stands-trumps/.

23 Ibid.

24 Ibid.

25 Michael McCaul, "Rep. McCaul: Yes, We Will Build a Wall, Put Mexico on a 'Payment Plan,' and Enforce the Law," Fox News, December 2, 2016, http://www.

foxnews.com/opinion/2016/12/02/rep-mccaul-yes-will-build-wall-put-mexico-on-payment-plan-and-enforce-law.html.

26 Abby Livingston, "Survey of Texans in Congress Finds Little Support for Full Border Wall," *Texas Tribune*, December 20, 2016, https://www.texastribune.org/2016/12/20/where-texas-congressional-delegation-stands-trumps/.

27 Chris Moody, "How a Bill Becomes a Wall," CNN, November 10, 2016, http://www.cnn.com/2016/05/09/politics/donald-trump-mexico-border-wall/.

CHAPTER NINE: TRUMP'S WAR TO RESTORE REAL SCIENCE

1 Robert Rapier, "Leonardo DiCaprio's Carbon Footprint Is Much Higher Than He Thinks," *Forbes,* March 1, 2016, http://www.forbes.com/sites/rrapier/2016/03/01/leonardo-dicaprios-carbon-footprint-is-much-higher-than-he-thinks/#2593666568a2.

2 James Varney, "Skeptical Climate Scientists Coming in from the Cold," Real Clear Investigations, December 31, 2016, http://www.realclearinvestigations.com/articles/2016/12/31/skeptical_climate_scientists_coming_in_from_the_cold.html.

3 Tony Heller, "The 100% Fraudulent Hockey Stick," Deplorable Climate Science blog, June 10, 2016, https://realclimatescience.com/2016/06/the-100-fraudulent-hockey-stick/.

4 Ben Guarino, "Thousands of Montana Snow Geese Die After Landing in Toxic, Acidic Mine Pit," *Washington Post*, December 7, 2016, https://www.washingtonpost.com/news/morning-mix/wp/2016/12/07/montana-snow-geese-searching-for-pond-land-in-toxic-minc-pit-thousands-die/?utm_term=.2afc67652b50.

5 Michael Scott, "Cuyahoga River Fire 40 Years Ago Ignited an Ongoing Cleanup Campaign," *Plain Dealer*, June 22, 2009, http://www.cleveland.com/science/index.ssf/2009/06/cuyahoga_river_fire_40_years_a.html.

6 Mridula Chari, "Bengaluru Lake Catches Fire Twice in Three Days, but Nobody Is Sure Just Why," Scroll In, December 15, 2016, http://scroll.in/article/728966/bengaluru-lake-catches-fire-twice-in-three-days-but-nobody-is-sure-just-why.

7 Brian Clark Howard and Robert Kunzig, "5 Reasons to Like the U.S. Environmental Protection Agency," *National Geographic*, December 9, 2016, http://news.nationalgeographic.com/2016/12/environmental-protection-agency-epa-history-pruitt/.

8 Michael Savage. *The Savage Nation* radio broadcast, October 6, 2015.

9 Kim Passoth, "CDC Director Pledges to Resign as Trump Sworn In," CBS 46 Atlanta, January 6, 2017, http://www.cbs46.com/story/34196534/cdc-director-pledges-to-resign-as-trump-sworn-in#ixzz4VbLj5R5y.

10 Michael Savage, *The Savage Nation,* January 30, 2015.

11 Ibid.

12 Arthur Allen, "RFK Jr. Says He'll Leave Environmental Group to Head Trump Vaccine Commission," *Politico,* January 12, 2017. http://www.politico.com/story/2017/01/robert-kennedy-jr-vaccines-trump-233547.

13 Maggie Fox, "Disney Measles Outbreak Came from Overseas, CDC Says," NBC News, January 29, 2015, http://www.nbcnews.com/storyline/measles-outbreak/disney-measles-outbreak-came-overseas-cdc-says-n296441.

14 "AFM in the United States," Centers for Disease Control and Prevention, https://www.cdc.gov/acute-flaccid-myelitis/afm-surveillance.html.

15 Ibid.

16 Nidhi Subbaraman, "US Ebola Czar Calls Trump 'Badly Misguided' on Diseases," *BuzzFeed News,* January 10, 2017, https://www.buzzfeed.com/nidhisubbaraman/

us-ebola-czar-calls-trump-badly-misguided-on-diseases?sub=4438148_10300458&
utm_term=.bgZAvbdrJ#.mx51WVvQ0.

CHAPTER TEN: TRUMP'S WAR FOR THE FIRST AMENDMENT

1 Daniella Diaz, "Sen. Barbara Boxer to Introduce Bill to End Electoral College,"
CNN, November 15, 2016, http://www.cnn.com/2016/11/15/politics/barbara-boxer-
electoral-college-donald-trump-2016-election/.

2 Craig Timberg, "Russian Propaganda Effort Helped Spread 'Fake News' During
Election, Experts Say," *Washington Post*, November 24, 2016, https://www.
washingtonpost.com/business/economy/russian-propaganda-effort-helped-spread-
fake-news-during-election-experts-say/2016/11/24/793903b6-8a40-4ca9-b712-
716af66098fe_story.html?utm_term=.b0d9b46a6b42.

3 Kevin Uhrmacher, "MAP: The Obama Voters Who Helped Trump Win,"
Washington Post, November 9, 2016, https://www.washingtonpost.com/politics/2016/
live-updates/general-election/real-time-updates-on-the-2016-election-voting-
and-race-results/map-the-obama-voters-who-helped-trump-win/?utm_term=.
a7cc6e67c6c1.

4 Liam Dillon, "Secessionists Formally Launch Quest for California's Independence,"
Los Angeles Times, November 21, 2016, http://www.latimes.com/politics/essential/
la-pol-ca-essential-politics-california-secession-calexit-htmlstory.html.

5 Thomas Jefferson, "First Inaugural Address March 4, 1801," Avalon Project, Yale
Law School, http://avalon.law.yale.edu/19th_century/jefinau1.asp.

6 Donald Trump. "FULL TEXT: Donald Trump's 2016 Election Night Victory
Speech," ABC News, November 9, 2016, http://abcnews.go.com/Politics/full-text-
donald-trumps-2016-election-night-victory/story?id=43388317.

7 Barack Obama, "Transcript: Obama's Victory Speech," CNN Politics, November
7, 2012, http://politicalticker.blogs.cnn.com/2012/11/07/transcript-obamas-victory-
speech/.

8 Ken Bensinger, Mark Schoofs, and Miriam Elder, "These Reports Allege Trump
Has Deep Ties to Russia," *BuzzFeed*, January 10, 2017, https://www.buzzfeed.com/
kenbensinger/these-reports-allege-trump-has-deep-ties-to-russia?utm_term=.
yfwAP9az3#.mrY9P56Ol.

9 Evan Perez, Jim Sciutto, Jake Tapper, and Carl Bernstein, "Intel Chiefs Presented
Trump with Claims of Russian Efforts to Compromise Him," CNN, January 12,
2017, http://www.cnn.com/2017/01/10/politics/donald-trump-intelligence-report-
russia/index.html.

10 "Donald Trump's News Conference: Full Transcript and Video," *New York Times,*
January 11, 2017, https://www.nytimes.com/2017/01/11/us/politics/trump-press-
conference-transcript.html.

11 Ibid.

12 Tyler Durden, "Obama Quietly Signs the 'Countering Disinformation and
Propaganda Act' into Law," Zero Hedge, December 26, 2016, http://www.zerohedge.
com/news/2016-12-24/obama-signs-countering-disinformation-and-propaganda-act-
law.

13 Gerald F. Seib. "In Crisis, Opportunity for Obama," *Wall Street Journal*, November
21, 2008, http://www.wsj.com/articles/SB122721278056345271.

14 Tyler Durden, "Propaganda Bill in Congress Could Give America Its Very Own
Ministry of 'Truth,'" Zero Hedge, June 7, 2016, http://www.zerohedge.com/
news/2016-06-07/propaganda-bill-congress-could-give-america-its-very-own-
ministry-truth.

15 "H.R. 5181—Countering Foreign Propaganda and Disinformation Act of 2016," Congress.gov, https://www.congress.gov/bill/114th-congress/house-bill/5181/text.

16 Rebecca Kaplan, "Obama Says 'Powerlessness' Behind Protests Across U.S.," CBS News, May 4, 2015, http://www.cbsnews.com/news/obama-says-powerlessness-behind-protests-across-us/.

17 Barack Obama, "Obama to Anti-Trump Protesters: March On," video, Fox News Politics, November 17, 2016, http://www.foxnews.com/politics/2016/11/17/obama-to-anti-trump-protesters-march-on.html.

18 George Soros, "Open Society Needs Defending," Project Syndicate, December 28, 2016, https://www.project-syndicate.org/onpoint/open-society-needs-defending-by-george-soros-2016-12.

19 Valerie Richardson, "Black Lives Matter Cashes In with $100 Million from Liberal Foundations," Washington Times, August 16, 2016, http://www.washingtontimes.com/news/2016/aug/16/black-lives-matter-cashes-100-million-liberal-foun/.

20 Asra Nomani, "Billionaire George Soros Has Ties to More than 50 'Partners' of the Women's March on Washington," New York Times, January 20, 2017, http://nytlive.nytimes.com/womenintheworld/2017/01/20/billionaire-george-soros-has-ties-to-more-than-50-partners-of-the-womens-march-on-washington/.

21 "Wow! HUGE List Of Organizations Funded by Evil George Soros," Distract the Media, November 13, 2016, https://www.distract101.com/2016/11/list-of-organizations-funded-by-george-soros33/.

22 Sarah Pulliam Bailey, "White Evangelicals Voted Overwhelmingly for Donald Trump, Exit Polls Show," Washington Post, November 9, 2015, https://www.washingtonpost.com/news/acts-of-faith/wp/2016/11/09/exit-polls-show-white-evangelicals-voted-overwhelmingly-for-donald-trump/?utm_term=.cc36da0d96dd.

23 Steven Ertelt, "Donald Trump: 'I Will Protect Religious Freedom and I Don't Care if That's Politically Incorrect,'" LifeNews.com, October 7, 2016, http://www.lifenews.com/2016/10/07/donald-trump-i-will-protect-religious-freedom-and-i-dont-care-if-thats-politically-incorrect/.

24 Todd Starnes, "Oregon Silences Bakers Who Refused to Make Cake for Gay Wedding," Fox News, July 6, 2015, http://www.foxnews.com/opinion/2015/07/06/state-silences-bakers-who-refused-to-bake-cake-for-lesbians.html.

25 Oregon State Constitution, 2015 version, https://www.oregonlegislature.gov/bills_laws/Pages/OrConst.aspx.

26 Samuel Smith, "Obama Can Force Coverage of Birth Control and Abortion Drugs on Churches, Admin. Lawyer Says," Christian Post, March 25, 2016, http://www.christianpost.com/news/obama-force-churches-cover-birth-control-abortion-drugs-lawyer-tells-supreme-court-160019/.

27 Robert Barnes, "Supreme Court Sends Obamacare Contraception Case Back to Lower Courts," Washington Post, May 16, 2016, https://www.washingtonpost.com/politics/courts_law/justices-send-obamacare-contraception-case-back-to-lower-courts/2016/05/16/84e5d6da-1b72-11e6-9c81-4be1c14fb8c8_story.html?utm_term=.246e392ea853.

28 Tyler O'Neil, "Why the First Amendment Defense Act Is Not Anti-Gay," PJ Media, December 16, 2016, https://pjmedia.com/faith/2016/12/13/why-the-first-amendment-defense-act-is-not-anti-gay/.

29 Emma Green, "The Religious-Liberty Showdowns Coming in 2017," Atlantic, December 28, 2016, https://www.theatlantic.com/politics/archive/2016/12/the-religious-liberty-showdowns-coming-in-2017/511400/.

30 Julie Hirschfield Davis, "Obama to Issue Order Barring Anti-Gay Bias by Contractors," *New York Times,* July 18, 2014, https://www.nytimes.com/2014/07/19/us/politics/obama-to-extend-protections-for-gay-workers-with-no-religious-exemption.html?_r=0.

CHAPTER ELEVEN: TRUMP'S WAR FOR THE SECOND AMENDMENT

1 "Federal Prosecutors File Charges Against Santiago, He Could Face the Death Penalty," Fox News, January 8, 2017, http://www.foxnews.com/us/2017/01/08/federal-prosecutors-file-charges-against-santiago-could-face-death-penalty.html.

2 Chris Sanchez, "Obama on the Fort Lauderdale Airport Shooting: 'These Tragedies Have Happened Too Often,'" *Business Insider,* January 6, 2017, http://www.businessinsider.com/obama-fort-lauderdale-mass-shooting-2017-1.

3 "Opinions on Gun Policy and the 2016 Campaign," Pew Research Center, August 25, 2016, http://www.people-press.org/files/2016/08/08-26-16-Gun-policy-release.pdf.

4 Jim Treacher, "Why Did Navy Yard Shooter Aaron Alexis Create a Website Called 'Mohammed Salem'?" *Daily Caller,* September 19, 2013, http://dailycaller.com/2013/09/19/why-did-aaron-alexis-create-a-website-called-mohammed-salem/#ixzz4WLB8yWMs.

5 Frances Martel, "FBI: We Have Not Found Jihadi Content on Ft. Lauderdale Shooter's Social Media," *Breitbart News,* January 9, 2016. http://www.breitbart.com/national-security/2017/01/09/fbi-not-found-jihadi-content-ft-lauderdale-shooters-social-media/.

6 "BREAKING: #FortLauderdale Terrorist #EstebanSantiago Joined Myspace as 'Aashiq Hammad,' Recorded Islamic Music," Got News, January 7, 2016, http://gotnews.com/breaking-fortlauderdale-terrorist-estebansantiago-joined-myspace-aashiq-hammad-recorded-islamic-music/.

7 Jack Billings, "Fort Lauderdale Shooting Reactions Fly Past Gunman and onto Gun Control," Guns.com, January 7, 2016, http://www.guns.com/2017/01/07/fort-lauderdale-shooting-reactions-fly-past-gunman-and-onto-gun-control/.

8 Ibid.

9 Walid Shoebat, "Photo Evidence Reveals Ft. Lauderdale Shooter Is a Muslim Terrorist," Shoebat.com, January 6, 2017, http://shoebat.com/2017/01/06/photo-evidence-reveals-ft-lauderdale-shooter-is-a-muslim-terrorist/.

10 Ibid.

11 "Inaugural Address: Trump's Full Speech," CNN, January 20, 2017, http://www.cnn.com/2017/01/20/politics/trump-inaugural-address/index.html.

12 Dan Roberts, "Every Mass Shooting Shares One Thing in Common & It's NOT Weapons," Ammoland, April 1, 2013, http://www.ammoland.com/2013/04/every-mass-shooting-in-the-last-20-years-shares-psychotropic-drugs/#axzz4WPhb61a1.

13 Ibid.

14 Ibid.

15 "Mental Health Medications," National Institutes of Health, https://www.nimh.nih.gov/health/topics/mental-health-medications/index.shtml.

16 Alison Leigh Cowan, "Adam Lanza's Mental Problems 'Completely Untreated' Before Newtown Shootings, Report Says," *New York Times,* November 21, 2014.

17 Allaine Griffin and Josh Kovner, "Lanza's Psychiatric Treatment Revealed in Documents," *Hartford Courant,* December 28, 2013, http://articles.courant.com/2013-12-28/news/hc-lanza-sandy-hook-report1228-20131227_1_peter-lanza-adam-lanza-nancy-lanza.

18 Brendan L. Smith, "Inappropriate Prescribing," *Monitor on Psychology*,43, no. 6 (June 2012), http://www.apa.org/monitor/2012/06/prescribing.aspx.

19 Will Self, "Psychiatrists: The Drug Pushers," *Guardian*, August 3, 2013, https://www.theguardian.com/society/2013/aug/03/will-self-psychiatrist-drug-medication.

CHAPTER TWELVE: TRUMP'S WAR AGAINST THE DEEP STATE

1 Donald Trump. "Trump News Conference (Video)," *New York Times*, January 11, 2017, https://www.nytimes.com/video/us/politics/100000004865278/watch-live-trump-news-conference.html.

2 Stephan Dinan, "Federal Workers Hit Record Number, but Growth Slows Under Obama," *Washington Times*, February 9, 2016, http://www.washingtontimes.com/news/2016/feb/9/federal-workers-hit-record-number-but-growth-slows/.

3 "Intelligence Report on Russian Hacking," *New York Times*, January 6, 2017, http://www.nytimes.com/interactive/2017/01/06/us/politics/document-russia-hacking-report-intelligence-agencies.html?_r=0.

4 Michael D. Shear and David E. Sanger, "Putin Led a Complex Cyberattack Scheme to Aid Trump, Report Finds," *New York Times*, January 6, 2017, https://www.nytimes.com/2017/01/06/us/politics/donald-trump-wall-hack-russia.html.

5 Donald Trump, Twitter, January 5, 2017, https://twitter.com/realDonaldTrump/status/817166353266262016.

6 "Comey: FBI Denied Repeated Requests to Access DNC Servers, Podesta's Device," Fox News Politics, January 10, 2017, http://www.foxnews.com/politics/2017/01/10/comey-fbi-denied-repeated-requests-to-access-dnc-servers-podesta-s-device.html.

7 Aaron Klein, "DNC 'Russian Hacking' Conclusion Comes from Google-Linked Firm," *Breitbart News*, January 6, 2017, http://www.breitbart.com/big-government/2017/01/06/dnc-russian-hacking-conclusion-comes-google-linked-firm/.

8 Ibid.

9 Atlantic Council website, http://www.atlanticcouncil.org/ukraine.

10 William Binney, "US Intel Vets Dispute Russia Hacking Claims," *Consortium News*, December 12, 2016, https://consortiumnews.com/2016/12/12/us-intel-vets-dispute-russia-hacking-claims/.

11 Peter Hasson, "Schumer: Intelligence Community May 'Get Back at' Trump for Tweet [VIDEO]," *Daily Caller*, January 4, 2017, http://dailycaller.com/2017/01/04/schumer-intelligence-community-may-get-back-at-trump-for-tweet-video/#ixzz4VmPSaNrv.

12 "Ukraine Crisis: Crimea Leader Appeals to Putin for Help," BBC News, March 1, 2014, http://www.bbc.com/news/world-europe-26397323.

13 Valerie Richardson, "Democratic Heads Roll After Video Shows Agitators Planted at Trump Rallies," *Washington Times*, October 18, 2016, http://www.washingtontimes.com/news/2016/oct/18/undercover-video-shows-democrats-saying-they-hire-/.

14 Curt Devine, "Trump's Foreign Business Interests: 144 Companies in 25 Countries," CNN, November 29, 2016, http://www.cnn.com/2016/11/28/politics/trump-foreign-businesses/.

15 Bradley Hope, Michael Rothfeld, and Alan Cullison, "Christopher Steele, Ex-British Intelligence Officer, Said to Have Prepared Dossier on Trump," *Wall Street Journal*, January 11, 2017, http://www.wsj.com/articles/christopher-steele-ex-british-intelligence-officer-said-to-have-prepared-dossier-on-trump-1484162553.

16 Sydney Ember and Michael M. Grynbaum, "BuzzFeed Posts Unverified Claims on Trump, Igniting a Debate," *New York Times*, January 10, 2017, https://www.nytimes.com/2017/01/10/business/buzzfeed-donald-trump-russia.html?_r=0.

17 "DNI Clapper Statement on Conversation with President-elect Trump," Office of the Director of National Intelligence, January 11, 2017, https://www.dni.gov/index.php/newsroom/press-releases/224-press-releases-2017/1469-dni-clapper-statement-on-conversation-with-president-elect-trump.

18 Matt Zapotosky and Sari Horwitz, "Justice Department Inspector General to Investigate Pre-Election Actions by Department and FBI," *Washington Post*, January 12, 2017, https://www.washingtonpost.com/news/post-nation/wp/2017/01/12/justice-department-inspector-general-to-investigate-pre-election-actions-by-department-and-fbi/?utm_term=.075dc320a1ff.

19 "Russia Hits Out at Biggest US Military Build-up in Europe Since Cold War," *The Week*, January 13, 2017, http://www.theweek.co.uk/74309/russia-hits-out-at-biggest-us-military-build-up-in-europe-since-cold-war.

20 Laura Smith-Spark and Atika Shubert, "Poland Welcomes US Troops as Part of NATO Buildup," CNN, January 14, 2017, http://www.cnn.com/2017/01/14/europe/poland-us-troops-nato-welcome/.

21 Krishnadev Calamur, "NATO Shmato?" *Atlantic*, July 21, 2016, http://www.theatlantic.com/news/archive/2016/07/trump-nato/492341/.

22 Ewan MacAskill, "Russia Says US Troops Arriving in Poland Pose Threat to Its Security," *Guardian,* January 12, 2017, https://www.theguardian.com/us-news/2017/jan/12/doubts-over-biggest-us-deployment-in-europe-since-cold-war-under-trump.

23 Ibid.

24 "Putin Discusses Trump, OPEC, Rosneft, Brexit, Japan (Transcript)," Bloomberg, September 5, 2016, https://www.bloomberg.com/news/articles/2016-09-05/putin-discusses-trump-opec-rosneft-brexit-japan-transcript.

25 "George W. Bush: The Bucharest Summit Will Be One 'Marked by Success,'" NATO Bucharest Summit website, 2008, http://www.summitbucharest.ro/en/doc_130.html.

26 "Nato Denies Georgia and Ukraine," BBC News, April 3, 2008, http://news.bbc.co.uk/2/hi/europe/7328276.stm.

27 Anatol Lieven, "Putin Versus Cheney," *New York Times*, May 11, 2006, http://www.nytimes.com/2006/05/11/opinion/11iht-edlieven.html.

28 Dean Parker. "In Hitler's Steps: Huge US Military Convoy to Advance from Germany to Russia's Border," *Russia Insider*, June 3, 2016, http://russia-insider.com/en/hitlers-steps-huge-us-military-convoy-advance-germany-russias-border/ri14784.

29 Ryan Teague Beckwith, "Read Donald Trump's 'America First' Foreign Policy Speech," *Time*, April 27, 2016, http://time.com/4309786/read-donald-trumps-america-first-foreign-policy-speech/.

30 Ibid.

CHAPTER THIRTEEN: THE BATTLE PLAN

1 "Inaugural Address: Trump's Full Speech," CNN, January 21, 2017, http://www.cnn.com/2017/01/20/politics/trump-inaugural-address/index.html.

2 Thomas Paine, *Common Sense*, from *Collected Writings*, edited by Eric Foner (New York: Literary Classics of the United States, 1955), p. 52.

3 "List of Trump's Executive Orders," Fox News, January 24, 2017, http://www.foxnews.com/politics/2017/01/24/list-trumps-executive-orders.html